LEARNING AND TEACHING

BES-123

For

Bachelor of Education [B.Ed.]

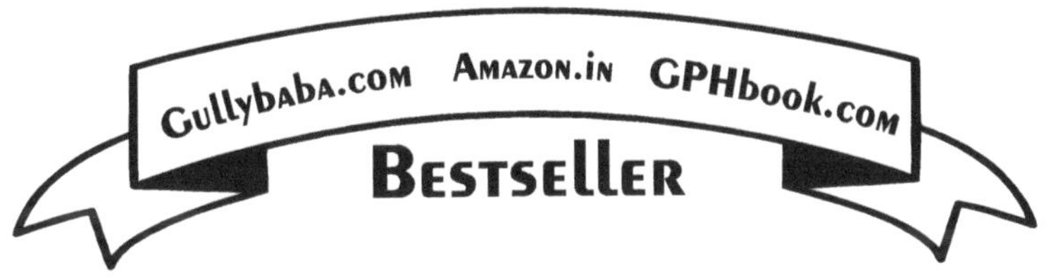

BASED ON TWO YEARS REVISED SYLLABUS RECOGNISED BY NCTE

Useful for

Magadh University (Bihar), Indira Gandhi National Open University (IGNOU), Kurukshetra University, Bihar University (Muzaffarpur), Nalanda University, Yashwantrao Chavan Maharashtra Open University, KSOU (Karnataka), Seva Sadan's College of Education (Maharashtra), Maharshi Dayanand University (Rohtak) and other Indian Universities

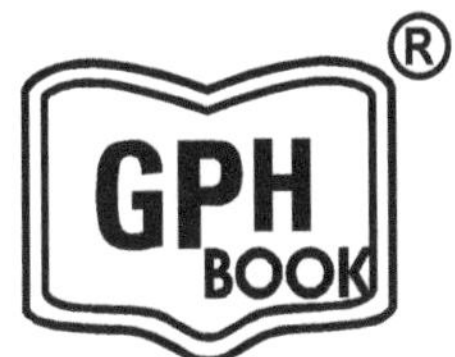

GULLYBABA PUBLISHING HOUSE PVT. LTD.

ISO 9001 & ISO 14001 CERTIFIED CO.

Published by:
GullyBaba Publishing House Pvt. Ltd.

Regd. Office:
2525/193, 1st Floor, Onkar Nagar-A,
Tri Nagar, Delhi-110035
(From Kanhaiya Nagar Metro Station Towards Old Bus Stand)
Call: 9991112299, 9312235086
WhatsApp: 9350849407

Branch Office:
1A/2A, 20, Hari Sadan,
Ansari Road, Daryaganj,
New Delhi-110002
Ph. 011-45794768
Call & WhatsApp:
8130521616, 8130511234

E-mail: hello@gullybaba.com, **Website:** GullyBaba.com

New Edition

Author: Gullybaba.com Panel

ISBN: 978-93-86276-63-6

Copyright© with Publisher
All rights are reserved. No part of this publication may be reproduced or stored in a retrieval system or transmitted in any form or by any means; electronic, mechanical, photocopying, recording or otherwise, without the written permission of the copyright holder.

Disclaimer: Although the author and publisher have made every effort to ensure that the information in this book is correct, the author and publisher do not assume and hereby disclaim any liability to any party for any loss, damage, or disruption caused by errors or omissions, whether such errors or omissions result from negligence, accident, or any other cause.

If you find any kind of error, please let us know and get reward and or the new book free of cost.

The book is based on IGNOU syllabus. This is only a sample. The book/author/publisher does not impose any guarantee or claim for full marks or to be passed in exam. You are advised only to understand the contents with the help of this book and answer in your words.

All disputes with respect to this publication shall be subject to the jurisdiction of the Courts, Tribunals and Forums of New Delhi, India only.

Home Delivery of GPH Books

You can get GPH books by VPP/COD/Speed Post/Courier.
You can order books by Email/SMS/WhatsApp/Call.
For more details, visit gullybaba.com/faq-books.html
Our packaging department usually dispatches the books within 2 days after receiving your order and it takes nearly 5-6 days in postal/courier services to reach your destination.

Note: Selling this book on any online platform like Amazon, Flipkart, Shopclues, Rediff, etc. without prior written permission of the publisher is prohibited and hence any sales by the SELLER will be termed as ILLEGAL SALE of GPH Books which will attract strict legal action against the offender.

Preface

Learning and teaching are the foundation of education and training. Most of us tend to place teaching first in the paradigm and say teaching and learning. It is as though there is a tacit belief that teaching is the more important of the two activities. Both learning and teaching are extremely important and generally go together but it can be easily argued that learning is more important than teaching. In fact, learning often occurs without teachers in situations where students learn by experience or by their own efforts.

This GPH book, *'Learning and Teaching (BES-123)'*, is conceptualized on the basis premise that learning and teaching should be viewed holistically. Through this book, it has been attempted to facilitate student teachers to understand learning and teaching as a process which works for construction of knowledge. Psychological and socio-cultural perspectives of learning have been discussed in this book. Various theoretical constructs of learning which will help to identify the appropriate learning strategies for facilitating construction of knowledge have been analysed critically.

This book is written specially in question & answer format to provide students the instant gratification of a correct answer. In this book, we have tried to solve all possible questions from the exams' point of view. Solutions of previous years' questions papers have also been included to help you to understand the unique examination structure. We hope that this book would not only be a favourite study material for the students but also can be a nice resource for teaching.

An attempt has been carefully made to present this book more useful and meet the requirement and challenges of the course prescribed by University/Institution.

We wish you a successful and rewarding career ahead. Feedback in this regard is solicited.

-GPH Panel of Experts

Acknowledgement

Our compliments go to the **GullyBaba Publishing House Pvt. Ltd.,** and its meticulous team who have been enthusiastically working towards the perfection of the book.

Their teamwork, initiative and research have been very encouraging. Had it not been for their unflagging support, this work wouldn't have been possible. The creative freedom provided by them along with their aim of presenting the best to the reader has been a major source of inspiration in this work. Hope that this book would be successful.

– GPH Panel of Experts

Publisher's Note

The present book BES-123 is targeted for examination purpose as well as enrichment. With the advent of technology and the Internet, there has been no dearth of information available to all; however, finding the relevant and qualitative information, which is focussed, is an uphill task.

We at **GullyBaba Publishing House Pvt. Ltd.,** have taken this step to provide quality material which can accentuate in-depth knowledge about the subject. GPH books are a pioneer in the effort of providing unique and quality material to its readers. With our books, you are sure to attain success by making use of this powerful study material. Provided book is just a reference book based on the syllabus of particular University/Board. For a profound information, see the textbooks recommended by the University/Board.

Our site **gullybaba.com** is a vital resource for your examination. The publisher wishes to acknowledge the significant contribution of the Team Members and our experts in bringing out this publication and highly thankful to Almighty God, without His blessings, this endeavor wouldn't have been successful.

We would like to thank also students and faculties that have used our books over the years and provided us with excellent feedback that has assisted us in writing better and more students-focused books.

– Publisher

Topics Covered

Contents

Question Papers

Learning: Perspectives and Approaches

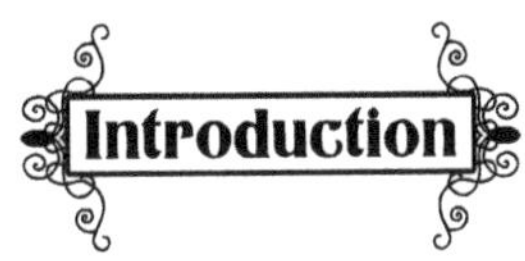

Learning is the act of acquiring new or modifying and reinforcing existing knowledge, behaviours, skills, values, or preferences which may lead to a potential change in synthesising information. Learning process helps us in solving the problems related to the education processes. Learning directs goal and takes place when an individual interacts with learning situation. Indian school education has transformed a lot and there is major emphasis on constructivist teaching learning or promoting learning for construction of knowledge by learners themselves. In facilitating constructivist learning, the role of Zone of Proximal Development, Scaffolding, Active Learning, Situated Learning, Cognitive Apprenticeship, Tutoring and Discovery learning among learners. Thus, learning remains a lifelong process.

Q1. What do you understand by learning? Discuss its nature.

Or

What is the meaning and nature of learning? Explain.

Or

Explain the nature of learning. [June-2017, Q.No.-3(c)]

Ans. Learning can be defined in a number of ways. From one point of view, it is a process of adjustment. Again, learning is modification of experiences, and not mere addition of experiences. Some define learning as the process of making suitable responses in order to satisfy one's need. Learning is also defined as acquisition of knowledge, skill and attitudes. Skinner includes in learning both acquisition and retention. Hilgard has defined learning as "the process by which activity originates or is changed through reacting to an encountered situation provided that the characteristics of the change in activity cannot be explained on the basis of native responses, tendencies, maturation or temporary states of organism like fatigue or effect of drugs."

Learning is a complex process. It is acquiring changes in behaviour as a result of experience. Learning is the process by which an organism, as a result of the interaction in a situation, acquires a new mode of behaviour, which tends to persist and affect the general behavioural pattern of the organism, to some degree. This definition suggests that learning takes place when an organism reacts in a situation. Learning consists in the acquiring of new modes of behaviour or adjustment. Such a change in behaviour is retained by the organism to some degree and is utilised in other situations to some extent.

Morgan and King (1971) stated that learning can be defined as any relatively permanent change in behaviour which occurs as a result of experience or practice. This definition shows the following three important elements of learning:

- Learning is a change in behaviour, for better or worse;
- It is a change that takes place through experience or practice, i.e. changes as a result of growth, maturation or injury cannot be considered as learned; and
- The change that occurs because of learning must be relatively permanent, i.e. it must last far a fairly long time. This rules out any change due to fatigue or adaptation to sensitivity by the organism.

Nature of learning: The nature of learning can be understood from the followings:

(1) **Learning is the change in behaviour:** Learning in its any form or shape is always associated with some change in the learner's behaviour. That is why learning is always directed or aimed at bringing changes in the learner's behaviour. However, these changes should always be desirable ones as the undesirable changes, if allowed to occur can prove detrimental to the welfare of the learner as well as to the society.

(2) **Change in behaviour is relatively enduring or permanent:** Change in behaviour caused by learning is neither too permanent (as caused maturation) nor too temporary (as caused by the factors like fatigue, illness etc.). They lie between these two states and are usually referred to as relatively permanent changes implying that although frequent or unwanted changes in the learned behaviour can't take place. Yet the needed changes can be introduced like getting rid of the bad habits or unlearning a wrong method of doing things etc.

(3) **Learning is a continuous life long process:** Learning though not inherited, can begin right from the conception of the child. The environment available in the womb of the mother may work as a facilitator for such learning. We have Abhimanyu as an example who learned the art of Chakravueh Bhedan from his father Arjuna in the womb of his mother Shubhadra. After birth, the process of learning picks up speed with the constant interaction and stimulation received from the physical, social and cultural environmental forces and it does not stop till one's death. Regarding its continuity we have enough evidence that one activity leads to another and the individual engages himself to learn more and more. Every day new problems are faced, new situation are created and the individual has to face these situations and bring essential changes in his behaviour. Thus it is a never ending process and so referred to as process which goes from womb to womb.

(4) **Learning is a universal process:** We, the living creatures on this earth, have the abilities and capabilities for learning irrespective of the nature of our species, caste, colour, sex, geographical location or some other such individual differences. Therefore, myths like members of the upper castes especially Brahmins have more ability of learning than the members belonging to the lower castes and untouchables, women have inferior learning capacity than men, or the blacks possess sub-normal capacities for learning in comparison to whites, etc., have no substantial ground. The truth remains that every living beings on earth has been favoured by the nature to possess the capacity to learn according to the species specific characteristics and environment as well as opportunities available for learning.

(5) **Learning is purposive and goal-directed:** All learning is goal-directed. It is the definiteness of the aim and clear understanding of the purpose which makes an individual immediately learn the techniques of performing a particular task. It is the purpose or goal which determines what he sees in the learning situations and how he acts there in. Therefore, the purpose or goal is the pivot around which the entire system of learning revolves. In cases where there is no purpose, there would hardly be any learning.

(6) **Learning involves reconstruction of experiences:** We learn something at a particular stage and it is stored in our learning experiences store in the form of past experience or learning for the learning of a future task. However, what has been learnt by us at a particular occasion always remains in the state of modification in the light of new or richer experiences gained by us in this respect. As a result old learning is replaced by new learning and our previous experiences are restructured and reorganized to give birth to a new structure composed of the reconstructed experiences. It is therefore education, i.e. the process of learning, that is often referred to as the process of continuous reconstruction of experiences.

(7) **Learning is the product of activity and environment:** The basic condition of the emergence of any learning essentially lies in one's responding activity to the stimuli present in his learning environment, he can't be persuaded to proceed on the path of his learning journey. More the learner will respond actively to the stimuli present in his learning environment, the more progress will he be able to make in terms of his learning outcomes. Therefore, the key to successful learning in any teaching learning-process always lies in the active responding of the learner to the stimuli present or the activities going on in the teaching-learning environment.

(8) **Learning is transferable from one situation to another:** Learning has a special characteristic of being transferred from one learning situation to another having positive as well as negative effect. In its positive transfer, learning in one situation helps the learning in another situation but in the case of negative transfer, we may observe the adverse effect when learning in one situation hinders or obstructs the path of learning in another situation.

(9) **Learning does not necessarily imply improvement:** Learning is often considered a process of improvement with practice or training. This means that all types of learning helps the child in the path of his process towards desired ends or results. But this is not always true, his goal. Habits like idleness, disrespect towards authority, truancy, developing poor handwriting and defective pronunciation and exposition are among these. Therefore, it should be known clearly that learning does not necessarily imply improvement (with respect to the achievement of an end).

(10) **Learning does not necessarily imply development in right direction:** In a similar way, while defining learning as a process of development, the word development should never be confined to mean 'progress in right direction to achieve certain ends or results'. Hence as Woodworth clarifies in his definition, as a result of learning, the pattern of development is free to

move in either direction—positive or negative. It is no guarantee that an individual will always pick up good knowledge, desirable habits, interest and attitudes. He has equal chances to be drifted to the debit side of the human personality.

(11) **Learning helps in bringing desirable changes in behaviour:** Learning is the process of bringing changes in behaviour. It can help in introducing desired changes in the behaviour of the learner in all its three domains, i.e. cognitive, conative and affective.

(12) **Learning helps in the attainment of teaching-learning objectives:** The teaching-learning objectives and teaching-learning situation can be effectively reached through the help of learning and consequently children can be made to acquire essential knowledge, skills, applications, attitudes and interests etc.

(13) **Learning helps in the proper growth and development:** Learning helps in reaching to one's maximum in terms of growth and development under their various dimensions, namely physical, mental (cognitive) emotional, social, moral, aesthetic and language.

(14) **Learning helps in the balanced development of personality:** Our educational efforts are directed to bring an all-round development in the personality of the child. The process of learning results in bringing such an all-round development of the personality.

(15) **Learning helps in proper adjustment:** Adjust is the key to success in life. Learning helps the individual to seek adjustment with his self and environment.

(16) **Learning helps in the realization of the goals of life:** Every man has his own philosophy and style of life and he strives to achieve the goals of his life. Learning process helps the individual to realize these goals.

(17) **Learning is a very comprehensive process, possessing a wide scope:** The world of learning is considered to limit itself in the narrow walls of the activities concerning intellectual and motor efficiency. It is often thought of as the acquisition of some knowledge and skills, memorization of certain facts and principles, development of reasoning and thinking power etc. These are some of the learning activities which formally go on inside the classroom or in any arranged learning situation. But learning is not only limited to these activities. It is a very comprehensive process that covers nearly all the aspects of the human personality. Its scope touches aspects like the formation of habits, development of interests, attitudes, a sense of appreciation and critical observation, acquisition of beliefs, perfection of values and ideals and setting of the goals and purpose.

Therefore, learning as a whole, is not confined to the formal classroom learning activities. Life presents enormous opportunities to learn and learning activities are so many that it is difficult to limit them in any specific categories.

Q2. Write short notes on followings:

(i) Learning and Maturation

Ans. Maturation is the process of becoming mature while learning is the act, process, or experience of gaining knowledge or skill. Maturation is the growth which takes place in the individual. The changes on account of maturation are the results of unfolding and ripening of inherited traits. They are relatively independent of activity, experience and practice. However, maturation and learning are closely interrelated. Sometimes it becomes difficult to say definitely as to which behavioural changes are the results of learning and which are the consequences of maturation. At a particular age, every child starts to sit, crawl, stand and walk. This is the result of maturation. But when the child dances, sings, plays football, drives scooter or a car and swims in the river, it is called learning. Learning is dependent on maturation to a great extent. Unless a particular stage in the process of maturation is reached, learning of any sort cannot be taken into hand. Maturation plays an important role in learning new skills. It prepares one physically and mentally to learn. So the relation between the two is so intimate that one is often misunderstood as the other. But they are two separate concepts and maturation fuels the organism with capability to learn.

(ii) Learning and Teaching

Ans. Teaching and Learning are two words that are to be used differently since there is a difference between the meanings. They should not be interchanged. The word teaching can be defined as the act of giving lessons on a subject to a class or pupils. For example, within a school a teacher carries out the process of teaching. On the other hand, the word learning is used in the sense of acquiring knowledge. Learning is undertaken by the student who wishes to broaden his understanding of various concepts pertaining to different fields. This is the main difference between the two words. Through this article let us examine the differences between teaching and learning.

Teaching is form of interpersonal influence aimed at changing the behavior potential of another person. It is a purposeful social and professional activity. The ultimate goal of teaching is to bring about development of a child. Teaching is a complex phenomenon as its nature is scientific as well as artistic. Gage (1979) has discussed teaching as a science to describe 'the elements of predictability' in teaching and as an art to describe 'what constitutes good teaching'. When one considers teaching as an art, s/he considers it loaded with emotions, feelings, values, beliefs and excitement and difficult to derive rules, principles or generalisations. When s/he considers teaching as science, then pedagogy is predictable to the extent that it can be observed and measured with some accuracy and research can be applied to the practice of teaching.

The total task of teaching is to provide a conducive environment to child for learning and helping him in exploring this potential. Joyce, Weil and Calhoun (2009) said that models of teaching are really models of learning.

According to Gage (1967), "Any valid conception of teaching must be integrally related to a conception of learning. How human beings learning should provide much of the basis for our derivations of how teachers should teach."

(iii) Learning and Imprinting

Ans. Imprinting refers to inherited tendencies or responses that are displayed by newborn animals when they encounter certain stimuli in their environment. Imprinting is an unlearned behaviour that is based on biological factors and that has great survival value: it increases the chances that newly hatched birds will remain with and follow their parent instead of wandering off into the waiting jaws of predators. Imprinting is quite dissimilar and distinct from the actual process of learning. It depends on an instinctive and inborn species-specific behaviour mechanism rather than the experience and training carried out during specific critical periods of the species life time soon after birth.

Q3. Identify the dimensions of learning.

Ans. There are five dimensions of learning which are as follow:

(1) **Attitudes and Perceptions:** Attitudes and perceptions affect students' abilities to learn. If students have negative attitudes about classroom tasks, they will probably put little effort into those tasks. A key element of effective instruction, then, is helping students to establish positive attitudes and perceptions about the classroom and about learning.

(2) **Acquire and Integrate Knowledge:** Helping students acquire and integrate new knowledge is another important aspect of learning. When students are learning new information, they must be guided in relating the new knowledge to what they already know, organising that information, and then making it part of their long-term memory.

(3) **Extend and Refine Knowledge:** Learning does not stop with acquiring and integrating knowledge. Learners develop in-depth understanding through the process of extending and refining their knowledge (e.g., by making new distinctions, clearing up misconceptions, and reaching conclusions). Some of the common reasoning processes used by learners to extend and refine their knowledge like: comparing, classifying, abstracting, inductive reasoning, deductive reasoning, constructing support, analysing errors, analysing perspectives etc.

(4) **Use Knowledge Meaningfully:** The most effective learning occurs when we use knowledge to perform meaningful tasks. When planning a lesson, make sure students have the opportunity to use knowledge meaningfully. In the Dimensions of Learning model, there are six reasoning processes around

which tasks can be constructed to encourage the meaningful use of knowledge: Decision making, problem solving, invention, experimental inquiry, investigation, systems analysis.

(5) **Habits of Mind:** The most effective learners have developed powerful habits of mind that enable them to think critically, think creatively, and regulate their behaviour. The metal habits for critical thinking are being accurate and seeking accuracy, being clear and seeking clarity, maintaining an open mind, restraining impulsivity, taking a position when the situation warrantsit and responding appropriately to others feeling and level of knowledge. Habit of preserving, pushing the limits of own knowledge and abilities, generating, trusting and maintaining own standards of evaluation enable in thinking creatively. Self-regulated thinking is enabled by the habits of monitoring own thinking, planning appropriately, identifying and using necessary resources, responding appropriately to feedback and evaluating the effectiveness of own actions.

Q4. Define construct. Explain learning as a psychological and social construct.

Ans. The *construct* is a proposed *attribute* of a person that often *cannot be measured* directly, but can be assessed using a number of indicators or manifest variables. The presence or absence of such an attribute is decided by the reflection of certain actions in an individual's behaviour. Learning is also a construct. It is characterised by certain behaviour.

Learning as a Psychological Construct: Learning as a psychological construct is defined as any activity that develops an individual, irrespective of being good or bad. Early schools of thought like behaviourist and cognitivist established learning as a psychological construct.

Behaviorist perspective focused on observable behaviour whereas cognitivists concentrated on role of internal cognitive processes in learning. Behaviorists believed that education is a mean to train individuals for desired behaviour. Cognitivists were concerned with internal processes of the brain and neryous system for learning. Internal mental processes include inputting, organising, storing, retrieving, and finding relationships between information are important for learning. Their focus was on how information is processed. Gestaltists also emphasised on learning a psychological construct however, they were of a different viewpoint. Gestalt theorists focus on role of perception, insight, and meaning as the key elements of learning. They perceived individual as a perceptual organism that organised, interpreted and gave meaning to the events.

Learning as a Social Construct: Learning as a social construct is characterised by development of socially desired behaviour, generally developed in a social environment by observation and self-regulation.

The outcome of interaction between people is learning as a social construct. These theorists believe that learning is based on observation of others in a social setting. In the 1960's, Bandura postulated that an observer can learn by observing without having to imitate what is being learned. He proposed four processes for observational learning i.e. attention, retention (memory), behavioural rehearsal, and motivation.

Q5. What do you mean by learning styles? Discuss its types.

Or

Discuss various learning styles with suitable examples.

[Dec-2017, Q.No.-3 (c)]

Ans. Learning styles are various approaches or ways of learning. They involve educating methods, particular to an individual that are presumed to allow that individual to learn best. Most people prefer an identifiable method of interacting with, taking in, and processing stimuli or information. Based on this concept, the idea of individualised "learning styles" originated in the 1970s, and acquired "enormous popularity".

Learning styles are simply different approaches or ways of learning. Proponents of learning styles contend that teachers should assess the learning styles of their students and adapt their classroom methods to best fit each student's learning style.

Learning styles are relatively more stable, though the same learner may resort to the use of a different learning style in a particular situation. Learning styles are thus relatively well-established response patterns in individuals compounded by one's learning and problem-solving processes.

Types of learning styles: VARK is an acronym that refers to the four types of learning styles: Visual, Auditory, Reading/Writing Preference and Kinesthetic.

- **Visual Learners:** Visual learners learn best by looking at graphics, watching a demonstration or reading. For them, it is easy to look at charts and graphs, but they may have difficulty foucussing while listening to an explanation. These learners need to see the teacher's body language and facial expression to fully understand the content of a lesson. They tend to prefer sitting at the front of the classroom to avoid visual obstructions.
- **Auditory Learners:** Auditory learners would rather listen to things being explained than read about them. Reciting information loud and having music in the background may be a common study method. Other noises may become a distraction resulting in a need for a relatively quiet place. These learners often benefit from reading text along and using a tape recorder.
- **Reading/Writing preference:** Learners with a strong reading/writing preference learn best through words. These learners are able to translate abstract concepts into words and essays.
- **Kinesthetic Learners:** Kinesthetic learning is a learning style in which learning takes place by the learner using their body in order to express a thought, an idea or an understanding of a particular concept. Kinesthetic learners process information best through a "hands-on" experience. Actually doing an activity can be the easiest way for them to learn. Sitting still while studying may be difficult, but writing things down makes it easier to understand.

Q6. Illustrate pace of learning. Discuss role of a teacher in it.

Ans. Everyone has his/her own pace of learning. For example, if we present any new concept and explain it in the classroom, some of our learners may grasp it immediately. For few of them, we may have to explain again with help of some examples. For some, we may design certain activities so that while doing those activities, learners can understand the concept, even for some, we may require repetitive drill and exercises and such learners can take much time. A learner is a learner; his/her pace may vary. Pace of learning is a kind of individual difference.

Khan defined the pace of learning "people learn at different rates. Some people seem to catch on the things in quick bursts of intuition; others grunt and grind their way towards comprehension. Quicker is not necessarily smarter and slower definitely is not dumber. Further, catching on quickly is not the same as understanding thoroughly. So, the pace of learning is a question of style, not relative intelligence".

In a class, learners learn in a different way, at a different pace and in a face-to-face class, it is almost impossible to cater to everyone's learning need but understanding of these concepts will help a teacher in accommodating diverse learning needs in the class.

Role of a Teacher: Teacher must have realised that every learner learns on his/her own pace but they cannot teach on different pace. Sometimes they may find it challenging to match with the pace of learners. There are following information teacher can try to facilitate learning for learners at different pace:

- Never present a lot of concepts at a time. Try to explain every concept and involve our learners to provide explanation of the concepts.
- Encourage learners to give examples based on their own experiences and observations; this will help the learners to link the concept with their own experiences and knowledge.
- Sometimes teacher may try time-limit or time-warning strategy to increase the pace of learners.
- If it is group work, teacher can assign time-keeper role to one of the learner who will encourage all to complete the task in given time.
- Teacher should analyse the activity/task before assigning to learners in terms of time required to complete the task and plan accordingly.
- Design some additional activities/exercises for learners who learn at comparatively slow pace.

Q7. Analyse various modes of learning.

Ans. There are four important modes of learning which are as follow:

(1) Learning by observation: By operating different things, a person discovers essential, but hidden, connections and relationships between different phenomenan and their features. The leaner performs actions not only on different things, but also on the content of his own psyche-sign, concepts and images. In learning by observation the student does not perform externally observed actions. However, he performs internal, mental actions. The student performs an observation in accordance with the goal of observation which can be regarded as a particular task-problem. The learner can actively interpret observed events and, in a similar situation, perform in a totally different way or use the same method in totally different situations. Observers develop interpretative strategies of performance. Learning by observation as an independent method is not effective in vocational training.

According to Bedny (1979), Subjects performed tasks that involved inserting pins into the holes of a pin-board. The behaviour in this task is overt. The actions and their sequence as performed by subjects may be precisely observed. Subjects were divided into two groups. One group used individual training by direct experience; the other used training through observation. Learning by direct experience was significantly superior to that of learning by observation.

(2) Learning by Imitation: Much of human learning is a function of imitating and observing the behaviour and action of others and these are also the main processes through which children acquire new experiences and behaviour. Imitation is copying or reproducing others' actions or behaviours. One does not imitate everybody one comes across. One chooses consciously or otherwise a person for imitating some of his/her behaviours or actions that attract him/her. Such a person becomes a model for imitation. The model can be a person with whom the child/individual has direct contact like the parents, siblings, teacher, or any other adult member with some quality to be imitated. There are other persons with whom the child has no direct contact but can be models for imitation. Examples of such models maybe great men from history and mythology like Ashoka, Shivaji, Akbar, Gandhi, Nehru, Mother Teresa or Sri Ram, Sri Krishna, Mirabai, Jesus or popular film stars, players, artists etc. Even the characters from popular comics are sometimes imitated by young children. Such models are called symbolic models. Very often, parents, siblings and teachers project before the child well-known persons of eminence. Such models either real or symbolic are called exemplary models.

(3) Learning by Trial and Error: The basic findings on trial and error learning have come from using laboratory animals in a variety of situations. Putting rats in a maze and recording the number of trials and errors for each test run has contributed much of the information important to trial-and-error learning. Take the price list again. If we had never seen the earlier list, we could not learn the new list by association. We would have to read through the list, remove it from sight, and try to repeat the details from memory. This is called recitation. If we could not recall certain points, we would continue memorising and reciting until we could repeat the list without a single error. The list would then have been learned by trial and error.

(4) Learning by Insight: Kohler, a German psychologist and a pioneer in Gestalt psychology, performed experiments with a chimpanzee that led to an awareness of the importance of insight. He placed the chimpanzee in a cage and put a banana outside it, beyond the reach of the animal. He furnished a potential tool in the form of sticks that could be joined together like a fishing pole. A single part would not reach the lure, hence the chimpanzee needed to get "insight" to see that by joining the pieces of the stick, the food could be reached.

The routing problem provides an example. We are not likely to solve it satisfactorily by either association or trial and error. The possibility of traveling the territory in a variety of ways is not feasible in terms of time, cost, and risk. The only realistic approach is insight. Armed with customer and prospect lists, as well as maps and perhaps a computer program, we can simulate and evaluate various solutions until we reach the best combination of calls. Insight is necessary to solve routing problems.

Q8. What is the meaning and nature of transfer of learning? Elaborate the types of transfer of learning and their classroom implication.

Ans. Transfer is basic to all learning. The relationship between the present learning task and what has already been learned constitutes the phenomenon of transfer of learning. Almost all the learned behaviour is inter-related and almost all learning is influenced by transfer. Hence, transfer of learning may be defined as the influence of prior practices or learning upon the learning and performance of new skills. That influence may improve, be detrimental or have no effect on the learning and performance of a new skill. Thus, when the learning of one task or skill influences the mastery of later task, the condition is called transfer of learning. It deserves careful consideration in the learning process.

Some of the definitions are as follows:

- According to Skinner, "Transfer of training is concerned with the question of whether or not the learning of material A–say mathematics-aids, hinders or does not affect the subsequent learning of material B-say Physics or Chemistry."
- In the words of *Crow* and *Crow,* "The carry-over of habit of thinking, feeling or working of knowledge or of skills from one learning area to another is usually referred to as the transfer of training."
- *Peterson* says, "Transfer is generalisation, for it is extension of idea to a new field."
- *Guthrie* and *Powers* state, "Transfer may be defined, as a process of extending and applying behaviour."
- *H.C. Ellis* in his book, *"The Transfer"* defines that "transfer of learning means that experience or performance on one task influences performance on some subsequent task." According to him, "transfer is the application or carry over of knowledge, skills, habits, attitudes or other responses from the situation in which they were initially acquired to some other situation for which they were not specifically learned."
- According to Hilgard, transfer of learning is possible only when a person develops the ability of finding out the identity of relationships and using it to solve solutions in new situations and for this, insight is necessary.

From the point of view of psychologists the following interferences concerning the nature of transfer of learning:

- Transfer of learning can also be viewed as problem solving, in which experience in one task influences the performance of another.
- Transfer of learning comes from similarity of contents, similarity of techniques, similarity of principles, or a combination of these.

Types of transfer of learning: Depending on the learning situations faced by the learners, the following three kinds of transfer can occur:

- **Positive Transfer of Learning:** When learning of one task facilitates the learning of second task, or the past learning of one activity helps in the learning of another activity, it is known as positive transfer of learning. A sportsman playing football plays hockey nicely. A bus driver can drive a truck also equally efficiently. It means that performance on one task may aid or facilitate performance of second task. When precious experience may help or promote the learning of a newly introduced skill or task, the situation is called 'positive transfer'. For example, if writing of English facilitates the writing of Hindi, transfer is positive in nature. A sportsman playing basketball plays volleyball also nicely. A bus-driver can drive a truck also equally efficiently.
- **Negative Transfer of Learning:** A situation may be called 'negative transfer' if it may impede or interfere with the learning of a new task. In this case, learning of one task makes the learning of a second task difficult. When the previously learnt activity interferes with the learning of another activity, it is known as negative transfer. For example, writing in Gurmukhi script hinders in writing Devanagari script. Negative transfer is also called habit interference as some form of interference called 'Retroactive Inhibition' occurs in the negative aspect of this process. Herein, learning of one task makes the learning of a second task harder. Learning shorthand by Danton method may cause interference in subsequent learning by Pitman method.
- **Zero transfer of learning:** Transfer is said to be 'zero' when learning or training in one situation does not have any significant influence over the learning or training in another situation. Such a situation may arise when the learning activities and subject areas have nothing in common between them. In such cases, it is quite natural that possession of knowledge and skill related to one area may have no or quite minimal effect on the acquisition of knowledge and skill related to another area.

Classroom Implications: Knowledge, skills and methods of learning which learners use in relation to definite school tasks remain available in the future and also applies to solve new problems. With this assumption in mind, the knowledge of nature of transfer of learning helps in finding answers to some crucial questions like - what type of learning in the school will help learners in solving problems in daily life. On the basis of the results of educationist investigations, they recommended that education must be life-centered to facilitate transfer of learning. School activities should have the tint and texture of the activities which the learners are expected to come across in his daily life. Problem-solving and discussion methods are more useful in promoting the power of transfer. Cramming should be replaced by meaningful learning. Learners should be trained to form generalisation and they should be made self-reliant in solving new problems.

Q9. What is learning approach? Examine various approaches to learning.

Ans. Learning approaches describe and explain the conditions under which learning does not does not take place. This movement is towards theorizing the process of learning. It attempts to provide a definite coherence to one particular subset of experimental findings in the field of learning.

Surface approach and Deep approach are two types of approaches prevailing in the world of learning.

Surface learners tended to concentrate on the writer's main point, and reproducing the main facts. Associated with anxiety in learning, the surface learners were dispassionate with the material. The students felt pressurised and rushed into retention of information; thus, they only memorised and did not understand the meaning behind the material. When it comes to recalling information, surface learning is not as effective because less information is remembered as efforts are placed on memorisation rather than understanding.

Deep learners transformed the knowledge they gained by exploring it beyond the main point. Deep learners aimed to understand the meaning behind the text, and interacted with the material by creating relevant arguments and examples related to their daily lives. Rather than memorisation, the learners engaged and thought critically about the information. They showed great interest and were calm in their learning of the information. As deep learners are more engaged information is more likely to be retained long-term.

Strategic learning, can be considered to be a balance between the two approaches. In this approach, the learner's intention is to get the highest possible marks or grades in the term-end examinations. To achieve this, s/he may choose either of the two approaches. But the most important characteristics of the strategic approach are well-planned and carefully organised study methods with the systematic management of time and efforts.

Q10. What is the concept of behaviouristic approach to learning? Explain its characteristics, limitations and educational implication.

Ans. Behaviorism is primarily concerned with observable and measurable aspects of human behavior. In defining behavior, behaviorist learning theories emphasise changes in behavior that result from stimulus-response associations made by the learner. Behavior is directed by stimuli. An individual selects one response instead of another because of prior conditioning and psychological drives existing now of the action.

Behaviorists assert that the only behaviors worthy of study are those that can be directly observed. Thus, it is actions, rather than thoughts or emotions, which are the legitimate object of study. Behaviorist theory does not explain abnormal behavior in terms of the brain or its inner workings. Rather, it posits that all behavior is learned habits, and attempts to account for how these habits are formed.

Characteristic of Behaviouristic Approach: Important characteristics of the behaviouristic approach are following:

- It chief emphasis is on environment. This approach considers environment more important than heredity in the determination of behaviour.
- The chief method of learning is condition.
- Behaviourists believe in the objective study of behaviour - animal and human being both (objectively observable behaviour).
- Behaviourists believe that one unit of knowledge gets associated with a new unit of knowledge by virtue of similarity, contrast or contiguity (closeness of occurrence in time or situation).
- Conditioning is the key to the understanding of behaviour, which is composed of stimulus and response links and can be successfully analysed by the objective scientific method.

Limitations of Behaviouristic Approach: Some of the limitations of behaviouristic approach are as follows:

- This approach explains emotions, thoughts and actions entirely with reference to only this over behaviour.
- It is argued that the behaviourists have ignored the structural and hereditary factors which are very important in the development of psychological process of language.
- The operant reinforcement system does not adequately take into account the elements of creativity, curiosity and spontaneity in the human beings.
- The approach considers human being as a machine which may not be true.
- Skinner's theory of learning dehumanises the learning process on account of its emphasis on the mechanisation of the mental process.
- Behaviourists argue that all human behaviour is acquired during the lifetime of the individual. Thus this theory gives no place to the importance of genetic inheritance.
- Operant theory of learning does not deal with the depth of mind and thus it is artificial in nature.
- It is doubtful if the results derived from controlled experimental studies on animals would yield the same results on human beings in social learning situations.

Educational Implications

One of the most important contributions to learning is the behaviouristic approach which throws light on habit formation, habit breaking and the role of incentives in learning. This approach is helpful in shaping the behaviour of students in the desired direction. Skinner has demonstrated in a number of ways how operant behaviour is shaped. The approach also helps the teacher in increasing the vocabulary of his students.

The most significant contribution to this theory in educational practice is the concept of programmed learning and introduction of teaching machines in teaching-learning.

Programmed instruction: Programmed instruction is a method of presenting new subject matters to students in a graded sequence of controlled steps. Students work through the programmed material by themselves at their own speed and after each step test their comprehension by answering an examination question or filling in a diagram. They are then immediately shown the correct answer or given additional information. Programmed Instruction is highly individualised instructional strategy and is an effective innovation in the teaching process. It is found quite useful for classroom as well as self-learning.

Teaching machine: The teaching machine is composed of mainly a program, which is a system of combined teaching and test items that carries the student gradually through the material to be learned. The "machine" is composed by a fill-in-the-blank method either on a workbook or in a computer. If the subject is correct, he/she gets reinforcement and moves on to the next question. If the answer is incorrect, the subject studies the correct answer to increase the chance of getting reinforced next time. Constructed-response and multiple-choice machines are the types of teaching machine.

Q11. Delineate Pavlov's classical conditioning.

Or

Discuss the process of classical conditioning.

Ans. Ivan Pavlov (1849-1936) demonstrated and articulated a form of learning known as classical conditioning. Pavlov was a behaviourist. This means that his theories focussed on observable behaviour. This is due to the reason that behaviour can be measured and thought cannot be measured. Pavlov viewed individual differences in personality as the result of learning and different environmental experiences.

Classical conditioning refers to a learning procedure in which a biologically potent stimulus (e.g. food) is paired with a previously neutral stimulus (e.g. a bell). It also refers to the learning process that results from this pairing, through which the neutral stimulus comes to elicit a response (e.g. salivation) that is usually similar the one elicited by the potent stimulus.

Pavlov identified four essential elements of the learning processes. They are as follows:

(1) **Unconditioned stimulus (UCS):** The natural stimulus that elicits a natural response. In Pavlov's experiment, the meat powder was the UCS.

(2) **Unconditioned Response (UCR):** The natural response elicited to the natural stimulus. In Pavlov's experiment, the salivation was the UCR.

(3) **Conditioned Stimulus (CS):** The neutral stimulus that does not naturally elicit the target response, but may do so after being associated with the UCS for a number of times. In Pavlov's experiment, the light or the sound of the bell was the CS.

(4) **Conditioned Response (CR):** The target response similar to the UCR that originally occurred to the UCS only, but after conditioning occurred to CS, even in absence of the UCS. In Pavlov's experiment, the salivation that occurred in response to the light or bell was the CR. The UCR and the CR are similar but not the same. Pavlov noticed that the amount of salivation was less in response to the light/bell in comparison to the original salivation in response to meat powder.

Process of classical conditioning: In Pavlov's experiment, a researcher first attached a capsule to a dog's salivary gland to measure salivary flow. A bell was rung, every time, the dog Sam was given the meat powder. This was repeated several times. Later, Pavlov observed that the dog salivated at the mere sound of the bell, without the meat powder being followed. Thus, the dog had been conditioned to respond to a new stimulus which was previously an unconditioned response.

The meat powder is the unconditioned stimulus (UCS); salivation is the unconditioned response (UCR) sound of the bell is the conditioned stimulus (CS) and salivation at the sound of the bell is the conditioned response (CR).

Before Conditioning

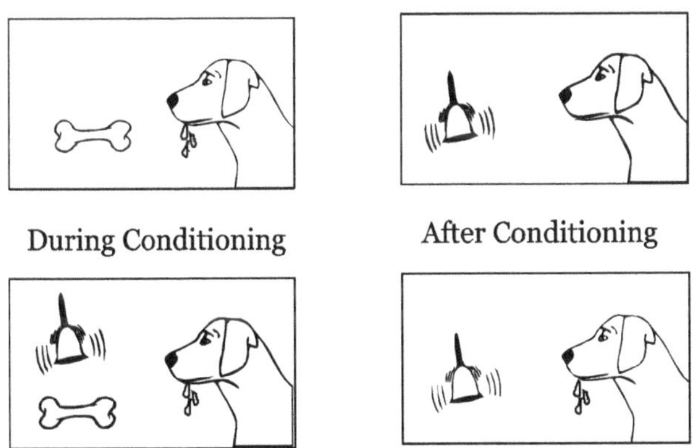

Fig 1.1: Pavlov's Classical Conditioning

Pavlov's theory is that CS (bell) simply as a result of pairing with the UCS (meat powder) acquires the capacity to substitute for the UCS in evoking the response. This means that an association is formed between the CS and the UCS, so that the CS becomes the equivalent of the UCS in eliciting response.

CS (Bell) ⟶ (Exploratory Responses)

UCS (Food) ⟶ CR (Saliva)

Pavlov believed that this association took place in the brain. Two areas of the brain, one for the UCS and the other for the CS became activated during classical conditioning and the activation of UCS area resulted in a reflex or automatic response.

Pavlov showed us how a significant internal process such as learning can be studied objectively.

Principles of Classical Conditioning: Some of the important principles of classical conditioning, which govern the following:

(1) Acquisition: Acquisition is the initial learning of the stimulus-response link, which involves a neutral stimulus being associated with the UCS and becomes the conditioned stimulus (CS) that elicits the CR. Two important aspects of acquisition are timing and predictability.

The time interval between the CS and the UCS is one of the most important aspects of classical conditioning (Kotani, Kawahara, and Kirino, 2002; Weidemann, Georgilas, and Kehoe, 1999). Conditioned responses develop when the CS and UCS occur close together. Often, optimal spacing is a fraction of a second (Kimble, 1961). In Pavlov's work, if the bell had rung 20 minutes after the presentation of the food, the dog probably would not have associated the bell with the food.

Robert Rescorla (1966, 1988) believes that, for classical conditioning to take place, not only must the time interval in the CS-UCS connection be brief but also the occurrence of one stimulus must be contingent on, or predictable from, the presence of another.

(2) Generalisation and Discrimination: Pavlov found that the dog salivated in response not only to the tone of the bell but also to other sounds, such as a whistle. Although Pavlov did not pair these sounds with the unconditioned stimulus of the food, he discovered that the more similar the noise was to the original sound of the bell, the stronger was the dog's salivary flow. Generalisation in classical conditioning is the tendency of a new stimulus that is similar to the original conditioned stimulus to elicit a response that is similar to the conditioned response (Jones, Kemenes and Benjamin, 2001). Generalisation has value in preventing learning from being tied to specific stimuli. For example, we do not have to learn how to drive all over again when we change cars or drive down a different road.

Stimulus generalisation is not always beneficial. For example, a cat that generalises from a minnow to a piranha has a major problem. Discrimination in classical conditioning is the process of learning to respond to certain stimuli and not to respond to others (Murphy, Baker, and Fouquet, 2001). To produce discrimination, Pavlov gave food to the dog only after ringing the bell and not after any other sounds. In this way, the dog soon learned to distinguish between the bell and other sounds.

(3) Extinction and Spontaneous Recovery: After conditioning the dog to salivate at the sound of a bell, Pavlov rang the bell repeatedly in a single session and did not give the dog any food. Eventually the dog stopped salivating. This result is extinction, which, in classical conditioning, is the weakening of the conditioned response in the absence of the unconditioned stimulus. Without continued association with the unconditioned stimulus (UCS), the conditioned stimulus (CS) loses its power to elicit the conditioned response (CR).

Extinction is not always the end of a conditioned response (Brooks, 2000). The day after Pavlov extinguished the conditioned salivation to the sound of a bell, he took the dog to the laboratory and rang the bell, still not giving the dog any meat powder. The dog salivated, indicating that an extinguished response can spontaneously recur.

Spontaneous recovery is the process in classical conditioning by which a conditioned response recurs after a delay without further conditioning. Consider an example of spontaneous recovery you may have had: You thought that you had totally forgotten about (extinguished) an old "love". Then, all of a sudden you are in a particular context and get a mental image of the person along with an emotional reaction to him or her from the past (spontaneous recovery).

Q12. Explain the Skinner's operant conditioning theory.

Ans. Skinner is regarded as the father of Operant Conditioning, but his work was based on Thorndike's (1905) law of effect. The theory of Skinner is based on the idea that learning is a function of change in overt behaviour.

Operant conditioning (or instrumental conditioning) is a type of learning in which an individual's behaviour is modified by its antecedents and consequences. It is a method of learning that occurs through rewards and punishments for behaviour. Through operant conditioning, an association is made between a behaviour and a consequence for that behaviour.

In the late 1930s, Skinner (a Harvard psychologist) created the operant box. It is a simple box in which the animal is reinforced by providing a food pallet/water arrangement. Hence, positive reinforcement enhances the lever pressing (rat). The lever (the CS) is presented just before the food pallet, i.e. the US, and then it is withheld until the next trail.

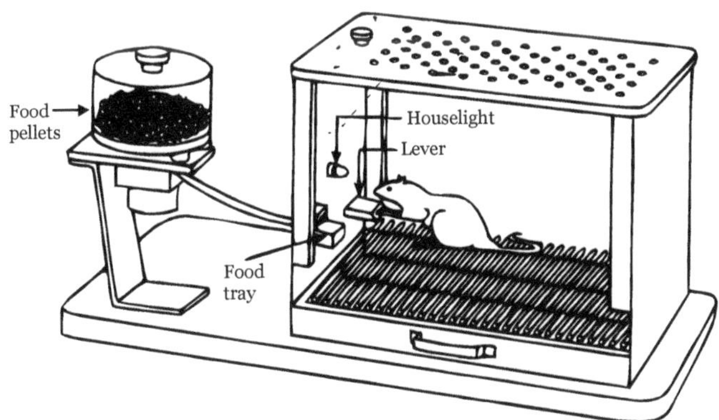

Fig 1.2: Skinner's Operant Conditioning

Components of Operant Conditioning: Some key concepts in operant conditioning are as follows:

(1) **Extinction:** This occurs when a behaviour (response) that had previously been reinforced is no longer effective. For example, a rat is first given food many times for lever presses. Then, in "extinction", no food is given. Typically the rat continues to press more and more slowly and eventually stops, at which time lever pressing is said to be "extinguished".

(2) **Schedules of reinforcement:** A schedule of reinforcement determines when and how often reinforcement of a behaviour is given. Schedules of reinforcement play an important role in the learning process of operant conditioning since the speed and strength of the response can be significantly impacted by when and how often a behaviour is reinforced (Van Wagner, 2010b). Two types of reinforcement schedules are: continuous reinforcement and intermittent reinforcement.

In continuous reinforcement, the desired behaviour is reinforce every single time it occurs. Once the response if firmly established, reinforcement is usually switched to a partial reinforcement schedule. In partial reinforcement, the response is reinforced only part of the time. Learned behaviours are acquired more slowly with partial reinforcement though there are more resistance to extinction.

According to Skinner's theory the following procedure is applied to ensure effective learning in students:

(i) For developing motivation among the students, the classroom reinforcers like praise, blames, grades, etc., should be used.

(ii) Learning objectives should be defined very specifically in terms of behaviour.

(iii) Reinforcers should be used periodically so that the possibility of extinction of the desired behaviour is resisted.

(iv) In the classroom, the principle of immediacy of reinforcement is very important. Praise for a job done well given immediately can be stronger reinforcer or motivator than a grade given much later.

(v) Objectives should be arranged in order of simple to complex.

(vi) Proper use of positive and negative gestures also serves as reinforcers to work.

Q13. Elaborate the concept of cognitive approach to learning. What is their educational implication?

Ans. In the cognitive approach, learning is considered as inner psychological functioning such as perception, concept formation, attention, memory and problem solving. The word "cognition" is derived from the Latin word 'cognoscrere' that means to know, or to perceive. Cognitive theories discuss how people gain an understanding of themselves and their environment and how, in using this, they act in relation to their environment.

Cognitive approach emphasises and gives importance to cognition in learning. According to this approach, learning is a complex process and it is viewed as acquiring changes in the cognitive structure. These changes take place generally in three ways, which are also basic in nature. They are: Differentiations, Generalisation and Restructurisation.

According to cognitive approach, learning is a complex process and it is viewed as acquiring changes in the cognitive structure. In other words, learning is the change in the cognitive structure. These changes take generally in three ways. They are: Differentiation, Generalisation and Restructuration.

(i) **Differentiation:** In this learning beings by differentiating specific aspects of oneself and of one's environment. For example, an infant perceives every woman as his/her mother. Later on, s/he differentiates between mother, aunt, sister, etc. Thus, the cognitive structure becomes more specific.

(ii) **Generalisation:** Concrete and particular instances are given and the children reach general conclusion or generalisation. After differentiating the concept, the child gradually categories the differentiated concepts on the basis of specific unifying characteristics known as generalisation. For example, the child first learns to differentiate between various things as men, women, animals, birds, etc. and later on s/he unifies these differentiated concepts to form a single concept- living things and thus generalisation is reached.

(iii) **Restructuration:** As the processes of differentiation and generalisation take place, the individual restructures his cognitive structure to accommodate these differentiated and generalised concepts to gain control of him/her and the world. The child learns that all living things do not behave as human beings do. Thus, the concept of living things is restructured.

Educational Implications: Important direct/indirect educational implications of Piaget's approach to cognitive development are as follow:

- Instructions must include action and should be brief.
- Students will not be able to follow instructions continuously, they need gaps.
- Visuals should be used for teaching.
- The teacher needs to understand that each student may have a completely different understanding about the concept being discussed in the class.
- Practical experience will help learners to involve more in teaching-learning processes.
- Play-way method is the most appropriate way to teach this age group. They enjoy playing house, dressing up and so on. Parents and teachers must use this idea while teaching them.
- Children should be allowed to explore as much as they can with toys, sand, water and so on. This will help them to learn conservation of various concepts.

- Children should be taught to relate their experiences with what they are being taught. They should be provided opportunities of authentic learning.
- Provide concrete experiences for learning. Simple experiments with concrete object will facilitate their cognitive development.
- Avoid giving too much to read. Provide limited reading. More focus should be given on concrete objects and their manipulation.
- Multi dimension modes should be used.
- Part learning and teaching should be more emphasised than mass practice.
- Complex ideas should be taught with simple examples.
- Use analogies to show the relationship of new material to already acquired knowledge.
- Children involve hypothetical reasoning in their thinking process. Abstract problems can be given to the learner.
- Imagination based task should be provided to learners and students encouraged to use their imagination to solve the problems.
- Teachers should provide space to learn and understand concepts, beyond rote recalling of facts.
- Developing abstract reasoning skills does not mean that the teacher should stop using concrete objects. The teacher should continue to use concrete experiences and objects.
- Ask students to formulate their questions and let them answer these questions.
- Discussion forms should be formulated to solve the problem scientifically.

Q14. What are the characteristics and limitations of cognitive approach?

Ans. Characteristics of Cognitive Approach: Characteristics of the cognitive approach are following:

- Earlier more emphasis was given of insight, while the modern cognitivists emphases more importance on the human mental process, which is similar to computer system in operation.
- Here, learning is considered as an active and dynamic process.
- The perceptions of the learner are processed through differentiation, generalisation and restructurisation, which help the learner in reacting to the specific cognitive structure to get a clear picture of the environment.
- The learner is purposive, and interacting within the field of his or her goals.
- This approach is represented by a dynamic system and most suited for concept formation, problem solving and other higher mental process.

Limitations of Cognitive approach: Piaget's approach to learning has some limitations also. The important limitations are as follows:

- More emphasis is on concepts of relationships and it does not investigate nominal concepts.

- Piaget's entire work lacks in use of scientific method in his study.
- It is lengthy and time consuming; no direct teaching is involved.
- Mathematics and Science cannot be thought in early childhood.
- Piaget does not seem to make his terminology very clear to his readers.
- He is too preoccupied with numerous epistemological considerations.
- Tailoring narrow exercises for individual children is both impractical and unnecessary.
- The child does not notice the contradictions in his or her own explanations.
- Children may lose confidence in their ability to figure things out.
- A child cannot engage in abstract thought and cannot perform any useful scientific activity.
- The preoperational child or even the concrete operational child is not yet ready for reading since his thought structures are as yet primitive.

Q15. Explain Jean Piaget's Cognitive approach to leaning.

Or

Discuss key concepts of Piaget's Theory

Ans. Jean Piaget (1896-1980) was one of the most influential theorists in the field of cognitive development. Piaget was a philosopher, biologist, educationalist and psychologist. He made the decision to study scientifically the way in which children develop knowledge.

It was Piaget who first noted that children were not just miniature replicas of adults, but in fact were different in the ways in which they thought about and interpreted the world. Piaget's idea was that adults did not simply know more than children, but that their knowledge was structured differently. Indeed, Piaget suggested that children at different stages of their development thought about and interpreted their worlds in different ways (Hummel, 1998). Piaget developed the idea of children as "little scientists" who were engaged in active exploration, seeking understanding and knowledge'.

Jean Piaget's theory of cognitive development redefines intelligence, knowledge and the relationship of the learner to the environment. Intelligence, like a biological system is continuing process that creates structures. In continuing interactions with environment, s/he needs intelligence. Similarly, knowledge is an interactive process between the learner and the environment. Knowledge is highly subjective in infancy and early childhood and becomes more objective in early adulthood.

Key concepts of Piaget's Theory: Jean Piaget viewed intellectual growth as a process of adaptation (adjustment) to the world. This happens through:

(1) **Schemas:** To Piaget, a schema is an organised system of actions or a mental representation that people use to understand the world and interact with it (Piaget, 1952). The child is born with simple schemas comprising basic reflexes

such as sucking. This schema obviously has adaptive value, since the infant needs to obtain nourishment from its mother's breast or the bottle by sucking.

(2) **Adaptation:** According to Piaget, adaptation is a process by which people adapt or change to function more effectively to meet challenges they face in the environment. Through adaptation, we adjust our schemas to meet the changing demands the environment imposes on us.

(3) **Accommodation:** Accommodation is the process of altering existing schemas or creating new ones to deal with objects or experiences that don't fit readily into existing schemas.

(4) **Assimilation:** Assimilation is the process of incorporating new objects or situations into existing schemas. For example, newborns will reflexively suck any object placed in their mouths, such as a finger or even a piece of cloth.

(5) **Equilibration:** This is the force which moves development along. Piaget believed that cognitive development did not progress at a steady rate, but rather in leaps and bounds. It occurs when a child's schemas can deal with most new information through assimilation. However, an unpleasant state of disequilibrium occurs when new information cannot be fitted into existing schemas (assimilation). Equilibration is the force which drives the learning process as we do not like to be frustrated and will seek to restore balance by mastering the new challenge (accommodation).

Stages of cognitive development: Piaget's four stages of cognitive (or intellectual) development are as follows:

(1) **Sensory Motor Stage (Birth to 2 years):** A period of time between birth and age two during which an infant's knowledge of the world is limited to his or her sensory perceptions and motor activities. As such, their behaviours limited to simple motor responses caused by sensory stimuli. At the start of this stage, children's behaviour is dominated by reflexes but by the end of it, they can use mental images. During this stage, children acquire the concept of object permanence, realising that objects still exist even when the objects are not present.

(2) **Preoperational stage (Ages 2 to 7):** At this stage, kids learn through pretend play but still struggle with logic and taking the point of view of other people. They also often struggle with understanding the ideal of constancy. For example, a researcher might take a lump of clay, divide it into two equal pieces, and then give a child the choice between two pieces of clay to play with. One piece of clay is rolled into a compact ball while the other is smashed into a flat pancake shape. Since the flat shape looks larger, the preoperational child will likely choose that piece even though the two pieces are exactly the same size.

(3) **Concrete operation stage (Ages 7 to 11):** This stage begins around age seven and continues until approximately age twelve. Kids at this point of development begin to think more logically, but their thinking can also be very rigid. They tend to struggle with abstract and hypothetical concepts. At this point, children also become less egocentric and begin to think about how other people might think and feel. Kids in the concrete operational stage also begin to understand that their thoughts are unique to them and that not everyone else necessarily shares their thoughts, feelings, and opinions.

(4) **Formal operational stage (11 Years and above):** Formal operational stage is characterised by abstract thinking and the beginning of adolescent thinking. During the formal operational stage, a child is engaged in abstract thinking. S/he does not take anything for granted. Formal operations consist of four overlapping logical abilities, namely: (i) Hypothetico-Deductive Thinking; (ii) Inductive Thinking; (iii) Reflective Thinking; and (iv) Interpropositional Logic (Dandpani, 2001).

Q16. State the social learning approach in brief.

Ans. The role of social interaction is very important in learning. Bruner (1986) said, "I have come increasingly to recognise that learning in most settings as a communal activity, a sharing of culture." To understand learning social perspective was considered as important one by Bandura in his social learning theory as well as by Lev Vygotsky in his social constructivist approach. These theories are as following:

(1) Social Learning Theory: Bandura and Walter developed social learning theory, which is different from S-R theory of Dollard and Miller. It is based on the premises that behaviour is learned and personality can be explained in terms of the cumulative effects of a series of learning experiences.

Bandura and Walter are also anti-Freudian and rejected psychoanalytic approach is incapable of explaining human behaviour. Most important component of social learning theory is reinforcement. An individual observes the actions of another person (model) who is reinforced or punished for his actions. They introduced the concept of vicarious reinforcement that follows modification of an observer's behaviour by reinforcement provided to the model, which is being observed.

They introduced the concept of self-reinforcement, which works in observational learning. Positive reinforcement and reward are important in social learning. This may be subject to stimulus properties of the model - age, sex and socio-economic status. Those high in socioeconomic status are imitated.

(2) Social-constructivist Approach: Vygotsky developed the social constructivist approach. He emphasised the critical importance of culture and the importance of the social context for cognitive development. Vygotsky's the Zone of Proximal Development is his best known concept. Vygostsky's the Zone of Proximal Development emphasises his belief that learning is fundamentally a socially mediated activity. Thinking and problem solving skills can according to Vygotsky, be placed in three categories. The child can perform some things independently. Others cannot be performed even with help. Between these two extremes are skills the child can perform with help from others. Those skills are in the ZPD. If a child uses these cognitive processes with help of others, such as teachers, parents, and fellow students, they will develop skills that can be independently practiced.

Q17. What do you mean by humanistic approach to learning? Explain its limitations and characteristics.

Ans. Humanistic approaches to learning are based on the principles of humanism and are founded most notably on the work of Abraham Maslow (1908–1970) and Carl Rogers (1902–1987). They center on the learner as an individual and consider that learning is not just about the intellect, but also about educating the "whole person," taking a person's interests, goals, and enthusiasm into account, so that full potential can be achieved. This approach to learning is student centered, with learners encouraged to take responsibility for their own learning and being intrinsically, rather than extrinsically motivated. The primary goal of a humanistic education is human well-being, including the primacy of human values, the development of human potential, and the acknowledgment of human dignity.

The humanistic approach makes use of creativity, belongingness, self-development, co-existence, mental health, values, etc.

Limitations of Humanistic approach: Some of the major limitations of a humanistic approach are as follows:

- To an even greater extent than the psychodynamic approach, humanistic psychology has generated theories and ideas that have proved very difficult to test by scientific investigation.
- Because the subject matter of humanistic psychology is the experience of the individual person, there is a logical problem of applying theories generated from one individual to another. We cannot for example assume that two people experience the same thing when they speak of a peak or spiritual experience.
- Many humanistic ideas (particularly those around the development of the self) are extremely culture bound, and cannot easily be applied to a range of societies or historical periods.
- The humanistic emphasis on the individual person means that the importance of external influences on people's lives have probably been underestimated. As Lerman (1992) has pointed out, battered wife can learn through humanistic psychology that she has a right not to be abused, but it does not in itself allow her to leave the situation safely.

Characteristics of Humanistic approach: The important characteristics of humanistic approach are as follow:

- This approach emphasises on learning in natural environment of human love, peace cooperation, freedom, equality rather than of physical values, money, wealth, etc.

- It believes in co-existence and considers the best learning as based on truth, good and beautiful.
- It is concerned with the welfare of all human beings.
- It increases learner's reactivity and develops interests in the arts.
- It emphasis on self-motivation for better learning.
- It emphasis is on learning at the higher level i.e. self-transcendence and self-actualisation.
- Learning is experience-based.
- To increase the learner's self-direction and independence.
- It believes that learning becomes effective when is need-based.
- It helps learners take more responsibility for determining what they are learning.

Q18. Examine the educational implication of humanistic approach.

Ans. The main implications of the humanistic approach to the learning process are following:

(1) **Place of the child in teaching-learning:** According to this approach student plays a central role in whole teaching-learning process. This approach believes in child-centered-education. This approach, considers that we should first understand the needs, interests, abilities, age level, attitudes, aptitude of students then try to organise teaching learning process according to these. It emphasises on reach, touch and teaches the child according to his nature, and interests. All teaching material and its process must be related to individual characteristics of students.

(2) **Emphasis on individuality:** In this approach, every individual has his own individuality. Teacher should respect and develop this individuality through education. Individual differences should be respected and internal virtues of individual be developed. Teacher should understand this individuality and organise his/her teaching-learning process according to this individuality.

(3) **Understanding the child:** According to humanistic approach, we should understand the child first of all, and then teach him. As a teacher, should know our students, their interest, personality, capabilities and background environment and use teaching methods and content accordingly. Because this approach believes in student centered education so before teaching, a teacher should understand students thoroughly.

(4) **Method of teaching:** In this approach, teacher should use methods of teaching which are based on psychological principles. Teacher should not use teacher centered and traditional methods of teaching in it. Teacher should emphasise on active learning which could consider the learner. Teacher should use the methods which could teach according to needs, interests, abilities and attitudes of learners.

(5) **Discipline:** Teacher should not force student to be disciplined. He/she should encourage self-discipline and self-control among students. Students should be given the responsibility of to be disciplined.

(6) **Place and role of the teacher:** According to this approach, student plays a central role in teaching learning process. Teacher acts as a guide, friend or helper of the students. "The tutor or lecturer tends to be more supportive than critical, more understanding than judgmental, more genuine than playing a role." Their job is to foster an engaging environment for the students and ask inquiry-based questions that promote meaningful learning.

Q19. Discuss Maslow's Hierarchy of human needs.

Ans. Maslow was humanistic psychologist. He set up a hierarchic theory of needs. Humans start with a very weak disposition that is then shaped fully as they grow. If the environment is right, people will grow, actualising the potentials they have inherited. If the environment is not 'right' (and mostly it is not), they will not.

Maslow set up a hierarchy of five levels of basic needs. However, they can be broadly classified into basic needs, psychological needs and self-fulfilment needs. Beyond these needs, higher levels of needs exist. These include needs for understanding, aesthetic appreciation and purely spiritual needs. In the levels of the five basic needs, the person does not feel the second need until the demands of the first have been satisfied, or the third until the second has been satisfied and so on. Maslow's basic needs are as follows:

(1) **Physiological Needs:** These are biological needs. They consist of needs for oxygen, food, water and a relatively constant body temperature. They are the strongest needs because if a person were deprived of all needs, the physiological ones would come first in the person's search for satisfaction.

(2) **Safety Needs***:* When all physiological needs are satisfied and are no longer controlling thoughts and behaviours, the needs for security can become active. Adults have little awareness of their security needs except in times of emergency or periods of disorganisation in the social structure (such as at the time of communal riots). Consequently, children often display signs of insecurity and the need to be safe.

(3) **Needs for Love, Affection and Belongingness:** When the needs for safety and physiological well-being are satisfied, the next class of needs is for love, affection and belongingness. Maslow stated that people seek to overcome feelings of loneliness and alienation. This involves both giving and receiving love, affection and a sense of belonging.

(4) **Needs for Esteem:** When the first three classes of needs are satisfied, the needs for esteem can become dominant. These involve needs for both self-esteem and the esteem in which a

person is held by others. Humans have a need for a stable, firmly based, high level of self-respect and respect from others. When these needs are satisfied, the person feels self-confident and valuable as a person in the world. When these needs are frustrated, the person feels inferior, weak, helpless and worthless.

(5) **Needs for Self-actualisation:** When all of the above mentioned needs are satisfied, only then are the needs for self-actualisation activated. Maslow described selfactualisation as a person's need to be and do that which the person was 'born to do.' 'A musician must make music, an artist must paint and a poet must write.' These needs make themselves reflect themselves in signs of restlessness. The person is on edge, feels tense, lacking something, in short, restless. If a person is hungry, unsafe, not loved or accepted, or lacking in self-esteem, it is very to know what the person is restless about. It is not always clear what a person wants when there is a need for self-actualisation.

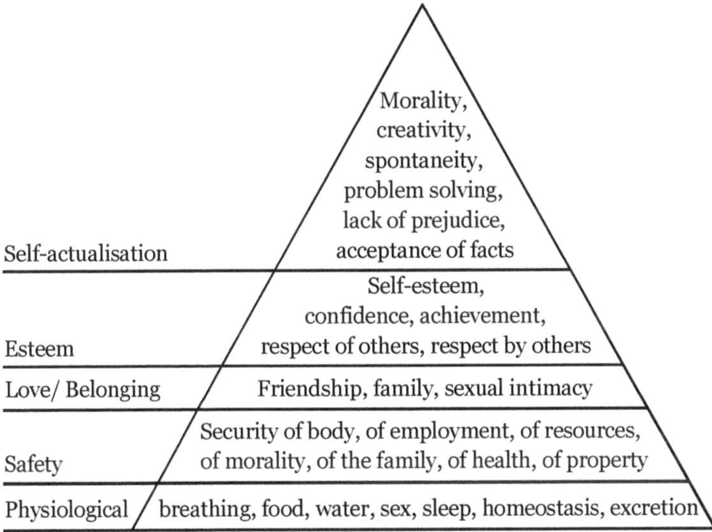

Fig 1.3: Maslow's Need Hierarchy

Q20. What do you mean by constructivism? Discuss the contribution of Dewey's in it.

Ans. Constructivism is a theory, which regards learning as an active process in which, learners construct and internalise new concepts, ideas and knowledge based on their own present and past knowledge and experiences. According to John Dewey, "Only by wrestling with the condition of the problem at hand, seeking and finding his own solution (not in isolation but in correspondence with the teaching and other pupils) does one learn."

Constructivist instructional practices, whether in the area of science, social studies, reading, writing, or any other have the following common characteristics:

- Learning and instruction is organised around important ideas;
- Adequacy of learner's prior knowledge is challenged and acknowledged;
- Learning is viewed as a Joint Cognitive Venture; and
- Learners are taught "how to learn" and their knowledge acquisition is assessed during the lesson itself.

Constructivist Theory of John Dewey

Learning is a process of construction based on the educational theory of John Dewey. Dewey, an early constructivist articulated a philosophy of education that would prepare students for work, citizenship, and life in a free society.

His most comprehensive work, Democracy and Education, first published in 1915, provides the foundation for inquiry learning. It incorporates the experience, action, and thinking of the whole child. Dewey explained that, "education is not an affair of telling and being told but an active and constructive process." He cautioned that, "The accumulation and acquisition of information for purposes of reproduction in recitation and examination is made too much of. Knowledge in the sense of information means working capital, the indispensable resources of further inquiry of finding out or learning more things" Guided Inquiry is based on this concept of information as "working capital" for constructing understanding and knowledge for each learner.

John Dewey emphasised that education should be based on real life experiences. According to him, "If you have doubts about how learning happens, engage in sustained inquiry: study, ponder, consider alternative possibilities and arrive at your belief grounded in evidence."

Q21. What are the views of Vygotsky's and Bruner's on constructivism?

Ans. Vygotsky's view on social constructivism

Vygotsky's theory of socio-cultural learning highlights the role of social and cultural interactions play in the learning process. Vygotsky's theory states that knowledge is co-constructed and that individuals learn from one another. It is called a social constructivist theory because in Vygotsky's opinion the learner must be engaged in the learning process. Learning happens with the assistance of other people, thus contributing the social aspect of the theory. A fundamental aspect of Vygotsky's theory is the **Zone of Proximal Development (ZPD)**. This is a "range of tasks that are too difficult for an individual to master alone, but can be mastered with the assistance or guidance of adults or more-skilled peers (Vygotsky, 1962)." Vygotsky believed that learning takes place within the Zone of Proximal Development. In this, students can, with help from adults or children who are more advanced, master concepts and ideas that they cannot understand on their own. This model has two developmental levels:

- The level of actual development – point the learner has already reached & can problem-solve independently.
- The level of potential development (ZDP) – point the learner is capable of reaching under the guidance of teachers or in collaboration with peers.

The ZDP is the level at which learning takes place. It comprises cognitive structures that are still in the process of maturing, but which can only mature under the guidance of or in collaboration with others.

Another part of this theory is **scaffolding,** which is giving the learner the right amount of assistance at the right time. If the learner can perform a task with some assistance, then s/he is closer to mastering it. This theory is relevant to healthy adolescent development because if students work in pairs, they are interacting with people and therefore can learn different academic ideas from one another. This theory shows that students learn from each other; they can assist one another and co-construct knowledge. Scaffolding is a process through which a teacher or a more competent peer helps the student in his or her ZPD as necessary and tapers off this aid as it becomes unnecessary, much as a scaffold is removed from a building after construction is completed. "Scaffolding is the way the adult guides the child's learning via focused questions and positive interactions." For example, Parents and driving instructors guide driving students along the way by showing them the mechanics of how the car operates the correct hand positions on the steering wheel, the technique of scanning the roadway, etc. As the student progresses, less and less instruction is needed, until they are ready to drive on their own.

Bruner's view on Constructivism

Bruner's theory of constructivism holds that students should be active in the learning process. Such experiential learning allows learners to better process their newfound knowledge and skills. Constructivism is also based on the idea that students construct their learning on past knowledge, and that reasoning plays an important role in the learning process.

Bruner (1915) is a psychologist who has made significant contributions to cognitive psychology and education philosophy. Similar to the other constructivists, Bruner believes that learners construct new ideas or concepts based on their prior knowledge. Learning involves processing information, deriving meaning from experience, forming hypotheses, and making decisions. Through his work, Bruner presents the idea that children are active problem solvers and are capable of exploring more difficult subjects of instruction. As a cognitive psychologist, Bruner is known for the term Scaffolding in educational instruction. Scaffolding is built on Vygotsky's concept of ZPD. A teacher uses scaffolding to assist a child to solve a problem that the child cannot solve alone. Scaffolding beings when a teacher motivates the child to take action and find solutions. With clues, supports, and interconnections, the child can begin, continue, and appreciate the significance of the journey and effort. Bruner believes that the teacher's efforts play an important role in helping the child to progress through the zone of proximal development.

According to Bruner, there are three stages of representation in learning – enactive, iconic, and symbolic. In the enactive stage, knowledge is largely represented in the form of motor responses. Learners may be able to perform a physical task better than describing the exact task that has just been accomplished. In the iconic stage, knowledge is more in visual images. When in the symbolic stage, knowledge is mostly in the form of abstract words, mathematical symbols, and other symbol systems.

Bruner proposes that learners' construct their own knowledge and do this by organising and categorising information using a coding system. Bruner believed that the most effective way to develop a coding system is to discover it rather than being told it by the teacher. The concept of discovery learning implies that students construct their own knowledge for themselves.

Q22. Enumerate Novak's contribution on human constructivism.

Ans. Novak's Theory of Human Constructivism, extends and applies Ausubel's ideas to the classroom by considering a framework of elements in education: the teacher, the learner, the content, the context, and evaluation. Novak says that the fundamental purpose of education is to enable learners to take charge of their own construction of meanings. Construction involves thinking, feeling and attitude; all aspects must be integrated to achieve a different and meaningful learning, especially to create new knowledge. In all educational situations, a share of actions as well as an exchange of meanings (and directions) between teacher and students occurs. The exchange is intellectually constructive and emotionally effective when it results in an improvement of the learner understanding of a part of the knowledge. In other words, when the two agents in the educational environment, teacher and learner, can successfully share or negotiate the meanings of a specific curricular content then meaningful learning occurs. Child tries to identify a relationship between his previous experiences and what is observed, this facilitates construction of new knowledge. According to him, "Knowledge is a human construction that is a natural outgrowth of the capacity of human beings for high levels of meaningful learning".

Novak's one more significant contribution to understand learning process is in form of 'concept maps'. He said that concept maps are the tools, which can help in meaningful construction of new knowledge by examining the existing relationships and deriving new relationships. Concept maps help a learner to organise the scattered views at one place and establish relationships. These maps help learners to learn how to think critically and more creatively. Concept map can also be used as assessment tool, which can help in improving the quality of learning. He said that a teacher should create an environment and help learners in sharing the materials. Learners should develop their own meaning from material. A teacher should appreciate what a learner is learning and tell them that their understanding is never complete. Learning should be an interactive process. He defined learning as:

"Learning is also an affective experience; it is the pain and anxiety of confusion, and the joy and excitement when one recognises that new meanings have been acquired. In my view, the construction of new knowledge in any field is no more than a special kind of meaningful learning."

Q23. What do you understand by constructive learning environment? Discuss its five key practices.

Ans. Constructivist learning environment (CLE) means "a place where learners may work together and support each other as they use a variety of tools and information resources in their guided pursuit of learning goals and problem-solving activities". A learning environment is a place where people can draw upon resources to make sense out of things and construct meaningful solutions to problems. Adding "constructivist" to the front end of the term is a way if emphasising the importance of meaningful, authentic activities that help the learner to construct understandings and develop skills relevant to solving problems.

According to Maor (August 1999), there are five key practices of constructive learning environment, which are as follow:

(1) **Personal constructions of reality:** Personal constructions of reality occur what each individual constructs within their own mind, is their reality. Knowledge comes from the creation of meaning that occurs because of life experiences. Knowledge does not come from someone else, but rather from experience.

(2) **Simulated authentic learning environments:** It occurs when instruction is designed to facilitate, simulate and recreate real-life complexities and occurrences. Authentic learning is concerned with depth of learning rather than the breadth of information sucked in and then spewed out; where memorisation is misdiagnosed as being well-informed. Authentic learning environments provide children with rich experiences and opportunities to construct knowledge in context, and in ways that make sense to their existing knowledge which is based on prior experiences. Also an important characteristic of authentic learning is contextualisation of learning.

(3) **Multiple perspectives:** A classroom committed to constructivist practices would not promote solely sequential, linear-based, didactic assignments or techniques. The teacher would not be seen as "the knower", but would depend upon a resource-based approach where students would generate their own investigations which would require access to varied and large amounts of current and static data. As students become more adept at gathering their own resource information, they must understand the importance of evaluating data for gender, racial, religious or political biases as well as authenticity, trustworthiness and credibility.

(4) **Active learning:** Active learning inherently implies a "doing". A classroom where the teacher has adopted a constructivist approach to learning expects performance and persistence from the learners. The students are expected and encouraged to generate their own ideas and knowledge by execution, exertion, and expansion of the known. Learners cannot construct knowledge just by passively receiving, acquiring, or accepting it; nor by inertly listening nor heeding. Knowledge is not formed during the transmission of it. Therefore the emphasis for

instruction must be on the creation of meaning and understanding while encountering new information or new contexts. Active learners need to be involved by partaking, participating, constructing and cooperating. Active learning must happen in order for knowledge to be owned by the learner. There are strategies, which promotes active learning like simulations, strategy and role-playing games, toolkits and phenomenaria, multimedia learning environments, intentional learning environments, storytelling structures, case studies, socratic dialogues, coaching and scaffolding, learning by design, learning by teaching, group cooperation, collaborative learning and holistic psychotechnologies, etc.

(5) **Collaboration:** The age-old adage of "iron sharpening iron" is indeed true for learners in a variety of guided situations. The natural reaction of mulling over a complex problem or situation with others allows for deeper levels of reasoning, new perspectives, shared responsibilities and greater motivation to remain focused on the task. Teachers need to recognise collaboration as a viable method of creating individual meaning, rather than viewing it as a means of acquiring information from someone else. This action of social negotiation (Vgotzky's) is beneficial and some essential to acquiring specific knowledge.

Collaboration should be used as a learning strategy in a constructivist classroom. A teacher will create such environment to facilitate construction of knowledge in classroom. They have to create such a learning environment where learners can collaborate, create, discuss and develop their own understanding, where they are free to experiment with existing ideas and get opportunity to explore on their own. Teacher's role will be of a facilitator only.

According to Brooks and Brooks (1993), there are some few characteristics of a constructivist teacher. A constructivist teacher is someone who will:

- use a wide variety of materials, including raw data, primary sources, and interactive materials and encourage learners to use them;
- encourage learner to engage in dialogue with the teacher and with one another;
- encourage learner inquiry by asking thoughtful, open-ended questions and encourage learners to ask questions to each other and seek elaboration of learners' initial responses;
- encourage and accept learner's autonomy and initiative;
- provide time for learners to construct relationships and create metaphors;
- assess learner's understanding through application and performance of open-structured tasks;
- engage learners in experiences that show contradictions to initial understandings and then encourage discussion;

- inquire about learner's understandings of concepts before sharing his/her own understanding of those concepts.

Q24. Write a short note on:

(i) Scaffolding

Ans. Scaffolding refers to a variety of instructional techniques used to move students progressively toward stronger understanding and, ultimately, greater independence in the learning process. The term itself offers the relevant descriptive metaphor: teachers provide successive levels of temporary support that help students reach higher levels of comprehension and skill acquisition that they would not be able to achieve without assistance. Like physical scaffolding, the supportive strategies are incrementally removed when they are no longer needed, and the teacher gradually shifts more responsibility over the learning process to the student.

Scaffolding is widely considered to be an essential element of effective teaching, and all teachers—to a greater or lesser extent—almost certainly use various forms of instructional scaffolding in their teaching. In addition, scaffolding is often used to bridge learning gaps—i.e., the difference between what students have learned and what they are expected to know and be able to do at a certain point in their education. For example, if students are not at the reading level required to understand a text being taught in a course, the teacher might use instructional scaffolding to incrementally improve their reading ability until they can read the required text independently and without assistance. One of the main goals of scaffolding is to reduce the negative emotions and self-perceptions that students may experience when they get frustrated, intimidated, or discouraged when attempting a difficult task without the assistance, direction, or understanding they need to complete it.

(ii) Tutoring

Ans. Tutoring is an age-old practice. Tutor as a person who gives additional, special, or basic instruction. The purpose of tutoring is to help students help themselves, or to assist or guide them to the point at which they become an independent learner, and thus no longer need a tutor. Tutoring may be of many kinds:

(1) **Mentor-Tutoring:** Mentoring is about guiding someone in the light of experience the mentor achieved during his/her life time. Mentoring is not only the task to be performed by teachers. Senior learners, retired teachers, some volunteer parents, can act as mentors for the learners, who need individual attention.

(2) **Peer-Tutoring:** Peer tutoring is an instructional strategy that consists of student partnerships, linking high achieving students with lower achieving students or those with comparable achievement, for structured reading and math study sessions. Peer tutor can explain things in a peer language understandable to the students. Same age peer tutoring is more beneficial and effective. The tutor and the tutee are of the same class, which helps them to understand each other better. This also facilitates individual learning.

Q25. Discuss cognitive apprenticeship. Also explain how to use cognitive apprenticeship in classroom?

Ans. Cognitive apprenticeship methods try to enculturate students into authentic practices through activity and social interaction. Cognitive apprenticeships are one of the earliest pedagogical designs to incorporate the theories of situated cognition. Cognitive apprenticeship uses four dimensions (e.g. content, methods, sequence and sociology) to embed learning in activity and make deliberate the use of the social and physical contexts present in the classroom.

Cognitive apprenticeship involves the modeling and coaching of various comprehension skills as teacher and students take turns in assuming the role of instructor. It is a synthesis of formal schooling and traditional apprenticeship.

In cognitive apprenticeship, instructors model the strategies and activities necessary to solve problems such as thinking aloud 'speaking out thinking' while solving a problem; while providing appropriate scaffolds (organisational strategies and other supporting materials) to support the students' own efforts. Coaching and correction are provided as the students work on increasingly complex problems, and then, support is withdrawn as the students develop competency.

The cognitive apprenticeship attempts to promote learning within the nexus of activity, tool and culture. Learning, both outside and inside school alliances through collaborative social interaction and the social construction of knowledge and collaboration. However, the notion of cognitive apprenticeship is related to situated cognition theory and stimulates or capitalises on real-world activities.

Around 1987, Collins, Brown, and Newman developed six teaching methods - modeling, coaching, scaffolding, articulation, reflection and exploration. These methods enable students to cognitive and metacognitive strategies for "using, managing, and discovering knowledge".

Table 1.1: Cognitive Apprenticeship in Classroom

Models	Meaning	Examples
Modelling	Observing the performance of an expert (teacher or more experienced peer)	Reading of various types of poems with modulation of voice and using body language.
Coaching	Giving external support to learner in form of hints, feedback, reminders, etc.	Observing learners while they are summarising any historical description or essay and giving them appropriate hints or feedback to bring out best from them.
Scaffolding	Helping learner in starting and gradually fading the support	Helping learner in learning how to use a chemical balance and slowing reducing support while progressing.
Articulation	Giving words to their understanding of the process and content	Asking learners to act as critic or moderator in a debate on some contemporary issue.
Reflection	Comparing their performance with expectations, reflecting on progress, improving their own performance	Recording the learner's activities in some role play or classroom leadership assignment and reply in front of him with comments from peers/teachers.
Exploration	Searching for new information, verifying to accept it as authentic knowledge	Asking learners to test the authenticity of a story on an historical event published in a newspaper through visiting a library and verifying with original authentic records.

Q26. Briefly describe the concept of discovery learning.

Ans. Discovery learning is an inquiry-based, constructivist learning theory that takes place in problem solving situations where the learner draws on his or her own past experience and existing knowledge to discover facts and relationships and new truths to be learned. Students interact with the world by exploring and manipulating objects, wrestling with questions and controversies, or performing experiments. Discovery learning was proposed by Bruner.

Discovery Learning is widely used in science and mathematics teaching. According to Bruner, issues or question that guides the discovery process must be personally and socially relevant. Curriculum should therefore, be organised in a spiral manner so that students can build upon what they have already learned. His concept of 'spiral curriculum' is based on the idea that any subject can be taught effectively in some intellectually honest form to any child at any stage of development.

The main times that discovery learning is used in the classroom are during problem solving exercises and educational programs. Students will undergo discovery learning when they are looking at their own experiences and knowledge in their studies, and enquiring about further information to improve their understanding. Discovery learning will also be used in terms of answering controversial and tricky questions, asking other people what they think, and generally discussing things. It is very good tool for learning in subjects like science, history, geography etc. It may be further developed as 'guided discovery learning', in which we can encourage learners to construct their understanding with your assistance and guidance.

There are few important processes associated with discovery learning which are as follow:

(1) **Inductive Reasoning:** According to Bruner, generally in classroom, principles should be formulated by the learners with the help of various examples in different contexts. Connections between different concepts can be established through this process.

(2) **Intuitive Thinking:** Bruner was of the opinion that teachers should encourage learners to think and guess with the help of some incomplete sentences, tasks or situations. Guesses of learners may be right or wrong but it should be promoted. Teachers should not discourage wrong guesses, because through guessing only we can develop intuitive thinking learners.

(3) **Guided Discovery:** It is an approach in which learners develop their understanding with the support of their mentor or teacher. Teacher provides some directions, which help learners to formulate hypotheses, to develop connections, and to draw conclusions.

Q27. Discuss the concept of active learning. Identify the main techniques for active learning in classroom.

Ans. Active learning is the intentional opportunity for students to engage in the learning process. It connects learners to the content through movement, reflection, or discussion, making students the center of the learning process as they take the initiative to learn. It can be behavioural or cognitive, supporting a variety of instructional objectives from recall through synthesis (Green & Casale-Giannola, 2011). Silberman (1996) addresses the question of what make learning active. He explains, "When learning is active, students do most of the work. They use their brains, study ideas, solve problems, and apply what they learn. Active learning is fast-paced, fun, supportive, and personally engaging". Often students are out of their seats, moving about, and thinking aloud. Active learning engages and motivates students while enhancing understanding and performance. It is important to make learning active because to learn something well, a student needs to hear it, see it, ask questions about it, and discuss it with others. Above all, students need to do it.

Techniques of active learning in classroom

Learners get opportunities, of reading, writing, discussion, problem solving, analysis, synthesis, evaluation, creativity, etc. in the methods of learning rather than listening come under Active Learning. Thus, Active learning modifies lecture method and includes active elements of learner. Thus, lecture method can be modified with the help of main techniques of active learning. The few technologies being used for modification of lecture are following:

(1) Pausing: Modifying a lecture to enhance students' learning by pausing at least three times to allow discussions among students puts the focus on clarifying and assimilating the information presented (Rowe, 1980), and empirical data support this contention (Ruhl, Hughes, and Schloss 1987).

In this method, during lecture, pausing can be used times of two minutes duration. There should be the interval of 12-18 minutes between two pausing. Learners are asked to divide themselves among two groups and note down the main points of lecture in these two minutes. Teacher does not interfere during this time. At the end of the lecture, three minutes are given to learners on the basic of memory for nothing down the main points of lecture.

(2) Test and Quizzes: During the lecture, informal Tests and Quizzes can help in keeping learners active. Verity of Quizzes can be used in the classroom on any topic, which not only helps in retention of knowledge, but also motivates learners to remain participative.

For instance, one way to modify traditional lectures to increase students' learning is to include an immediate mastery test of the subject material covered.

Research conducted in the 1920s, often replicated, details students' "forgetting curve" for lecture material, finding that the average student had immediate recall of 62 percent of the information presented but that recall declined to approximately 45 percent after three or four days and fell to only 24 percept after eight weeks. If students were asked to take an examination immediately after the lecture, however, they retained almost twice as much information, both factual and conceptual, after eight weeks (Menges 1988).

These results suggest that short quizzes and hour-long examinations are powerful influences upon, if not the major determinant of, what students study and how students learn (Milton and Eison 1983).

(3) Demonstration: Demonstrations during a lecture, particularly in the sciences, can be used to stimulate students' curiosity and to improve their understanding of conceptual material and processes, particularly when the demonstration invites students to participate in the investigative process through the use of such questions as "What will happen if we...?" Demonstrations can also serve as a vehicle for instructors to share attitudes about the tentative and changing nature of knowledge in their discipline, with a goal of motivating students to engage in experimentation on their own (Shakhashiri 1984). A caveat is necessary, however. One study has clearly shown that students who actively engaged in laboratory experiments designed to illustrate specific principles of physics had less difficulty learning those principles than students who merely saw a similar demonstration illustrating the principle given during a lecture (Okpala and Onocha 1988)

(4) Alternatives of Lecture Method: According to researchers few alternatives to lecture method, like Feedback Lecture, Guided Lecture, Learner Generated Questions and Responsive Lecture, etc. These are as follow:

(i) **Feedback Lecture:** Feedback lecture is conducted through supplementary study guide in which study materials, pre and post the test, aims of study and format of comments for lectures are already given. This includes two small lectures of 20 minutes of each, which are divided into small group study sessions. During these sessions, learners respond to questions for discussion in two divided groups on the basis of lecture materials provided by teachers.

(ii) **Guided Lecture:** Guided Lecture is another alternate. Teacher spells out the aim of the lecture, makes instruction likes stop writing and listen carefully, which are being stated. This follows a lecture of 25-30 minutes. Learners are asked to write the points from the lecture in 5 minutes on the basis of their memory. It is followed by small group discussion through which they elaborate all the points. They can take help from teacher for detailed explanation of any point during this time. Then, the learners are asked for thinking and at the same day, they are suggested to describe the main points of lecture without reference. Thus, this method develops listening and information synthesis skills.

(iii) **Learner Generated Questions and Responsive Lecture:** The responsive lecture was designed to provide feedback about the study material as per the needs of each learner. There should be one class assigned in every week for such lecture, in which self-made open ended questions on any aspect of textbook can be asked by learners and responded to by the teachers. There are certain conditions associated with this lecture, i.e. inclusion of all aspects of textbook, all learners should ask question necessarily and explain the importance of the particular question.

Active Learning in Large Classes: Anyone who has taught a large class is aware of the physical and emotional constraints upon both instructor and students. The situation is impersonal —perhaps even overpowering— when students fill hundreds of seats rising tier after tier in a large amphitheater that seemingly dwarfs the instructor. It is not surprising that, in these circumstances, professors who might otherwise use methods encouraging active learning revert to presenting formal 50-minute lectures without significant discussion.

Thus, in a large classroom, creating active environment is very difficult. Assuring active participation of all learners is more challenging, when numbers is 100 or more in one class. Researchers have shown that when active learning environment is created in large classroom, then the achievement of learners is more is small group presentations, written report, oral presentation, etc. as compared to learners from a small class. Active learning environment can be created easily group discussion by making group of 5 to 10 learners in each group, followed by presentation the learners.

Q28. Analyse the strategies for promoting active learning.

Ans. There are few strategies, which can be used to promote active learning environment in classroom:

(1) **Visual-Based Instruction:** To create an active learning environment, instructions are planned, assisted/based on stagnant projection film, multimedia presentation, TV, Video, etc. Teacher may have experience in their classroom that such visual based instructions enhance interest in learning and make them more active during the class.

(2) **Creative Writing:** Creating supportive environment for critical and creative writing comes under this method. Writing related works, like writing comments on sides of research journals, writing thoughts on any specific title, writing summary of a lecture, writing summary on any given study material, essay writing and other creative like writing for all magazines, newspapers etc. can help in developing active learning environment. Writing and creative play a very effective role in developing deep understanding on any subject.

(3) **Problem Solving:** A teacher should train learners to use problem solving method in order to find out the solutions of various problems, so that they actively find out the way to solve their problem on their own. Popular instructional approaches being used for problem solving are case study and Guided designs.

(4) **Computer-Based Instruction:** In this method, individualised instructions are given through computer. Learners learn according to their pace. Present day initiatives like MOODLE (Modular Object Oriented Dynamic Learning Environment) and MOOCs (Massive Open Online Courses) are mainly computer based instructions. Teacher can also develop their own computer based instructions to make active learners active.

(5) **Co-operative Learning:** Learners have different kinds of abilities and characteristics. If they develop understanding on any subject and find out solution of any problem together with the help of each other, they achieve the best result. They get opportunities to develop social skill as well like decision making ability and communication etc.

(6) **Drama:** Drama is also a very interesting method, in which learners are active and involved. Remember that childhood days when story with dialogue retained itself for long time in memory. If drama is used as a medium of instruction to develop understanding of the subject, then surely learners will participate actively in the learning process.

(7) **Role Playing, Simulations and Games:** These are also very interesting methods, where learners get involved with interest. These methods will be very beneficial in instruction subjects like History, Mathematics, Science; Languages can integrate these methods very easily.

Q29. Write short note on the following:

(i) Obstacles in active learning

Ans. To address adequately why most faculties have not embraced recent calls for educational reform, it is necessary first to identify and understand common barriers to instructional change, including:

- The powerful influence of educational tradition;
- Faculty self-perceptions and self-definition of roles;
- The discomfort and anxiety that change creates;
- The limited incentives for faculty to change.

But certain specific obstacles are associated with the use of active learning:

- The difficulty in adequately covering the assigned course content in the limited class time available;
- A possible increase in the amount of preparation time;
- The difficulty of using active learning in large classes;
- A lack of needed materials, equipment, or resources.

Perhaps the single greatest barrier of all, however, is the fact that faculty members' efforts to employ active learning involve risk—the risks that students will not participate, use higher-order thinking, or learn sufficient content, that faculty members will feel a loss of control, lack necessary skills, or be criticised for teaching in unorthodox ways. Each obstacle or barrier and type of risk, however, can be successfully over come through careful, thoughtful planning.

(ii) Roles of stakeholders in active learning

Ans. Change in conceptual understanding assistance, initiations and initiations and systematic attempt by teachers, teacher trainers, researches, policy makers, management and administrators of schools are very important in eliminating the mentioned obstacles in the part of active learning. Roles of all stakeholders related to education process needs to be ascertained for the development of environment, teachers needs to understand deeply the study and training of new strategies and techniques for creating active learning environment.

Stakeholders should be free from prejudice and old concepts. They should practice low risk techniques initially followed by other techniques. Teacher-trainers should train teachers in all strategies, methods and techniques as well as collect experience based data related to concerned experiments, so that a confidence can be developed. This training may be given as pre-service and in-service. The role of researchers should be for collecting experience based data through research related to various aspects of active learning environment. Policy makers should create positive environment towards these innovative experiments and give appropriate place in curriculum. Campus managers and administrators should provide patronage for experiments of these innovations in their institutions as well assure the arrangement of needful resources.

Q30. What do you mean by observational learning? What are the various elements and significance of observational learning?

Or

Explain various elements of observational learning.

[Dec-2017, Q.No.-3 (d)]

Ans. Observational learning refers to the process of change in the behaviour of one person simply by being exposed to another person's behaviour. This second person is known as the model. Here, modelling refers to the behaviour of the observed person and not to the behaviour of the person who follows. The child observes parents behaviour and parents are role models. The child imitates the parent's behaviour. In Bandura's version, the parents model a specific behaviour and the child imitates. Observational learning is a complex process more complex than mere imitation. In our society, there are plenty of examples of this learning such as, many criminals, caught by police, confessed that they committed crime by viewing a particular movie or a serial of the same type. Many researches are available in the literature, which reveal that young people learn aggression through watching the actions of others.

Elements of observational learning: The four elements, which can influence observational learning, are as follows:

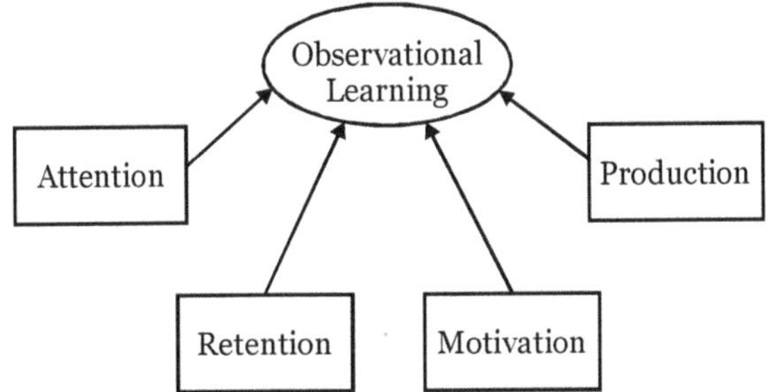

Fig 1.4: Elements of Observational Learning

(1) **Attention:** In order to learn, one needs to be paying attention. Anything that detracts his/her attention is going to have a

negative effect on observational learning. If the model is interesting or there is a novel aspect to the situation, s/he is far more likely to dedicate his/her full attention to learning. Thus, if s/he is going to learn anything, s/he has to be paying attention. Likewise, anything that puts a damper on attention is going to decrease learning, including observational learning. If, for example, s/he is sleepy, groggy, drugged, sick, nervous or "hyper", s/he will learn less well.

(2) **Retention:** The ability to store information is also an important part of the learning process. Retention can be affected by a number of factors, but the ability to pull up information later and act on it is vital to observational learning. Thus, one must be able to retain and remember what s/he has paid attention to. This is where imagery and language come in. We store what we have seen the model doing in the form of mental images of verbal descriptions. When so stored, we can later "bring up" the image or description, so that we can reproduce it with our own behaviour.

(3) **Production:** Once we have paid attention to the model and retained the information, it is time to actually perform the behaviour we observed. Further, practice of the learned behaviour leads to improvement and skill advancement. Through the reproduction processes, we have to translate the images or descriptions into actual behaviour. So we have to have the ability to reproduce the behaviour in the first place. Another important tidbit about reproduction is that our ability to imitate which improves with practice at the behaviours involved. And also it has been noted that our abilities improve even when we just imagine ourselves performing! Many athletes, for example, imagine their performance in their mind's eye prior to actually performing.

(4) **Motivation**: And yet, with all this, we're still not going to do anything unless we are motivated to imitate that is, until we have some reason for doing it. Hence, in order for observational learning to occur and be successful, we have to be motivated to imitate the behaviour that has been modelled. Reinforcement and punishment play an important role in motivation. While experiencing, these motivators can be highly effective, one can also observe other experiences such as some type of reinforcement or punishment that others are being subjected to. For example, if we see another student rewarded with extra credit for coming to class on time, we might start to show up a few minutes early-each day.

Significance of observational learning

- Observational learning is helpful in introduction of new behavior.
- Teachers can use observational learning in the subjects like mathematics, science, geography, etc. very effectively as in these subjects many concept are introduced with the help of observation.

- Selection of model (i.e. the person or instrument) to represent the skill or behaviour is very important. Appropriateness of model is the key of success in observational learning.
- Peers can also be used as an effective model. Especially rewarding desired behaviour of a learner can motivate other to imitate him/her.
- Teacher can identify the people to whom most learners assume their models. Their good acts, movies, videos, etc. can be used in their class.
- Teacher can identify the models from community, who can be good learning resources for learners. For example, they can organise a visit of skilled person in painting/drawing/dancing to demonstrate his/her skill or they can arrange a visit of learner to his/her workplace.
- Teacher himself/herself could be a good model. Many behaviour/skills a learner learn through imitating his/her teachers.

Q31. Define situated learning. What are the elements and conceptions of situated learning?

Or

How does situated learning take place? Give suitable examples. [June-2017, Q.No.-3(d)]

Ans. Situated learning is an instructional approach developed by Jean Lave and Etienne Wenger in the early 1990s, and follows the work of Dewey, Vygotsky, and others (Clancey, 1995) who claim that students are more inclined to learn by actively participating in the learning experience. Situated learning essentially is a matter of creating meaning from the real activities of daily living where learning occurs relative to the teaching environment.

Social situation, context, social involvement and participation are very important for a learner in this technique, because knowledge can be introduced in authentic situations and its practical aspects can be learnt thought social participation. Lave believed that learning should not be observed as abstract concepts and communication of non-contextual knowledge rather it should be observed as a social process in a specific social and physical environment, where knowledge should be created by circulative efforts.

The following are examples of situated learning activities:

(1) Field trips where students actively participate in an unfamiliar environment

(2) Cooperative education and internship experiences in which students are immersed and physically active in an actual work environment

(3) Music and sports (physical education) practice which replicate actual setting of these events, e.g., orchestras, studios, training facilities

(4) Laboratories and child-care centers used as classrooms in which students are involved in activities which replicate actual work settings

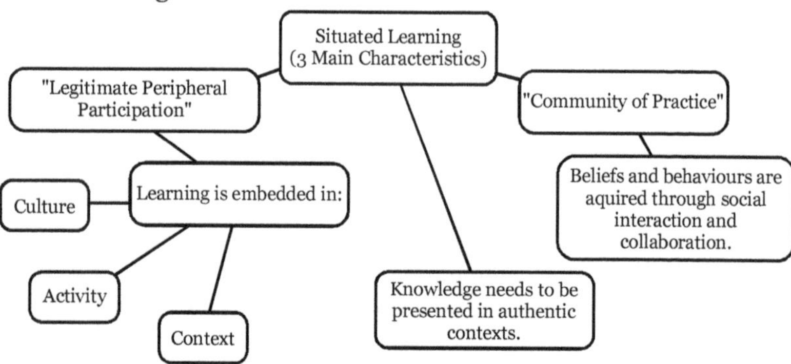

Fig 1.5: Situated Learning

These examples illustrate that students are actively involved in addressing real world problems. As the practice implies, the student is "situated" in the learning experience and knowledge acquisition becomes a part of the learning activity, its context, and the "culture in which it is developed and used" (Oregon Technology in Education Council, 2007). Students form or "construct" their own knowledge from experiences they bring to the learning situation; the success of situated learning experiences relies on social interaction and kinesthetic activity.

Situated learning involves students in cooperative activities where they are challenged to use their critical thinking and kinesthetic abilities. These activities should be applicable and transferable to students' homes, communities, and workplaces (Stein, 1998). While immersed in the experience, students reflect on previously held knowledge and by challenging the assumptions of other students.

Elements of situated learning: Following are the major elements of situated learning:

(1) Content: Situated learning emphasises higher-order thinking processes rather than the acquisition of facts independent of the real lives of the participants. The facts and the processes of the task.

(2) Context: Learning in context refers to building an instructional environment sensitive to the tasks learners must complete to be successful in practice. The situations, values, beliefs, and environmental cues by which the learners gains and masters content.

(3) Community: Learners interpret, reflect and form meaning. Community provides the setting for social interaction needed to engage in dialogue with others to see various and diverse perspectives on any issue. The group with which the learner will create and negotiate with the others situation.

(4) Participation: Describes the interchange of ideas, attempts at problem-solving, and active engagement of learners with each other and with the materials of instruction. The process by which the learners working together and with experts in a social organisation solve problems related to everyday life circumstances.

Conceptions about situated learning

(1) Knowledge is not a thing and memory is not a place, rather it is created socially.

(2) Knowledge reflects through behaviour and work of individual or group of individuals. With new situation, knowledge develops naturally through participation of individuals and adaptation.

(3) Learning, knowing and cognition develop socially through tasks performed by person or other interaction with others. There is takes shape and get expressed.

(4) Meanings are developed through affiliation with specific context and objectives.

(5) Cultural model does not exist within person rather is alive in social practices. The way people are associated, the instruments they use and the specific cultural context in which they work, cultural model develops in that. Learning takes place within this cultural model.

(6) "As situation shapes human's cognition and thinking similarly a person's actions create the situation" (Wilson & Myers, 2000). Situated learning is very important for the betterment of our school education. They can make a visit with their learners to the post office, police station, railway station, airport, power grid, bank, judiciary, etc. where they get opportunities in real situations and learning becomes effective and interesting.

Q32. What is collaborative learning? Explain its strategies and significance.

Or

Discuss the concept of collaborative learning.

Ans. Collaborative learning is an educational approach that involves groups of learners working together to solve a problem, complete a task, or create a product. It is based on the idea that learning is a naturally social act. Learning occurs though active engagement among peers, either face-to-face or online. Peers learning, or peer instruction, is a type of collaborative learning that involves students working in pairs or small groups to discuss concepts, or find solutions to problems. This often occurs in a class session after students are introduced to course material through readings or videos before class, and/or through instructor lectures. Similar to the idea that two or three heads are better than one, many instructors have found that through peer instruction, students teach each other by addressing misunderstandings and clarifying misconceptions.

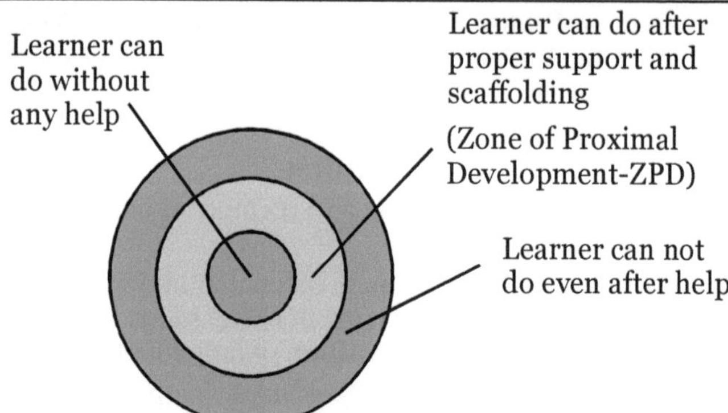

Fig 1.6: Zone of Proximal Development

Collaborative learning is similar to, but not the same as, cooperative learning. In cooperative learning the task is divided vertically (i.e., members work more or less concurrently on different aspects of a project), whereas in collaborative learning the task is divided horizontally (i.e., members work together more or less sequentially on different aspects of a project).

Strategies for collaborative learning: In classroom and at workplace, collaborative learning can be practices in many ways, which are as follows:

(1) **Think-Pair-Share:** A problem related to higher order thinking ability like analysis, synthesis, evaluation and construction, etc. is introduced before learners. All learners are provided five minutes so that they can respond properly to the solution of problem. After it, they are given time for sharing their thinking with peers in small groups. Also, they have to listen to others and discuss with other classmates. At least, they have to have a consensus on appropriate method for solution of problem. All groups share related processes and outcomes of discussion during follow-up discussion.

(2) **Catch UP:** During the lecture, teacher stops suddenly and ask learners to compare their notes with other classmates and to ask questions on doubtful points to clarify. Teacher should start question- answers session after sometime and motivate the learners from another group to answer.

(3) **Fishbowl debate:** Teacher can make three groups of learners. Those who are sitting on the right side may be in support and the left side group may be in opposition or vice-versa. The group which is sitting in the middle row is asked to note down the thoughts of both groups and determine who has put facts, strong reasons effectively, etc. In the end, they are asked to present the report before the class.

(4) **Case Study:** Teacher should prepare four to five case study proposals of same difficulty level. These may be assigned to learners dividing them in groups. Groups should be provided

time for analysis, teacher may ask for progress report during this period. It should be presented before class, after completion of work.

(5) **Team Based Learning:** In this method, learners are divided in groups by teacher and assigned some specific work i.e. a book for study, a laboratory work or to find out solution of some specific problems. Learners are asked to appear in a group examination after completion of the work. Quiz is very popular for it. They have to answer on the basis of consensus in the group and also name the member who has suggested the answer. At last, teacher needs to explain the difficulties and resolve the misconceptions among learners. After many such settings, learners may be assigned some challenging problems also to find out the solution.

Significance of collaborative learning: In imparting training of skills, collaborative learning is very effective. Many institutions have emphasised on collaborated learning as a method of training for the development of technical and managerial skills at work place. Providing opportunities to the group of trainees for learning among experienced persons and in real situation is more effective as compared to other methods. After such type of learning, learners may be deployed in real situations and higher order thinking abilities, like, analysis, synthesis, evaluation, construction, etc. can be developed among learners in such an environment and also problem solving ability develops due to their place and encounters with real situation. There are some problems at workplace, which learners may face like difference of cultural background, lack of awareness about cultural norms, generation gap and age gap, etc. But there, problems are improved during training and counseling session and new knowledge and skills can be developed through concerted effort.

- New dimensions of collaborative learning have emerged in this new age of modern information and communication technology. People living in remote areas can work together through technology at virtual platforms and solve the problems. Very effective and attractive learning environment can be created for classroom and workplace though it. Some ways are as follows:
  - **Collaborative Networked Learning (CNL):** Creating a learning environment with the help of electronic equipments.
  - **Computer Supported Collaborative Learning (CSCL):** Creating an environment with the help of Computer and Internet.
  - **Wikipedia Supported Collaborative Learning (WSCL):** A good example of collaborative learning is Wikipedia, where many people are involved together in knowledge creation and problem solving.
  - **Collaborative Learning in Virtual World:** Skype, 3D model, Mind mapping tools, etc.

- In collaborative learning, understanding the cultural diversities and modification of behaviour should be emphasised. It should be taught in various ways in the context of different learning situations in different cultural backgrounds. Resources should be used according to cultural background at in classroom. One method may be effective in one cultural situation, but it may not be effective in another cultural situation. There may be a need of another method. It should be considered carefully.

Q33. Discuss the conceptual understanding of 'learning out of schools'. What is the difference between learning inside the school and outside of the school?

Ans. In modern society, schools are working as an institutional center for the learning of various knowledge, skills and attitude. But the people attached with educational process and various social activities believe that opportunity for the preparation of life and society, life skills education is decreasing continuously. Life of a learner is like a prisoner within the boundaries of school. Burden of subject knowledge is diverting them from practical life, i.e.: social issues, essential life skills, ambition for the preparation of better civil society and knowledge society, reflection on future challenges of life, as they have to do with social concerns, etc. School and Institutions are like islands in the society. It is not good to be dependent on schools or institutions in this situation and it is necessary to look out of the schools for construction of knowledge. So that it could be related with the needs of society and nature.

Along with people of society, behaviour can be modified. Education was never bounded with in schools or gurukuls. In traditional Indian education, rather a large section of education was within the society. Excursion, Bhikshatan and other social activities were the means for development of social relationships in the society. It was also the means of life skill development. These days, learners are deprived of experience related to real world, which are out of school and more emphasis is on subject knowledge. Learners should be provided with the opportunities for experiencing the social life outside the school.

There are various learning situations out of school. According to Resmick, there is difference between learning inside the school and outside of school in following ways:

(1) Learning takes place individually in school but develops as shared cognition outside the school.

(2) School motivate to work with pure consciousness without help of equipment (book, note, calculator and other tools) followed by examination. (For example, we must have felt that minimum tools are allowed to use during examination) but in real situation, we have to accomplish any task with the help of many such tools and help of others.

(3) In school, due to lack of real situations, maximum learning happen in form of symbols, outside of school, whereas opportunities are available more for learning and discussion in specific context.

(4) Generalised learning takes place in schools, whereas skills related to a specific situation develop outside of it.

Teacher can practice such experiments in their school. Plan for an excursion and say that locally available resources will be used. Opportunities to learn to live in nature may be provided to learners.

Q34. State the theories/dimensions of learning out of the school.

Ans. There are following theories have been proposed about learning out of school in the book 'Learning in and out of school' by James A. Bank, *et al.* (1997) which are as follow:

(1) Learning takes place in socio-economical and historical contexts according to local culture, customs and perspective.

(2) Learning does not take place in school only, but it continues in many contexts, activities and social behaviour,

(3) There is a need to provide help to every child for personal intellectual development in every institution.

(4) Learning will be more effective, when learners are motivated to use their language of home and community, culture and society. This extends their language and understanding.

According to Bank *et al.* (1997), learning in and out of school apart from subject teaching and suggested that it is essential for a development of better individual and society. These three dimensions are as follows:

(1) Life-long Learning: Curiosity of learning new knowledge and skills useful for life through situation and events and communication and interactions in relation to it needed lifelong. It begins at childhood and continues till death.

(2) Life–wide Learning: Developing skills to adjust and accommodate according to time, place and situation comes under it. Living with equivalence in human relationship despite various favorable as well as bitter experiences is also a part of it. It is basically the preparation of life and future.

(3) Life–deep Learning: Religion, values, morality, ethics-these control our faith, behaviour and belongingness and help in decision making for self and others are part of it.

To learners out of school opportunities should be provided, like community organisation and civil society for experiencing various aspects of life as well. School may also create such an environment for example.

- Appointment of experienced counselor and mentor for learners outside of school with the help of guardian.
- Study club: It should not be bound by curriculum rather extends it.
- Social meeting for various communities and groups.
- Residential activities: Weekend residential meet for extensive learning, residential study week, residential summer workshop and excursion (museum, zoo, library, historical place, natural diver cities).
- Community based homework and homework club for assistance.

BACHELOR OF EDUCATION (B. Ed.)

Available

Ist Year

BES-121: Childhood and Growing Up

BES-122: Contemporary India and Education

BES-123: Learning and Teaching

BES-124: Language Across the Curriculum

BES-125: Understanding Disciplines and Subjects

Optional

BES-141 Pedagogy of Science

BES-142 Pedagogy of Social Science

BES-143 Pedagogy of Mathematics

BES-144 Pedagogy of English

BES-145 Pedagogy of Hindi

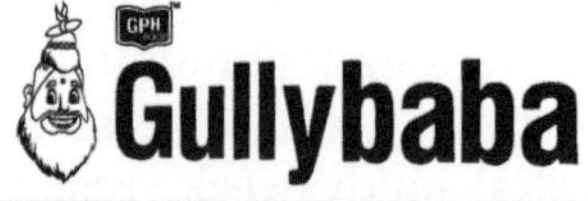

Understanding The Learner

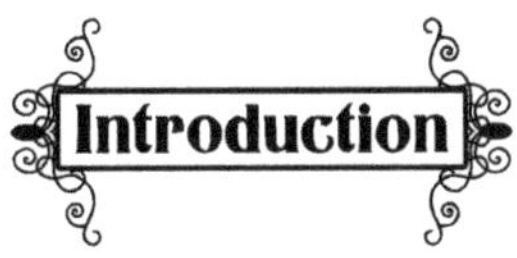

Learning begins from the birth of the child and continues till his death. Learning is not possible unless the different desirable factors do not contribute to the process of learning. A learner learns from his family, society and school who can deal well or behave effectively may be said as having good personality and social intelligence. A learner having high abstract intelligence has the mental capacity for knowing how to deal effectively with others. There are a number of elements in social abilities that are not abstracted in nature. A learner's personality, his Intelligence Quotient, Emotional Quotient & Spiritual Quotient are all important factors in determining how well he will get along with others.

Q1. Explain how the socio-cultural factors affecting learners.

Ans. Socio-cultural factors are the larger scale forces within societies and culture that affects the thoughts, behaviours and feelings of individual members of those societies and cultures. The socio-cultural environment has an essential impact on child learning. The socio-cultural factors include family, neighbourhood, community, class, caste, religion and ethnicity.

- **Family** is the foundation from which learning activities of any child take off. The family can significantly affect children development and school achievement. It is in family that child undergoes conscious, subconscious and subliminal learning. It is within the family that the individual learns behaviour patterns for survival, social attitudes, skills, interpersonal skills, social norms, the do's and don'ts of his culture and community, acquires a sense of right and wrong, a value orientation, etc. Thus, we can say that the family is the school of all learning.
- **The neighbourhood and community** in which one lives also have an important impact on what one learns and acquires. Many attitudes, habits, beliefs, perceptions, stereotypes and social roles and responsibilities are shaped directly or indirectly by our experiences with the persons in our neighbourhood. These persons include our peer and age-mates and all the elders around us.
- **Caste, class and religion** also play a predominant role in shaping our identity, self-concept, attitudes, value-orientation, goals and achievement patterns. For example, the socio-economic status of the group to which we belong can be directly linked with the degree of stimulation or enrichment available to us in our learning environment. It has been seen that an adequately enriching and stimulating environment provides the learner with more learning opportunities, and greater control over the environment than an impoverished or needy environment.
- Learning is also seen to vary across **religious and ethnic groups**, owing to the distinction in their beliefs, values, attitudes and practices. For instance, in many Islamic countries, women lead a very sheltered and restricted life and are taught to be submissive and obedient. In the Pan Indian culture, children are encouraged to develop a sense of autonomy, independence and control over their own lives. In many orthodox Hindu communities, the social learning of girls is fraught with biases and injunctions which are justified in the name of religious beliefs. The kind of experiences which a learner is exposed to differ across regions and geographical locations as well.

Q2. Identify changing perceptions about learners.

Ans. In schools, teacher should create an atmosphere where they give more importance to a learner rather than to a student. In classrooms, children compare themselves to other children. It is a natural phenomenon that every child compares themselves with other children during the learning process. Traditionally, in schools, a teacher gives appreciation to those children who are good, meaning those who follow directions, complete their homework, get high marks and grades.

About learner, teachers have to change their perception by finding a learner in every child and by helping them to learn best. For this purpose, a teacher should have learner's personal profile which may be helpful for a teacher to understand how each learner engage himself/herself with the content, how s/he express his/her previous knowledge and how s/he understands new knowledge.

There is a need to develop for appreciating good learners such a learning environment where every child can be recognised as a learner, a learning environment that can give direction to the learners to think in depth about their learning. On one side, it may be helpful for learners in setting their learning goals to support their learning while on the other side, it may also be helpful for teachers in creating an understanding of tools, strategies and resources which will be helpful for learning of learners. To develop such an environment, teachers should talk with the learners to know how they are learning with them. This type of conversation will open a door to maximise learning. Teachers should appreciate their learner's interests so that they are able to think about their future.

Q3. List and clarify the various types of learners. Explain their role of teacher.

Ans. The types of learners are as follows:

(1) Auditory Learners (Learn through listening and hearing): Auditory learners would rather listen to things being explained than read about them. Reciting information loud and having music in the background may be a common study method. Other noises may become a distraction resulting in a need for a relatively quiet place. They learn best through verbal lectures, discussions, talking things through and listening to what others have to say. Auditory learners interpret the underlying meanings of speech through listening to tone of voice, pitch, speed and other nuances. Written information may have little meaning until it is heard. These learners often benefit from reading text along and using a tape recorder.

Role of Teacher: Following are the some common strategies which a teacher may use to help these learners:

(i) Encourage the learners to participate in discussions.

(ii) Recorded lectures may be used to present learning material.

(iii) Traditional teaching methods, where lecture is considered as the least effective method but auditory learners learn best by listening.

(iv) Present the information verbally by interacting with learners.

(2) Visual Learners (Learn through seeing): Visual learners learn best by looking at graphics, watching a demonstration or reading. For them, it's easy to look at charts and graphs, but they may have difficulty foucussing while listening to an explanation. These learners need to see the teacher's body language and facial expression to fully understand the content of a lesson. They tend to prefer sitting at the front of the classroom to avoid visual obstructions (e.g. people's heads). They may think in pictures and learn best from visual displays including figures, illustrated textbooks, overhead transparencies, videos, flipcharts and handouts. During a lecture or classroom discussion, visual learners often prefer to take detailed notes to absorb the information.

Role of Teacher: A teacher can help a visual learner in following manners:

(i) Teacher may use charts, diagrams, pictures, videos, overhead transparencies, etc.
(ii) Teacher may encourage the learners to use color pens or colored highlighters when they read and take notes.
(iii) Teacher may use concept mapping method for teaching.

(3) Tactile/Kinesthetic Learners (Touch): Kinesthetic learning is a learning style in which learning takes place by the learner using their body in order to express a thought, an idea or an understanding of a particular concept (which could be related to any field). Kinesthetic learners process information best through a "hands-on" experience. Actually doing an activity can be the easiest way for them to learn. Sitting still while studying may be difficult, but writing things down makes it easier to understand.

Role of Teacher: When tactile/kinesthetic learners are engaged in activities they learn best. Teacher can help them in following ways:

(i) Teacher may use problem solving method and project method as teaching methods
(ii) Teacher may provide opportunities to learn by doing
(iii) Teacher may encourage them for participating in exhibitions, club activities drama, dance, skit and field trips, etc.

Q4. What is mental retardation? Discuss features of of children with mental retardation. Also explain some common and practical steps a teacher should take to help such children in classroom.

Ans. Intellectual disability (ID), also called mental retardation or generally learning disability, is characterized by below-average intelligence or mental ability and a lack of skills necessary for day-to-day living. According to AAMR (2002), "Mental Retardation is a disability characterised by significant limitation in intellectual functioning and in adaptive behaviour as expressed in conceptual ,social and practical adaptive skills. This disability originates before age 18".

Features of children with this type of category include:

- Displays poor academic achievement,
- Forgets learning after a short time,
- Is inattentive and distracted,
- Shows too much reliance on presentation of concrete objects,
- Has poor self-image,
- Lacks in self-confidence,
- Seeks repetition and practice,
- When the child is asked to do something, s/he seems to have a problem in understanding what s/he has been asked,

- Appears dull or slow in mannerisms,
- Difficulty in learning to do things,
- Difficulty in understanding abstract things, and
- Overdependence on concrete examples/objects.

For educational purposes teacher can classify learners with mental retardation into three categories:

- **Educable:** learners who have an IQ approximately 50-70
- **Trainable:** learners who have an IQ approximately 20-49
- **Custodial:** learners who have an IQ below 20

All the above categories are based on the level of functioning of the learner with mental retardation. It helps us to decide which type of education or support should be provided to the learner.

Some common and practical steps teachers can take to help such children in class are as follows:

(1) They have to provide more concrete experiences for these children. These experiences can be provided by available standard or improvised materials. Direct experiences from the local environment may be provided through field trips.

(2) These children require repetition and practice more than other normal children.

(3) The learning task has to be presented in small steps and their attention needs to be drawn to important points of the learning task because they have comparatively very small attention span.

(4) While they are engaged in learning, simple questions may be asked to give them a feeling of success.

(5) Immediate reward in terms of verbal or material reinforcements should be the watchword for these children.

(6) These children need to be provided with training on communication skills through practice in social situations.

(6) Curriculum for these children has to be transacted through simple and interesting learning experiences.

Q5. Give analyse on learners with hearing and visual impairment. Also discuss the role a teacher has to play.

Ans. Children with hearing impairment

Hearing loss, also known as hearing impairment, is a partial or total inability to hear. According to Individual with disabilities Education Act, 1992, "An impairment in hearing, whether permanent or fluctuating that adversely affect the child's educational performance."

Hearing impaired child will not develop language without extensive training. It is difficult to measure such children on intellectual abilities which further makes it complicated to design and educational programme for them. Five basic educational options are available to students with hearing impairment:

(1) Full time placement in a regular classroom

(2) Part time placement in a regular classroom and part time placement in a special educational classroom

(3) Special class placement in a regular school
(4) Separate day school placement
(5) Separate residential school placement.

For educational purposes hearing impaired learners can be classified into four categories:

(1) Mild hearing loss - 25 - 50 db
(2) Moderate hearing loss - 51 - 70 db
(3) Severe hearing loss - 71 - 90 db
(4) Profound hearing loss - 91 db and above

Role of Teacher: With the help and support of the teachers, learners with mild and moderate hearing loss may be admitted into the regular schools and educated. Some common strategies which a teacher may use to help these learners are:

(1) Allow use of appropriate modern hearing aids
(2) Provide teaching notes in advance to these learners so that they can read them before the topic is discussed in the class
(3) Arrange seats in front, closer to the teacher and with other learners
(4) Providing new information using pictures and emphasising on demonstration.

Learners with visual impairment

The term 'visual impairment' is used to refer to not only those who are blind, but also those who have low vision. We tend to think that people who are blind have no vision at all. This is not always the case. While some blind individuals do not receive any meaningful input through the visual sense, and may be able to differentiate only between light and dark, it is not as if all blind persons suffer from total absence of sight. Many blind individuals have some remaining sight, or residual vision. When the person has residual vision above a certain level, he is said to have low vision or poor vision.

Most children with visual impairments will need extra support to succeed in school. Ideally, students will have received early intervention which includes the involvement of a Teacher of Students with Visual Impairments. Students with visual impairment may look like typical children, but early-signs can indicate a problem. It is important to identify these signs at a young age in order to take advantage of early-intervention. Learn the early-signs of visual loss in children and what can be done for them in school.

Role of the Teachers:

(1) Allow the student with visual impairment to use a computer with a speech synthesiser. Braille printer may be useful for proofreading.
(2) Teachers should eliminate the clutter in the classroom so that the students can move without hurdles. Make tactile map of the classroom, school and other places so that the student will know how to easily move through the areas.

(3) Teacher should learn some Braille. Students do not spell words in letter to letter correspondence with English.

(4) Recognise that some vocabulary words men nothing to a person who has never seen them.

(5) Other students can read assignments for visually impaired that are not available in Braille. Audio tapes can also be prepared for such assignments.

(6) If the student has some vision, use large print with lots of contrasts such as black letters on yellow paper.

Q6. Classify the types of specific learning disabilities. Explain the role a teacher play in these.

Ans. A specific learning disability refers to a disorder in one or more of the basic learning processes involved in understanding or in using language, spoken or written, that may manifest in significant difficulties affecting the ability to listen, speak, read, write, spell, or do mathematics. A specific learning disability does not include learning problems that are primarily the result of a visual, hearing, motor, intellectual, or emotional/behavioral disability, limited English proficiency, or environmental, cultural, or economic factors. There are four types of specific learning disabilities, which are as follow:

(1) Dyscalculia: Dyscalculia is a specific learning disability in math. Kids with dyscalculia may have difficulty understanding number-related concepts or using symbols or functions needed for success in mathematics. For example, learner with dyscalculia may:

- Shows difficulty understanding concepts of place value, and quantity, number lines, positive and negative value, carrying and borrowing
- Has difficulty understanding and doing word problems
- Has difficulty sequencing information or events
- Exhibits difficulty using steps involved in math operations
- Shows difficulty understanding fractions
- Displays difficulty recognising patterns when adding, subtracting, multiplying, or dividing
- Has difficulty putting language to math processes
- Exhibits difficulty organising problems on the page, keeping numbers lined up, following through on long division problems.

Role of Teacher: Following are the some common strategies, which a teacher may use to help the learner with dyscalculia are:

(i) Play mathematics related games which may connect numbers to everyday activity and the learner could feel more comfortable with mathematics.

(ii) Use problem solving method to solve a mathematics problem

(iii) Use such examples of mathematics which connect mathematics to real life. For example, counting fruits, counting household objects, counting flowers, etc.

(iv) Use visual aids while solving the problem.

(2) Dyslexia: Dyslexia is a specific learning disability in reading. Kids with dyslexia have trouble reading accurately and fluently. Dyslexia is not due to mental retardation, brain damage or a lack of intelligence. It is caused by an impairment in the brain's ability to translate images received from the eyes or ears into understandable language. The severity of dyslexia can vary from mild to severe. For example, learner with dyslexia may:

- Read and write very slowly
- Confuse the order of letters in words
- Put letters the wrong way round – such as writing "b" instead of "d"
- Have poor or inconsistent spelling
- Understand information when told verbally, but have difficulty with information that's written down
- Find it hard to carry out a sequence of directions
- Struggle with planning and organisation

Role of Teacher: There are following strategies which a teacher may use to help learner with dyslexia:

(i) Refer the learner to a reading specialist

(ii) Encourage the learner to read different books of his own choice like comics, story books, newspaper articles on sports, movies etc. and in school provide a quiet area and extra time for reading

(iii) Allow the use of computer in classroom

(iv) Use books with large print and having big gaps between lines

(v) Present reading material in small units

(vi) Allow the use of word processor and spell checker which will be helpful for these learners who have trouble with reading and spelling

(3) Dysgraphia: Dysgraphia is a learning disability that affects writing abilities. Signs and symptoms of dysgraphia include:

- Handwriting that is illegible
- Letter sizes and shapes are irregular
- Incomplete letters
- Difficulty using writing as a means of communication
- Missing or incomplete words in sentences
- Trouble with grammar and sentence structure
- Have trouble in thinking and writing at the same time.

Role of Teacher: Some common strategies which a teacher may use to help the learner with dysgraphia are as follows:

(i) Instead of written examinations conduct oral examinations

(ii) Instead of writing lecture notes, allow use of tape recorders as an alternative

(iii) Provide preprinted notes to reduce writing work

(iv) Avoid criticising the learner for careless work

(v) Allow use of specially designed writing aids

(vi) Give the learner additional time to finish schoolwork or take tests

(4) Dyspraxia: Dyspraxia is a disorder that is characterised by difficulty in muscle control which causes problems with movement and coordination, language and speech, and can affect learning. Although not a learning disability, Dyspraxia often exists along with Dyslexia, Dyscalculia or ADHD. Learner with dyspraxia may:

- exhibits poor balance; may appear clumsy; may frequently stumble
- shows difficulty with motor planning
- demonstrates inability to coordinate both sides of the body
- has poor hand-eye coordination
- exhibits weakness in the ability to organise self and belongings
- shows possible sensitivity to touch
- be distressed by loud noises or constant noises like the ticking of a clock or someone tapping a pencil
- break things or choose toys that do not require skilled manipulation
- has difficulty with fine motor tasks such as coloring between the lines, putting puzzles together; cutting accurately or pasting neatly
- irritated by scratchy, rough, tight or heavy clothing

Role of Teacher: A teacher can adopt following strategies to help the learners:

(i) First of all, any teacher needs to ensure that instructions are broken down and simplified. It is important to maintain eye contact when giving instructions to an individual dyspraxic child. This will help them to concentrate.

(ii) Explain things in a simple uncomplicated way. Make sure our instructions remain constant and unchanged.

(iii) In these circumstances, patience is a virtue. Be prepared to repeat ourselves calmly and frequently.

(iv) Offer encouragement and keep reminding the class of the task and the sequence.

(v) It is always helpful to establish a predictable routine and firm guidelines. Sudden changes in routine can cause major problems for a child with dyspraxia.

Q7. Define intelligence. What are the misconceptions about intelligence and how it relates with learning?

Ans. Intelligence consists in ability to solve problems, that is, to deal with situations that are new to the person, as against merely carrying out well-practiced response to familiar situations. It consists of grasping the essentials in a given situation and responding appropriately to them.

The history of research on learning and on intelligence the prevailing view of the interaction between these aspects of mental function has been one-sided, learning and the products of learning being conceived as prerequisites for intelligent performance in such activities as problem solving.

There are few misconceptions on intelligence as given below:

(i) Can intelligence be tested exactly

(ii) An individual's intelligence level is fixed

(iii) Intelligence quotient does not measure intelligence

(iv) Nothing can be done to become more intelligent

These issues and their bearings on learning are as follows:

(i) Factors basic to effective learning and personal success such as achievement drive, emotional health, cultural background and curiosity should be kept in mind when the factor of mental capacity is given primary consideration.

(ii) Standings on intelligence tests correlate only moderately with marks in the academic subjects because of differences in learners' study habit, inaccuracies in making and unreliability of test scores.

(iii) Correlations between intelligence-test standings and special subjects such as art, textile, woodwork and other skill subjects are low.

(iv) Intelligence quotients and mental ages obtained for school entrants by means of individual mental examinations are helpful in guiding the child and for predicting his progress in learning.

(v) Intelligence test standings indicate what a learner should be able to do and school marks indicate what s/he has done and therefore will probably do again. Learners who are high in both usually progress, dropout generally lacks in both capacity and achievement.

In several areas, describing intelligence as involving effective behaviour, it is not valid to make complete distinctions between the areas, for they are interrelated. Thus, there in an abstract thought component is most motor, mechanical and social activities. A learner is said to have little capacity, aptitude, talent or potential for a given activity when, after earnest effort, s/he has acquired few abilities in that activity. For example, every learner with very few expectations has had a number of opportunities to play baseball, basketball and other games. Some continue to be poor in these games because they have little aptitude for athletics; others make rapid progress and become good players because they have high aptitude. Similarly, quick success in academic subjects indicates a learner's aptitudes for them.

Prime indication of capacity of course is the age at which a child show her/his abilities. Children who learn to walk early, who know how to read before they start school, do anything at younger than average than age are demonstrating high capacity.

Q8. What do you understand by intelligence quotient (IQ), emotional quotient (EQ), spiritual quotient (SQ)? Also discuss the relationship among them.

Ans. Intelligence Quotient (IQ): In 1912, adaptation of Stern's concept of an intelligence quotient (IQ) in the Stanford-Binet Intelligence Scale was the most important development in the area of intelligence testing. Stern put forth the notion that to derive an IQ and Terman incorporated this concept into the 1916 version of Stanford-Binet Scale. To obtain the IQ, a person's mental age is divided by his/her chronological or real age. This product is further multiplied by hundred to avoid decimal fractions.

$$IQ = \frac{\text{Mental Age}}{\text{Chronological Age}} \times 100$$

Emotional Quotient (EQ): The term Emotional Quotient (EQ) may be defined as a relative measure of one's emotional intelligence possessed by him at a particular period of his life. Emotional Quotient represents the relative measures of a person's emotional intelligence similar to intelligence quotient (IQ). This level or potential of one's emotional intelligence is relatively measured through some tests of situations in life, resulting in one's emotional quotients (EQ), a relative measure of one's emotional intelligence or potential.

Cooper and Sawaf (1997) define Emotional intelligence as the ability to sense understand and effectively apply the power and acumen of emotions as a source of human energy, information, connection and influence.

Spiritual Quotient (SQ): Spiritual Intelligence was defined as the ability to apply, manifest, and embody spiritual resources, values, and qualities to enhance daily functioning and wellbeing.

Spiritual Intelligence is "The ability to act with Wisdom and Compassion while maintaining inner and outer peace (equanimity), regardless of the circumstances." Spiritual intelligence is an innate human intelligence – but like any intelligence it must be developed. This means that describe and measure it by looking at the skills that comprise Spiritual Intelligence. It is only Spiritual intelligence that set humans apart from machines and animals. Spiritual intelligence is about compassion and creativity, self-awareness and self-esteem, flexibility and gratitude.

Spirituality is an exercise in Holistic Management of one's integrated-self, in togetherness with the higher pool of energy. So, it is a dynamic process, which gives direction to the human resource building through our conscious efforts. The fruits to follow would be a sustained qualitative growth on the strength of enriched intrinsic energies; a well ordained thought process; and a healthy body. What emerges then is the very best in a person, laying the ground for a successful and fulfilling life.

Relationship among IQ, EQ and SQ

There are some major groups who see the relationship among IQ, EQ and SQ in the following manner:

(1) One group assumes an individual sharing all the three quotients up to some extent. The success and failure, dealing with life situations and leading towards a happy life is the result of interaction of these three quotients.

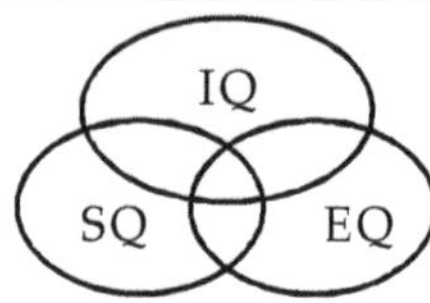

Fig. 2.1

(2) This group assumes the three quotients in hierarchical manner where IQ is at base, above to which is EQ and on top of the triangle is SQ. IQ is a prerequisite for EQ and EQ is a prerequisite for SQ.

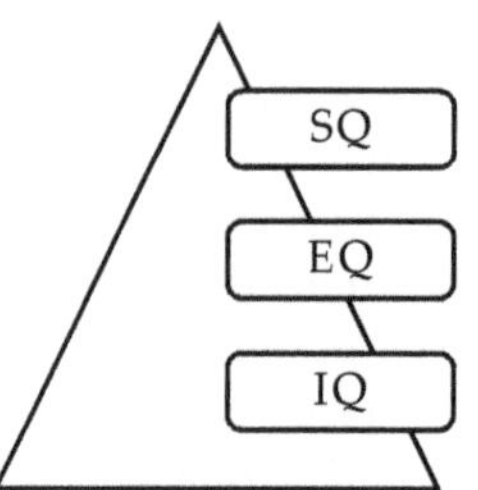

Fig. 2.2

(3) This group assumes that Spiritual Quotient is a sum total of intelligence Quotient and Emotional Quotient.

IQ + EQ = SQ

Fig. 2.3

Comparative understanding of IQ, EQ and SQ

Table 2.1: Comparison of IQ, EQ and SQ

Intelligence	Operations
IQ	Knowledge, Understanding, Application, Analysis, Planning, Execution
EQ	Teamwork, Leadership, Awareness, Action, Relationship Management, Emotional Well-being, Physical Well-being, Optimism, Skills, Experience
SQ	Evaluation, Synthesis, Judgment, Insight, Creativity, Problem Solving, Intuition, Breakthrough Thinking, Inspiration, Vision, Commitment, Resilience, Self-Belief, Happiness, Flow

Q9. Explain the theory of multiple intelligences as identified by Gardner.

Or

Explain the various types of intelligence identified by Gardner with suitable examples. [June-2017, Q.No.-3(a)]

Ans. Multiple intelligences theory allows one to assess the talents and skills of the whole individual rather than just his/her verbal and mathematical skills. Indeed, the theory of multiple intelligences provides a more holistic, natural profile of human potential than an IQ test.

Multiple intelligence theory challenges the notion of IQ in at least three significant ways. MI maintains that: (1) several intelligences are at work, not just one; (2) intelligence is expressed in our performances, products and ideas, not through a test score; and (3) how the intelligences are expressed is culturally defined. Gardner's definition claims that intelligence represents potential that will or will not be brought to bear, depending on the values, available opportunities, as well as personal decisions made by individuals of a particular culture.

To qualify as "intelligence" the particular capacity under study was considered from multiple perspectives consisting of eight specific criteria drawn from the biological sciences, logical analysis, developmental psychology, experimental psychology and psychometrics.

Using biological as well as cultural research, he formulated a list of seven intelligences. This new outlook on intelligence differs greatly from the traditional view which usually recognises only two intelligences, i.e. verbal and computational. Gardner initially proposed that there are at least seven areas of intelligence. Later, he added an eighth intelligence, naturalist intelligence, and a ninth, existential intelligence, both of which have since been analysed (Kane, 1999).

(1) **Linguistic Intelligence ("word smart"):** This involves sensitivity to spoken and written language, the ability to learn languages and the capacity to use language to accomplish certain goals. This intelligence includes the ability to effectively use language to express oneself rhetorically or poetically; and language as a means to remember information. Writers, poets, lawyers and speakers are among those that Howard Gardner sees as having high linguistic intelligence.

(2) **Logical-mathematical intelligence ("number/ reasoning smart"):** It consists of the capacity to analyse problems logically, carry out mathematical operations and investigate issues scientifically. In Howard Gardner's words, it entails the ability to detect patterns, reason deductively and think logically. This intelligence is most often associated with scientific and mathematical thinking.

(3) **Musical intelligence ("music smart"):** This involves skill in the performance, composition and appreciation of musical patterns. It encompasses the capacity to recognise and compose musical pitches, tones and rhythms. According to Howard Gardner, musical intelligence runs in an almost structural parallel to linguistic intelligence. People with a high musical intelligence normally have good pitch and may even have absolute pitch and are able to sing, play musical instruments and compose music. Since, there is a strong auditory component to this intelligence, those who are strongest in it

may learn best via lecture. Language skills are typically highly developed in those whose base intelligence is musical.

(4) **Bodily-kinesthetic intelligence ("body smart"):** It uses the body effectively, like a dancer or a surgeon. Keen sense of body awareness–they are like movement, making things, touching. They communicate well through body language and be taught through physical activity, hands-on learning, acting out and role-playing. Tools include equipments and real objects. Careers that suit those with this intelligence include athletes, dancers, musicians, actors, surgeons, doctors, builders, police officers and soldiers. Although these careers can be duplicated through virtual simulation, they will not produce the actual physical learning that is needed in this intelligence.

(5) **Spatial intelligence ("picture smart"):** It is taken in terms of physical space, as do architects and sailors–very aware of their environments. They like to draw, do jigsaw puzzles, read maps, daydream. They can be taught through drawings, verbal and physical imagery. Tools include models, graphics, charts, photographs, drawings, 3-D modeling, video, videoconferencing, television, multimedia, texts with pictures/charts/graphs.

(6) **Interpersonal intelligence ("people smart"):** It relates with an understanding of interacting with others. These students learn through interaction. They have many friends, empathy for others and also, they are street smarts. They can be taught through group activities, seminars and dialogues. Tools include the telephone, audio conferencing, time and attention from the instructor, video conferencing, writing, computer conferencing and e-mail.

(7) **Intrapersonal intelligence ("self smart"):** It relates with an understanding of one's own interests and goals. These learners tend to shy away from others. They are in tune with their inner feelings; they have wisdom, intuition and motivation, as well as a strong will, confidence and opinions. They can be taught through independent study and introspection. Tools include books, creative materials, diaries, privacy and time. They are the most independent of the learners.

(8) **Naturalistic Intelligence ("nature smart"):** This involves understanding the natural world of plants and animals, noticing their characteristics and categorising them; it generally involves keen observation and the ability to classify other things as well.

(9) **Existential Intelligence:** This involves sensitivity and capacity to tackle deep questions about human existence, such as the meaning of life, why do we die, and how did we get here.

Q10. Define and discuss the concept of personality.

Ans. The term "personality" is derived from the Latin word *'persona'* that means "mask". Among the Greeks, actors used a mask to hide their identity on stage. This dramatic technique was later adopted by the Romans to whom *persona* denoted "as one appears to others" not as one actually is. *Persona* literally means, "mask", although it does not usually refer to a literal mask, but to the "social masks", all humans supposedly wear. Thus, personality is used in terms of influencing others through external appearance. Sum total of ways in which an individual reacts and interacts with others.

Personality is an internalised system, which includes all those aspects of a person that are inherited as well as those that are learned. These two internal aspects are interdependent and cannot be isolated.

According to Gordon Allport, "Personality is the dynamic organisation within the individual of those psychophysical systems that determine his unique adjustments to his environment".

According to Munn, "Personality is the most characteristic integration of an individual's structures and activities".

According to Carl Rogers, "Personality is self-organised, permanent, subjectively perceived entity which is at the very heart of all our experiences".

According to Erickson, "Personality is the outcome of a series of psychological crises".

According to Ruch, personality should include:

- external appearance and behaviour or social stimulus value;
- inner awareness of self as a permanent organising force; and
- the particular pattern or organisation of measurable traits, both inner and outer.

In other words, personality refers to the total person in his overt and covert behaviour. It includes many factors of his being as well as his social, mental, emotional, cultural and physical aspects. His personality is the reflection of his inner self. His behaviour causes others to respond to him favourably or unfavourably. Hence, his effectiveness as an individual depends upon the extent to which he develops his potentials and how he utilises his talents, capacities and intelligence in dealing with other people. Also, he must know how to adjust equally well to various life situations that confront him with full satisfaction for him and for the people around him.

One who impresses other people is considered as a person having good personality with the ability to get on well with others, whereas those who does not possess such ability is said to have relatively poor personality. However, if one considers personality from a scientific point of view, being attractive to others is not a true concept of personality. In fact, psychologists consider any attempt to define personality in terms of social attractiveness as inadequate because of the following two reasons:

(1) It limits the number and types of behaviours considered important and worthy for incorporation into the study of personality.

(2) Such a notion implies that some people who have unique abilities, temperament and traits are devoid of having a personality.

Psychologists have attempted to explain the concept of personality in terms of individuality and consistency. We often observe that people differ a great deal in the ways they think, feel and act and that too to different or even same situations.

This distinctive pattern of behaviour helps one to define one's identity. Commenting upon the notion of individuality, it has been said that each of us in certain respects is like all other persons, like some other person and like no other person who has been in the past or will be existing in the future.

Another important notion in defining the concept of personality is consistency. In other words, it can be stated that the concept of personality also rests on the observation that a person seems to behave somewhat consistently in different situations over different time. From this observation of perceived consistency comes the notion of personality traits that determine the way of responding to one's world.

In other words, it can be said that personality refers to all those relatively permanent traits, dispositions or characteristics within the person that give some measures of consistency to the person's behaviour. These traits may be unique, common to some groups or shared by the entire species but their pattern will be different from individual to individual.

The thoughts, feelings and actions that are perceived as reflecting an individual's personality typically have the following three characteristics:

(1) The behaviours of the person seem to have organisation and structure.

(2) Thoughts, feelings and actions are considered as behavioural components of identity that make distinction between individuals

(3) Behaviours are viewed as being primarily caused by internal rather than environmental factors.

Q11. How will you overcome the myths about personality in order to facilitate learners?

Ans. The myths may be inferred, in following manner:

(i) Personality cannot be developed: Nature Vs Nurture

(ii) There are successful and unsuccessful personality: Learning background

(iii) Personalities can be typified: Uniqueness Vs Labeling

- Following issues may be taken care so far as learning is concerned:
- Children of the same age differ so much in their personalities, abilities, interests and general adjustment that is highly desirable to adapt the school to these individual differences.
- Within heterogeneous group appeal can be made to the individual child by having him take appropriate parts in different classroom activities.
- A learner has personality, physical and educational weaknesses and strengths. As a rule a learner will benefit most by developing his individual talents and interests and simultaneously overcome his weaknesses sufficiently so that they will not handicap him.

- Ideally, learners of about the same social, intellectual and educational maturity should be in the same groups and taught according to their needs and ability to learn.
- The bright learners who achieve well and wishes to work hard should be accelerated accordingly. High-achieving bright learners generally benefit both academically and socially by acceleration.

Mostly every learner wants to be successful at their various school tasks and is happy when he is able to do them will; though he wants to be challenged by his tasks, he does not want the tasks to be difficult that they setup feelings of frustration and defeat. At the same time, every ordinary group of learners is comprised of individuals who differ widely in their personalities, motivations, capacities and abilities. Thus, tasks that are easy for some learners will be too difficult for others and some will grasp lessons much faster than other. Learners will therefore be happiest and do their best work in classes where the experiences are suited to them as individuals and the school must guide each child so that his experiences will satisfy the needs.

Q12. Define learner preparedness. What a teacher can do to enhance learners preparedness for learning?

Ans. Preparedness means readiness to learn anything which is new for an individual. The readiness means that when a learner is ready for a modifiable connection and is ready to act and to do so is satisfying; whereas lack of readiness leads to dissatisfying act. Readiness is dependent upon both maturation and experience. It is supposed that without readiness for acquiring new knowledge the speed of learning will be slower than having readiness. This propagates importance of preparedness for learning.

There are few steps a teacher can do to enhance learners preparedness for learning which are as follows:

- Teacher should know when the learner is prepared to learn. If any learner is not prepared then teacher should provide him/her with such experiences through which s/he becomes ready to learn.
- Teacher should analyse the factors which may be hindering the preparedness of the learner. Indentify those factors and try to overcome those.
- One of the important factors affecting learner's preparedness is interest of the learner in the subject/content. Identify his/her interest and prepare him/her accordingly.
- Sometimes, learners with different learning styles are asked to learn with similar methodology taught by the teacher. Their learning styles and learning preferences affect their preparedness to learn. Teacher should be aware of their styles and introduce flexibility in teaching-learning process which can be adapted to all kind of learners.
- The classroom environment should be made learner centered so that learners may become more inclined towards acquiring new knowledge and skill.

Q13. What do you mean by motivation? Discuss its types and approaches.

Ans. The word motivation is derived from Latin word 'motum', which means to move, motor or motion. Motivation is the inner force, which drives one's behaviour towards goal. Some learners learn the same subject matter or task more efficiently than others, some find it more rewarding and interesting than others; and some enjoy it more than others. At any given time, learners vary in the extent to which they are willing to direct their energies to the attainment of goals, due to difference in motivation. According to Blair and Simpson, "Motivation is a process in which the learner's internal energies are directed towards various goal objects in his environment."

Some psychologists have explained motivation in terms of personal traits or individual characteristics. According to them, some students have a strong need to achieve, the fear of tests, or an enduring interest in art as part of their personality make-up and will thus spend hours or engage in considerable hard work to achieve, to avoid tests and visit art galleries. Other psychologists see motivation more as a state, a temporary situation. For example, students studying only to pass their exam next day. Here motivation is determined by the challenge of the situation. In reality, in any given situation and at any point of time, motivation is usually a combination of trait and state.

Most of the psychologists are of the opinion that three key factors are associated with motivation which are needs, drive and incentive.

(1) Needs: For our physiological well-being food, drink and sleep are really essentially. Our body cannot survive without these things. So while there is want of food, the man becomes victims of hunger. Apart from this, there are also psychological and social motives. For e.g. it is very difficult to remain in the society without love and praise. So, needs may be physiological and psychological. Need is the first step in the motivation.

The feeling of lack of something is called the need. Every individual has basic needs and in order to gratify, he activates. The basic physiological needs are those of food, water, sleep and sex, etc. and the mental or social needs include fame, affection, security, adequacy, social approval, etc. Maslow has presented a clear hierarchy of needs. According to him, if the basic physiological needs are well met, the individual is able to meet the higher level needs more efficiently.

(2) Drive: Drive originates from needs and is in fact the psychological consequence of a need. The drive set in motion the compensatory activities whenever the internal physiochemical balance is threatened by unfavorable temperature, lack of food, water, excess of waste products, toxins' etc. Drive of any nature can be divided into two categories:

(i) Biological or Primary Drive: Hunger, thirst, sex etc.

(ii) Socio-Psychological Drive: Fear, anxiety desire for approval, aggression, etc.

Whether a need is physiological or psychological, each individual tries to satisfy his/her need. The innate tendency to satisfy the need is drive which forces one to act accordingly. Drive directs a person to act for satisfaction of need. Intensity of drive depends upon nature of need.

(3) **Incentives:** Incentive is an object or response of others that can fulfill the need and decrease the tension due to drive condition. Food in case of hunger, water in case of thirst and member of the opposite sex in case of sex drive are said to be incentive which satisfy their respective physiological need. When incentive is achieved, the severity of drive gets decreased, the mental tension withers away and balance of body and mind is restored.

Types of Motivation: There are basically two types of motivation, i.e. intrinsic motivation and extrinsic motivation.

(1) **Intrinsic Motivation:** Intrinsic motivation is a drive that comes from within the child. It is an aspect of the child's nature or personality. This type of motivation can be encouraged or discouraged by a number of factors including the structure of the classroom, the teacher, class size, the responsiveness of the parents to the child and many other factors. Many children never lose their intrinsic motivation because of their personality and the positive nature of the aforesaid circumstances. More often, motivation only becomes a factor in the education of a child when it is lost. At that point, placing blame is disputable, and motivation must be re-established by extrinsic factors.

(2) **Extrinsic Motivation:** Extrinsic motivation is external. It is motivation that comes from the possibility of a 'reward' or acknowledgment. The very nature of our educational system in this country is based on extrinsic or external rewards: report cards and grades, honour rolls, standardised test scores, medals and so on. This grade-based system may actually shade a child's natural, intrinsic motivation. That is why parents and educators must work to ensure that such a blurring of motivational factors does not occur. Once intrinsic motivation is lost, extrinsic motivational techniques must be utilised in order to encourage a child to take responsibility for academic success or failure.

Approaches of Motivation: There are following approaches of motivation:

- The **behaviourists** tend to emphasise extrinsic motivation caused by incentives, rewards and punishment. They believe that if we are consistently reinforced for certain behaviours, we may develop habits or tendencies to act in certain ways. For example, if a student is repeatedly rewarded with affection, money, praise or privileges for playing cricket for his school, but receives little recognition for his studies, he will work much longer and harder at cricket than the studies.

- The **humanistic** view stresses intrinsic motivation created by the need for personal growth, fulfilment and self-determination. These theorists believe that people are continually motivated by the inborn need to fulfil their potential. To motivate students means, thus trying to encourage them to use their inner resources-their sense of competence, self-esteem, autonomy and self-actualisation.
- The **cognitive approach** stresses a person's active search for meaning, understanding and competence as the basis of motivation. They believe that our behaviour is determined by our thinking and not simply by whether we have been rewarded or punished. In fact, behaviour is initiated and regulated by plans, goals, schemes, expectations and attributions. Thus, cognitive theories emphasise intrinsic motivation. Individuals are seen as active and curiously searching for information to solve personally relevant problems and concerns.
- The **socio-cultural** views of motivation emphasise participation in communities of practice. They believe that people engage in activities to maintain their identities and interpersonal relations within the community. Students are motivated to learn if they are members of a classroom or school community that values learning. When we see ourselves as artists, or engineers, or teachers, or students of class IX, we have an identity within a group and are motivated to contribute to the group.

Q14. What is the relationship between need, drive and intensive?

Ans. Need and drive are the internal stages of the organism whereas intensives exit in the external world. Drive is created thanks to need. Because of the drive condition, tension is felt. To avoid this tension, the organism is put to action. By virtue of this action, the intensive is obtained.

As soon as the incentive is obtained, the need no longer remains and the drive and the tension are decreased. Like this, any activity that is caused due to some need ends only when the need is fulfilled by the achievement of incentive. Thus, need, drive and incentive are factors involved in the process of motivation. This process starts with the achievement of the incentive. This is called need-drive-incentive formula.

Q15. What is the role of motivation in learning? Discuss the role of a teaching in motivating a learner.

Ans. Motivation plays a great role in accelerating learning in the child. It is a kind of force generation in the learners, sustaining, directing and controlling the various activities of the pupil till the goal is achieved. Motivation may be regarded as something which prompts, compels and energizes an individual to act/behave in a particular manner, at a particular time for attaining some specific goals. It may also be formally defined as an internal state that arouses, directs and maintains behaviour. A teacher should know various techniques to motivate the learner. S/he should also be careful to draw the attention of the student by devising suitable mechanisms or methods.

In the learning process, the learner who responds to the external stimulus so that to acquire changes in the behaviour needs motivation. It is the factor that influences the improvement and achievement of the learners. No learning is possible without motivation. In the learning process, the source of motivation may be complex. It may be either intrinsic or extrinsic.

Motivation leads to self-actualization in learning. It helps in satisfying the needs of the learner. It develops an individual to acquire competencies like independent, democratic, adaptable approaches and creative, interpersonal, problem solving skills.

Brophy defined motivation "to learn as 'a student', tendency to find academic activities meaningful worthwhile and to try to drive the intended academic benefits from them.

Key characteristics of motivation to learn are:

- It involves more than wanting or intending to learn.
- It includes the quality of the learners' mental effort.

Every teacher assumes that his/her learners are motivated to learn but it is never true. Teachers have to achieve certain goals:

(1) Involve their learners productively in all the activities of class, i.e. create a state of motivation to learn.

(2) Develop a habit of being motivated to learn among their learners. Their learners should be ready to learn lifetime from various sources, whenever they get an opportunity to learn.

(3) Make them thoughtful so that they can think deeply about what they study. For this, activities like summarising, elaborating the basic ideas, outlining in their own words, diagrammatically representing the relationships etc. can be practiced with them.

Role of a Teacher: To motivate, there are few strategies, which a teacher can try or can devise to his/her own too:

- Make children's academic work more enjoyable and interesting.
- Teacher can develop some learning centers like, for languages, mathematics, science, social sciences, etc. where they can encourage learners to work individually or collaboratively on some projects of their own choice. Teacher can also create some interest groups.
- Create an environment in classroom, where learners feel free to express, share, debate and discuss their views. Promote critical thinking and develop a habit of acceptance of criticism too.
- Set those learning goals, which are possible to achieve. Our clear, specific and possible to reach goal will motivate the learners. A sense of progress in aching small goals will motivate children to achieve bigger goal.
- Develop a habit of problem solving among their learners. They should be encouraged to analyse the problems, identify the solutions and apply to know which one will be the best solution.
- Encourage a habit of self-comparison among learners i.e. they should develop a habit of listening what is wrong and reflect on

their own that why it is wrong. Avoid comparing children's work among themselves.

- Teachers' enthusiasm, confidence, competence in subject area and presenting ourselves as an intrinsically motivated teacher affects learners positively. They should build up the confidence level of children's abilities and skills.
- Begin their teaching from learners' level and gradually move upwards in small steps.

Q16. What is meant by aptitude and what are its components? Do individual differ in aptitude? Discuss instructional strategy for handling individual differences.

Ans. The set of abilities essential for acquiring knowledge and skills specific to an area of performance is called aptitude. Precisely, it denotes the set of abilities required to perform a specialised activity. For example, when we say aptitude for engineering and aptitude for art, the set of abilities involved in learning performing in engineering is different from that of art. The same is true for medicine, mathematics, science, music, teaching or athletics.

Components of aptitude: There are following components of aptitude:

(1) Intellectual processes – Intellectual processes are a major component of aptitude. It refers to multiple cognitive processes related to thinking such as memory processes, restructuring symbols and ideas, perception of relations and patterns between ideas, spatial comprehension or orientation, reasoning, problem solving, judgement, etc. These cognitive processes are important for recognition of information and for innovation, invention or discovery while performing a task.

(2) Sensory components – Sensory component refers to the abilities related to sensory process such as vision and audition. Vision implies the ability for visual sensitivity. Audition means the ability to hear tones at different pitch levels (pitch discrimination, loudness discrimination, etc.).

(3) Psychomotor component – Psychomotor component refers to the kind of abilities involved in the gross body movements or its parts-trunk, limbs, hands, etc. The kinds of abilities involved are strength, impulsion, speed, precision and flexibility. Strength means strength of body parts-leg, trunk and hand (e.g. hand grip). Impulsion refers to the rate of initiation of a movement and can be identified using reaction time to light or sound (e.g. time taken to start at the signal in an athletic event). Speed means the rate of movement (e.g. hand or finger or leg speed while performing an act). Precision implies steadiness in performing an act or movements (e.g. putting pins through tiny holes rapidly). Flexibility refers to the looseness of the joints (e.g. touch toes with fingers without bending knees).

Intelligence vs. aptitude: Aptitude is differ from intelligence. While intelligence refers to a set of mental abilities and skills, the term aptitude refers to the set of those abilities which directs individual performance in certain specific areas, such as teaching aptitude, mechanical aptitude, etc. One may like to know the difference between aptitude and academic achievement. Though both are important for determining future learning, academic achievement reflects the effects of learning of a specific subject or a set of subjects during a given period of time. Aptitude reflects the cumulative influence of a combination of a set of abilities and a multiplicity of experiences (including learning subjects) in daily life. For example, a student of your class may be very intelligent but that student may not have an aptitude for public speaking or dancing for that matter.

Individual Differ in Aptitude: Individuals in differ aptitude. An individual may have a mechanical aptitude. Another individual may have an aptitude for mathematics or yet another may have an aptitude for logic. Such differences are due to the differences in the combination of abilities which are related to the cognitive process and the sensory and psychomotor components for instance, mechanical aptitude is connected with ability for spatial relations, ability to acquire information on mechanical matters and ability to comprehend mechanical differences in aptitude using aptitude tests. Aptitude tests for areas such as mechanical skills, science, language, music and graphic art can be used to identify the aptitude of students in each area of performance. The aptitude test, in fact, provides a measure of the candidates promise or teachability in a field of study, say law. In other words, the test would tell whether the candidate possesses the required aptitude or readiness to profit from studies in the concerned field of study.

Instructional Strategy for Handling Individual Differences

In instructional strategy, at least two alternative instructional treatments are needed to ensure academic success, which is the most appropriate instructional treatment for the student depends upon his or her existing level of aptitude (learning readiness). Students with high aptitude may choose unstructured instructional strategy. With minimum guidance from teacher, they may be encouraged to learn through the discovery oriented approach. Teacher may use the inductive process but instructional treatment is essentially learner-centered.

For low aptitude learners, highly structured instructional treatment is designed in small units through sequential steps and feedback. Frequent summary and review with simplified illustration, analogy and precise explanation of concepts and principle to be learned will facilitate progressive learning. Periodic achievement and aptitude assessments and comparison of these scores with the aptitude scores obtained at the start of instruction would tell degree to which each learner in the specific treatment group has achieved.

However, compensatory aptitude training is suggested for those who are unable to profit from either of the alternative treatments presented above. This consists of directed reading skills, study habits, self-learning skills, note taking and related activities. The main aim of compensatory aptitude training is to develop readiness for entry into structured treatment. Periodic monitoring should be formulated to identify the students who reach the required level for entry into alternative treatment.

Implications of Aptitude for teachers:

(1) Aptitude includes both inborn capacity and the effects of environment on the individual.

(2) Learning in any area is conditioned by the leaner's readiness to learning.

(3) A specific aptitude in the form of talent may show itself early and respond readily to training in future.

Q17. Discuss the nature of attitude. How are they learnt or acquired? What are the reasons of different attitude?

Or

How can a teacher facilitate learning for attitude? Briefly discuss.

Ans. Personality tract which indicates towards individuals likes or dislikes is called attitude. Attitude influences the way an individual behaves towards an object, institution or a person. Attitude towards a particular object is influenced by parents, teachers, school and society in which the individual lives.

Nature of Attitude

Environment around us consists of all kinds of objects, people, groups and institutions. An individual does not always react, to these experiences a fresh in every encounter. The cognition, feelings and response dispositions that these objects recurrently evoke, get organised into a unified and enduring system. Attitudes predispose the individual to act in particular ways towards these objects, persons, situations or ideas and there is a degree of consistency in his response to these.

According to G.W. Allport, "Attitudes is a mental and neutral state of readiness. Organised through experience, exerting a directive and dynamic influence upon an individual's response to the objects and situations with which it is related." Thus, the attitudes of a student are formed due to his experience and interaction with real situations.

Attitudes provide the frame of reference for a person's life. Attitude involves organisation of motivational, emotional, perceptive and cognitive processes. In this way, attitudes are reinforced by information (the cognitive component) and often generate strong felling (the emotional component) that may lead to a particular form of response (i.e. the action-tendency component).

Harrison (1976) has identified three components in attitudes as under:

- Beliefs
- Emotions
- Behaviour

These are explained as under:

(1) Beliefs are what one considers desirable and undesirable.

(2) Attitudes are accompanied by emotions they influence each other, the resultant behaviour is always a complete interplay of both.

(3) The individual displays his likes as dislikes (attitudes) through his action (behaviour).

Attitudinal information is governed in the following way:

(1) On the one hand, by socio-cultural influences operating on the individual.

(2) On the other, the nature of experiences that the individual has and the information he is exposed to.

Positive and Negative Attitudes: Many attitudes cannot be neutral so children acquire or learn positive as negative attitude from their parents, peers and schools.

A brief description of them is as under:

(1) Negative Attitudes: They lead to avoidance, disagreements, arguments, conflicts or other confrontations. Prejudice is a premature or snap judgement that is made before examining the facts.

(2) Positive Attitudes: They can induce an individual to assist other people, to be at peace with his word.

Acquisition of Attitudes and Attitude Change: Initially, all the children imitate the attitude of parents. Later, in school, teachers and peers contribute to the formation of attitudes.

Unchangeable Nature of Attitudes: Attitudes, once formed, are resistant to change. Explanation, unconditioning or rational analysis of errors in perception or fallacies cannot change attitude. Attitudes, whether good or bad, do change. Many attitudinal changes are accompanied by changes in the personality.

Facilitating Learning of Attitude

To facilitate learning of an attitude, it is necessary to identify the attitude to be acquired and clarify the meaning of the attitude. After getting it done a person should share his experiences about attitude building. It would be better if he can arrange appropriate contexts for practice and reinforcement of the attitude. For this, one can also use group techniques to facilitate understanding and acceptance of that attitude.

Dealing with Extreme Attitudes: We should not emphasise on agreement upon all attitudes and values. However there must be a sufficiently large core of common attitudes and value for people to live together reasonably well.

Causes of Individual Differences in Attitude

One can see individual differences in attitudes in students. This is due to variety in maturity levels, planned and random experiences, extent of warmth physical surroundings, exhibited, democracy and indulgence in home environment, schooling, playmates and exposure to media. An object liked by one may be disliked by others and vice-versa. The result would be attitudinal differences among individuals.

An intellectually mature individual can change and modify his attitudes, if he happens to realise that his attitudes are narrow, biased or even wrong. On the other hand, the intellectually immature individual will cling to his attitude even though there is enough evidence to indicate that it is desirable. A young child is reverent in his attitude towards religion. Adolescence children are reported to be skeptics and agnostics. Adolescents differ in their attitude towards authority (teachers, principals, leaders, and parents) the difference depends on the satisfaction or figures of dissatisfaction which they derived during the course of their interaction with them.

Q18. What is creativity? Do individuals differ in creativity? Can creativity be fostered?

Or

Discuss the various ways to foster creativity among learners. [June-2017, Q.No.-3(b)]

Ans. The ability to create or discover something that is novel and has some value for the society is called creativity. For example, the discovery of penicillin, formulation of the concept of relativity, creation of television, Tagore's work Gitanjali and the link are acts of creativity. The definition of creativity stated that something that is created should be novel and of some value. Novel means the unusual nature of the thing that is created whether it is penicillin, the concept of relativity or Gitanjali. The emphasis is on the production of something new. Equally important is the value which means that products of creativity should be of some value to humanbeings. For instance, the discovery of penicillin, formulation of the concept of relativity and creation of television have been turning points in the development of knowledge as well as for human beings and society. Further, Tagore's writings speak certain basic truths about humanity and seem as powerful now as when he conceived them. Psychologists in general, to name a few, Guilford, Hayes, Taylor, Torrance, Wallach and Kogan, accept the novelty and value aspects of creativity.

Do Individual Differ in Creativity

The major component of creativity is divergent thinking which refers to the thinking process involved in generating alternative ideas or answers to a given problem. Creativity involves a cluster of abilities based on the divergent thinking process. They are as under in a hierarchical order.

(1) **Ability to sense problems** i.e. an awareness of the defects needs and deficiencies in the environment. For example, sensing the need to improve the telephone.

(2) **Fluency** i.e. the ability to express or generate multiple solutions of a given problem or concept. For example, list the number of uses of the newspaper.

(3) **Flexibility** i.e. the ability to state a variety of solutions or answers to a problem and reflects the ability to change the direction of one's thinking. For example, variety of uses of the newspaper can be identified as source of news, packing material.

(4) **Originality** i.e. the ability to produce unique or new ideas. Inventions are the most common example of this aspect of creativity. For example, ability to suggest a new title of a poem.

(5) **Elaboration** i.e. the ability to develop well an idea or insight. For example, the idea that by providing only information to students does not develop their competencies rather the task or activity-based approach would ensure students involvement in learning and development of competencies.

(6) **Redefinition** i.e. the ability to improvise operations in situations where a familiar function is performed with an object which is not normally used to perform such a function. For example, using a bangle or a cold drink can draw circles. Though creativity is essentially based on the ability of divergent thinking, psychologists opine that components such as intelligence, knowledge and motivation are linked to creativity. In fact, intelligence involves, cognition and convergent thinking i.e. form of thinking which is needed in a situation where there is only one acceptable answer.

Psychologists opine that a certain level of intelligence is required for creativity. For instance, Machinnon had studied highly creativity individuals link (biologists, mathematicians, architects and social scientists. These person had IQs ranging from 120 to 177. The study indicates that highly creative individuals had higher than average level of intelligence. Yet they were not brighter than their noncreative colleagues. It means that there is no difference in the IQ scores of say, the highly creative architect and the non-creative architect. Thus, if a person possesses higher than average level of intelligence alone it does not guarantee or give assurance of creativity. It implies that creativity is essentially divergent thinking process but there is a place for cognition and convergent thinking too.

The reality is that creativity is directly linked to knowledge and motivation. A biologists or a musician cannot become creative until he acquires a great deal of knowledge in the field of biology or music. By devoting study over a long period of time one becomes able to gain knowledge in the field. Motivation to produce original work is another factor. Motivational factor, consist of the following.

(1) A desire to question.

(2) High intellectual persistence.

(3) Tendency to put up with frustration of not being able to find solution.

(4) Delight in trying with ideas and curiosity.

Thus, divergent thinking abilities, intelligence, knowledge and motivation are helpful in understanding creativity and in identifying individual differences in creativity. The fact is that individuals do not possess the same level of divergent thinking abilities, knowledge, intelligence and motivation. Such differences create difference in creativity. Such individuals, besides some other traits link the ability to sense problem fluency, originality, flexibility, elaboration and redefinition, are not found in the equal level in the same individual. Again, differences in intelligence, knowledge and motivation strengthen, the difference in creativity. Thus, differences in divergent thinking abilities, intelligence, knowledge and motivation, are responsible for differences in creativity in the field of study or work chosen by individuals.

Can creativity be fostered

Creative abilities can be enhanced if appropriate, supportive behaviour and classroom practices are provided. Following are the techniques of attaining this:

(1) **Encourage unusual or odd questions:** Teacher should encourage their student's curiosity and accept unusual question. For example, a student may ask teacher, how does a cloud form? The teacher takes a half-filled beaker with boiling water and closes the top with an ice piece. Students are asked to observe what happens. They notice evaporation and a cloud-link formation in the upper portion of the beaker. In the ensuing discussion they relate water, heat, evaporation, temperature, cloud, and rain all this leads further to the concept of different states of matter. Teacher acceptance of the questions encourages the student's curiosity to know. Quite often teachers dismiss such questions by saying, 'you find for yourself'. An indifferent or negative attitude of a teacher damages a student's thinking process and creative effort.

(2) **Provide activities to promote creative thinking/abilities:** For example, by following things, ask students to list unusual uses they can:

Ball pen Paper Rope

Shoe Book Candle

Discuss the answers and help each student to understand his or her fluency, flexibility and originality. Continue the exercise using different items.

(3) **Organise brainstorming sessions:** This is a strategy where each member of the group generates ideas to find solutions to a given problem. The teacher presents the problem to the brainstorming group and directs each member of the group to state one idea at a time. After one round, the session moves on to the second and is on leading to several rounds. One is encouraged to generate an idea based on another's idea (hitch hiking) but not allowed to criticise another member's idea. Ideas thus generated, are further scrutinised by members for choosing the idea with the most potential to solve the problem.

(4) **Use synectics:** This strategy is based on analogies to generate ideas. Analogies provide a structure to generate ideas by connecting a familiar content with a new content, or looking at a familiar content from a new perspective. Teacher can use direct analogy or personal analogy. In direct analogy, they compare two objects or ideas. To help students get an insight into the mechanics of a car, for instance, compare it (the mechanics of a car) with the movement of a bird. The students list the connections they see between a car and a bird.

Bird	Car
Brain	engine
Food	petrol
Nervous system	mechanical connections
Sick	breakdown

Now students can be asked to write a short paragraph indicating the analogical connections. In personal analogy, an individual is asked to empathies with an object or an idea to be compared. If the discussion is about air, ask students to imagine themselves to be in the air and express what they feel.

(5) **Provide students situations to evaluate their own ideas or thinking:** Students who make evaluation of their own thinking are less likely to be inhibited in future questioning.

(6) **Extra credit for creative thinking:** While evaluating student's performance in their subject, look for creative ideas. Students exhibiting creative effort should be recognised and rewarded by extra credit. Well, creativity cannot be fostered unless a teacher display originality in his/her classroom behaviour.

Q19. Describe the term interest. What are the individual differences in interest?

Ans. The term interest is used to designate a concept pertaining to factors within an individual which attract him to or repel him from various objects, persons and activities within his environment. Interest is viewed in different ways:

(1) Webester defines interest as excitement of feeling accompanying special attention to some object or concern, such as, an interest in Botany.

(2) An interest is something with which the child identifies his personal wellbeing. Interest is a source of motivation which drives people to do what they want to do when they are free to choose. They specify a condition or cause of attention. We read a book, or attend a lecture on religious discourse, because we are interested in them.

(3) The term 'interest' is also used to connote the felling of pleasure resulting from giving attention to something.

(4) Interest is defined as a feeling of pleasure resulting from attending to something not a cause but a result. Interests become stable by the time development and growth reaches a level of maturity in an individual. Slow maturers have interests in children while their other age mates develop interests those of adolescents.

Interests are influenced by cultural factors and are emotionally weighted. Interest is weakened by an unpleasant emotion (likewise it is) strengthened by pleasant emotion.

Aspects of Interest: Interest has both subjective and objective aspects as under:

(1) **Subjective:** In the subjective aspect, the emphasis in on the feeling component.

(2) **Objective:** In the objective aspect, the emphasis is on the motor behaviour of the individual.

All interests have cognitive, affective as well as motor aspects. The components that make up the cognitive aspects of interest are based on personal experiences gained from various means of communication at home, at school, and in the country. Interests give rise to certain activities. The attitude towards these activities is part of the affective domain. It is developed from personal experiences as well as from the attitudes of others especially parents, teachers and peers towards the particular activities.

Individual Differences in Interest

In the case of all students, physical and psychological characteristics, socio-economic backgrounds; the familial and environmental support, social pressures, attitudes, access and exposure to information and learning opportunities are not the same. Therefore, individuals differ among themselves in their interests.

In interest of children and adolescents, clear-cut differences are discernible in sports and games, school activities and various areas of subject matter at the school level and in almost every classroom. Their interests range from very low to very high. For example, some children may like playing most of the time while others prefer reading.

Infants present evidence of interest in the form of attention. Exploratory activities are the interests of the child during first two or three years. Nursery school children between 2-5 years of age are interested in toys. This interest in movement seems to increase with age for boys and shows a decline for girls.

At the age of five or six patterns of likes and dislikes are not the same. Marked sex differences are observed in what children like or dislike. Girls avoid physical activities, and seldom exhibit aggression. Boys dislike anything called inappropriate.

Before and after childhood the sexuality characteristics differ. Small children play with children of both sexes. Pre-school group turns to unusual friendships. Children of the age group five to eight feel neither embarrassment in playing with opposite sex nor do they feel embarrassed in getting physical affection from adults. During adolescence both sexes shows interest in heterosexual group activities. Adolescents are more interested in sex, personal attractiveness and getting along with other sex.

Q20. Write short note on the following:

(i) Growth and Development of Interest

Ans. In born and acquired are two kinds of interests. Interest grows out of three kinds of learning experiences:

- Trial and error learning.
- Identification with people they love or admire, and
- Guidance and directions they receive from others.

The child's physical and mental development closely parallels to the development of interest. Limitations in his physical and mental capacities or in his experience set limits on his interest. Interests develop through:

- Contact with wide range of desirable activities,
- Activities proportionate to capacities, and
- Presence of conditions insuring satisfaction.

(ii) Identification and Importance of Interest

Ans. Children's interest can be identified through:

- Observation of their activities
- The questions they ask
- The topics of their conversation
- The books they read
- Their spontaneous drawings
- Their wishes, and
- Their self-reports of what is of interest of them.

Interests are a contributing factor in motivation to learn. Students who are interested in an academic activity, whether it is through play or work, put more effort in learning than those students who are less interested. It affects their aspirations and lends enjoyment in getting engaged in the activity of their interest. Failure to understand student's interest reduces effectiveness of teaching.

(iii) Role of interest in adolescent development

Ans. Interests plays an important role in adolescent development. Interests lead one to choose activities of his/her choice and acquire knowledge about them. Wide ranges of wholesome interests tend to ensure breadth of experience and personality. Interests facilitate substitution in case of thwarting and help in maintaining mental health. Intense and abiding interests are desirable for efficiency.

Q21. What is curiosity? Also discuss the strategies to promote curiosity.

Ans. Curiosity is a quality related to inquisitive thinking such as exploration, investigation, and learning, evident by observation in humans and other animals. Curiosity is heavily associated with all aspects of human development, in which derives the process of learning and desire to acquire knowledge and skill.

Curiosity may be a great thing that readies the brain to learn sincerely. Many researchers suggest a link between motivation, learning and curiosity. It's no secret that curiosity makes learning more effective and enjoyable. Curious learners not only ask questions, but also actively seek out answers.

John Dewey said, "The curious mind is constantly alert and exploring, seeking material for thought, as a vigorous and healthy body is on the qui vive for nutriment. Eagerness for experience, for new and varied contact, is found where wonder is found. Such curiosity is the only sure guarantee of the acquisition of the primary facts upon which inference must base itself.

In word of Albert Einstein, "The important thing is not to stop questioning. Curiosity has its own reason for existing."

Instilling students with a strong desire to know or learn something is what every teacher lives for, and research has even shown that curiosity is just as important as intelligence in determining how well students do in school.

Strategies to promote curiosity

(1) **Curiosity prepares the brain for learning:** While it might be no big surprise that we're more likely to remember what we've learned when the subject matter intrigues us, it turns out that curiosity also helps us learn information we don't consider all that interesting or important. The researchers found that, once the subjects' curiosity had been piqued by the right question, they were better at learning and remembering completely unrelated information. One of the study's co-authors, Dr. Matthias Gruber, explains that this is because curiosity puts the brain in a state that allows it to learn and retain any kind of information, like a vortex that sucks in what you are motivated to learn, and also everything around it.

(2) **Curiosity makes subsequent learning more rewarding:** Aside from preparing the brain for learning, curiosity can also make learning a more rewarding experience for students. The researchers found that when the participants' curiosity had been sparked, there was not only increased activity in the hippocampus, which is the region of the brain involved in the creation of memories, but also in the brain circuit that is related to reward and pleasure. This circuit is the same one that lights up when we get something we really like, such as candy or money, and it relies on dopamine, a "feel-good" chemical that relays messages between neurons and gives us a sort of high.

(3) **Asking the Right Question:** Naturally, about curiosity's role in learning, there are still few things that remain unclear. For one thing, scientists have yet to determine its long-term effects. For example, if a student's curiosity is stimulated at the beginning of a school day will it help them better absorb information all day long? Another thing the researchers are keen to investigate is why some people are more naturally curious than others and which factors most influence how curious we are. So rather than jumping straight into the answers, one should try to start students off with the sort of questions that encourage them to do their own seeking.

(4) **Be curious yourself:** Curiosity is contagious. Try a new sport, start a new hobby or take an online course in an unfamiliar subject. Seek out people with different backgrounds and viewpoints, and then actively listen to what they say. Teacher take on these new challenges, share our experiences with their leaner-the excitement, the rewards and the challenges. In this process, teacher will inspire their learner to tackle new subjects

and persevere through the initial discomfort that often comes with learning something unfamiliar.

(5) **Ask questions and answer the questions:** Teachers have heard the saying. "It's the journey, not the destination." When it comes to curiosity, it's the question, not the answer that engages learners. The destination has value and will reward a leaner's hard work. The journey, however, makes that end result more exciting and satisfying. Curiosity starts the journey and motivates a learner to keep going, no matter how rocky the path is.

To draw learners in, teacher need to ask open-ended questions that encourage them to seek out their own answers-questions that cannot be answered with a yes or a no or a shrug of the shoulders. Open-ended questions can begin with phrases like:

(i) What would happen if ....

(ii) What would it be like to ....

(iii) Why did ...

(iv) How do we know that ...

(v) What did you think when ...

(6) **Practice and encourage active listening.** If no one is listening great questions are pointless. When teacher actively listen to their learner, they are also demonstrating how he or she can live curiously and communicate effectively. By example, show their learner how to listen with full attention, how to play back or paraphrase the speaker's comments, and how to ask questions that generate more information and maybe even more questions.
Best source for IGNOU help books—Gullybaba dot com.

(7) **Present new information in chunks.** For arousing curiosity, information should be presented in small chunks. The learner will be forced to think about the next chunk, if information is presented in small chunks.

For Sure Success Best Read GPH Books
Order Now 9312235086

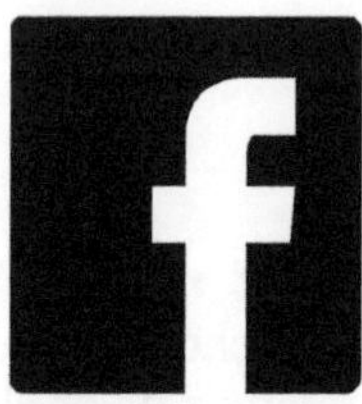

WE'D LOVE IT IF YOU'D LIKE US!

/gphbooks

We're now on Facebook!

Like our page to stay on top of the useful, greatest headlines & exciting rewards.

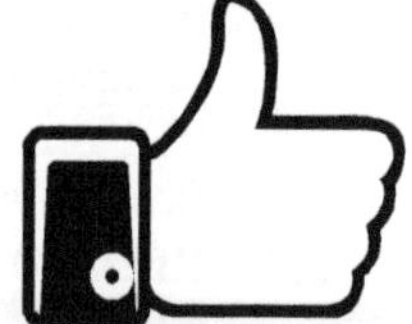

Our other awesome Social Handles:

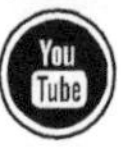

gphbooks
For awesome & informative videos for IGNOU students

9350849407
Order now through WhatsApp

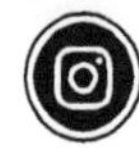

gphbooks
We are in pictures

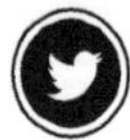

gphbook
Words you get empowered by

Teaching-Learning Process

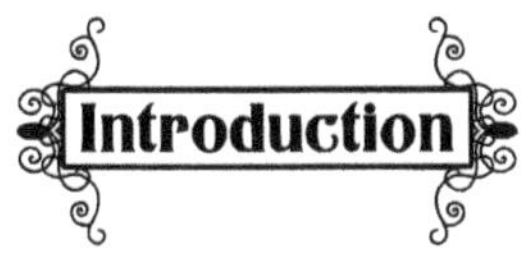

Teaching has a wide spectrum all around it. A teacher has certain responsibilities, duties and rights towards his/her profession that have been taken up. The teaching must inculcate the values and prepare an overall developed individual who can adjust in the society. Teaching is directed towards certain desired learning in learners to unlock their potentials. Effective teaching is planned activity. Planning is a vital component of the teaching learning process which provides a complete structure and context for both teacher and learners to accomplish the educational goals. Teaching always remains a planned behavioural activity which may be controlled more by teachers. The teachers should plan classroom time in such a way that it facilitates learner learning and solve a number of managerial problems.

Q1. Discuss the dual nature of teaching.

Or

Is teaching an art or a science? Explain.

Ans. Teaching is both a science and an art. In its simplest form, effective teaching can be seen as the art of applying education research (Makedon). A teacher cannot be effective unless they are able to integrate both the science and the art of teaching. One may be a genius, but if s/he is unable to communicate his/her knowledge effectively, s/he cannot impart that knowledge onto others. Conversely, one may be an excellent orator, able to mesmerise an audience, yet s/he needs to have a knowledge of the subject matter, learning theories and teaching strategies, as well as an understanding of the needs of his/her own students' in order to gain the trust that is essential to creating an effective learning environment.

Teaching as art: Art is an act of performing by hands. As an art, teaching implies the presence of the teacher who through his/her hands moulds learners. Everyone has a complex set of behaviour and judgments, all of which is based on personal experiences. Consequently, teaching as an art is expected to assist learners to discover.

Every individual teacher teaches according to her aptitude, ability, personality and knowledge. For example, during teaching of the 'structure of flower', one teacher may explain in traditional method that it consist of four whorls viz: calyx, corolla, androecium and gynoecium. Another teacher may explain in a more aesthetic way to explain it in an interesting manner. The teacher shows a flower of hibiscus to the children. The colour and beauty of the flower will attract learners' attention. One by one, each part can be shown and explained by visual beauty of the flower. Thus, the structure can be explained aesthetically.

In teaching, the kinesics of teacher can be effective too. The voice, gestures, facial expression, body language and appealing personality of teacher adds beauty to the teaching process. Artists are who excel in their art; similarly, a teacher highlights her strengths instead of teaching in a traditional manner. The teacher uses her positivity and talents to teach the learners successfully.

Teaching is flexibility. There is freedom of expression for both teacher and learners. The teacher accepts criticism and appreciation both and gives scope for creativity. It has more of personal touch or humanistic approach is observed.

Teaching as science: To say that teaching is a science is to say that it is a rational activity, subject to general principles and laws that are discoverable through research. So, teaching can become more systematic, structured and stable.

The approach to teach is based on scientific inquiry, logical sequencing of content and systematic dissemination of it. The objectives are set as goal of teaching. The teaching plan revolves round the achievement of these objectives. For this, the activities are logically arranged and taught in traditional systematic manner. Since teachers are accountable for the result of the teaching, they rarely try to deviate from the sequential teaching pattern. There are some reasons that teaching is science as:

- It is systematic, logically planned and executed in the class
- Before teaching begins, the objectives are fixed to bring desired behavioural changes in the learner.
- All the tools, techniques and strategies are planned beforehand.
- It has an impersonal touch to it.
- All the content of class level has to be transferred within limited time so approach of teaching is justified.
- Humanistic approach may create excitement and interest but good systematic teaching too can do the same.
- Recently new pedagogical approaches which are scientific in nature are also equally beneficial as aesthetic approach.

Teaching observes dual role and a teacher must balance both of them so that the main objective of education is fulfilled successfully. Whenever and wherever required, the role of teaching should be interchanged.

Q2. Examine the morality behind teaching profession.

Ans. According to McClellan 1999, the development of character has been an explicit aim of education ever since the emergence of common schools and the rise of systems of education. The education aims at overall development of a child. Thus, the teacher has an important role to play to attain this aim. In other words, teaching is a morally laden profession. There is a struggle going on within the teacher as well as within the society where the comments like teaching profession has become a business where only money is reaped and morality is neglected, teachers do not teach properly in class so that they can earn money through private coaching, teachers do not work hard in school as they are paid low salary by the management etc.

In the classroom, the environment has totally become academic and moral development has taken a backseat. The learners also need teachers who impart them content knowledge properly and nothing else. The affective domain states that the final achievement is characterisation but that level is reached rarely. The classroom teaching should be a value laden activity i.e. they form intrinsic part of education. The teacher has to decide by what methods it can be achieved. Any content that is taught in class should also have some value based on look or explanation. This can be incorporated during teaching, interaction between teacher-learner or peer discussion. It is a real challenge for teachers to keep in consideration the moral aspect during teaching process. It may vary like use of moral language, to judging right and wrong deeds, attendance, regularity and respecting relations in the class. Thus, a teacher has a huge responsibility while teaching a class. Teacher can be adopted to achieve these following strategies:

- This can be taught during training period of trainee teachers. During lesson planning and its implementation, this fact should be taught by teacher educators.

- To attain the above objective, the teacher educators should themselves be equipped with this character. But before this the curriculum is too designed such that moral and-ethical aspect is integrated in it.
- Teaching should be made effective so that character development is one of the behavioral outcomes of the learners.
- It is the responsibility of teacher educators and teacher training institutions to mould the trainees into effective teachers.
- Only teachers can help the learners to develop the bond with their school similar to that they have for their home i.e. a sense of belongingness is to be developed.
- School is miniature representation of our society or community. Through teaching the norms, ethics and expectations of the society can be inculcated in learners.
- The feeling of brotherhood, communal unity, and strength and community service can help to drive youth towards positivity and thus reduce vices and delinquency in them.
- The learners who acquire the above mentioned values excel academically, too.
- Teacher has the moral responsibility of taking into consideration the ability and aptitude of learners and guide them accordingly.
- Teacher should try to make the class an environment which motivates learners to fare according to their capability and capacity. The learners in the class must have respect and trust for each other.
- Teaching should incorporate such activities which shall strengthen the bonding between all in the classroom and all get equal opportunity of expression. Teacher must teach that character building is higher than academic achievement. Good morality is a precursor for a successful life.
- Teacher should not avoid the inquisitiveness of learners related to sex, attraction, drugs, stress, abuse, suicide, bribery etc.
- Teacher should arrange workshops on 'life-skills'.
- Learners dislike direct lectures on morality. It is upto teacher to try different interesting ways to convey these messages.

In a class, teaching involves cognitive, affective and psychomotor aspects. In our country, we are more bothered about the cognitive gain only. NCERT has taken a good step in designing curriculum where teaching involves moral value dissemination with the content.

Q3. Elaborate Gagne's steps of instructional process.

Ans. Robert Gagne proposed a series of events which follow a systematic instructional design process that share the behaviorist approach to learning, with a focus on the outcomes or behaviors of instruction or training. There are nine steps of instructional process are following:

(1) Gaining attention: Pose a question, present a case, or find an interesting or controversial issue in the class reading. The point is to stimulate learner curiosity.

(2) **Informing learners of objectives:** Learners want to be made aware of what they are to glean through their learning efforts. Be sure to include cognitive, behavioural, and affective objectives if this is what you intend, then later be sure to evaluate learning according to the domain and level of the unit objectives.

(3) **Stimulating recall of prior knowledge:** Help the learner to recall that they know something and that new learning will build on what is already known. In addition, recalling previous learning stimulates short-term and long-term memory.

(4) **Presenting the stimulus:** Use various tactics to present content so, that it feeds curiosity and motivates participation.

(5) **Providing learning guidance:** Assist the learner with strategies and resources for learning at the intended level.

(6) **Eliciting performance:** Provide opportunities for learner elaboration, for learners to build on learning by drawing them out, or through seeking learning transference to a similar but not identical situation.

(7) **Providing feedback:** Wherever required during instructional process feedback should be provided so that there is minimum deviation from the path of right understanding.

(8) **Assessing performance:** Instructors need to know if learners reached the intended learning objectives and if course instruction helped or hindered this process; therefore, summative and formative assessment techniques should be built into each learning activity, unit, and course.

(9) **Enhancing retention and transfer:** Sequence instruction and learning outcomes so that learners can build from a solid base; encourage socialisation real-life problems; assess at a level appropriate to moving the learner forward in the program.

Q4. What is pedagogy? Discuss its relation with teaching, learning and instruction.

Ans. Pedagogy is an encompassing term concerned with what a teacher does to influence learning in others. It is the discipline concerned with theory as well as practical aspect of education. It elaborates that how best a teaching can occur in a classroom for complete development of the learners. John Dewey said, "Pedagogy involves the organic relation between curriculum and teaching, and it entails study based, socially just and ethically sound practices resulting from negotiations among the teachers, learners and others".

According to Herbart, 'pedagogy' is assumptions by a teacher and a specific set of capabilities with a fixed aim. He stated that there is a correlation between personality development and the final outcomes which will benefit the society and mankind as a whole. According to him, there are five elements which are as follows:

(1) **Preparation**, a process of relating new material to be learned to relevant past ideas or memories in order to give the pupil a vital interest in the topic under consideration;

(2) **Presentation**, presenting new material by means of concrete objects or actual experience;

(3) **Association**, thorough assimilation of the new idea through comparison with former ideas and consideration of their similarities and differences in order to implant the new idea in the mind;

(4) **Generalization**, a procedure especially important to the instruction of adolescents and designed to develop the mind beyond the level of perception and the concrete; and

(5) **Application**, using acquired knowledge not in a purely utilitarian way, but so that every learned idea becomes a part of the functional mind and an aid to a clear, vital interpretation of life. This step is presumed possible only if the student immediately applies the new idea, making it his own.

Pedagogy involves steps which begin the moment is assigned the work of teaching any subject. It can be represented as follows:-

(1) **Teacher**: Personality, content knowledge, communication skill, behaviour, style, conduct and character etc.

(2) **Organising various activities**: Planning the format of teaching, logical arrangement of content, use of supporting aids etc.

(3) **Dissemination of the content**: Teaching the content according to the step (ii), using reinforcement and motivation, increasing interaction, giving stimulus variation to maintain interest, creativity.

(4) **Evaluation of achievements of learners:** Thorough oral or written test, observation or continuous class evaluation to see the positive change in behaviour.

Relationship amongst teaching, learning, instruction and pedagogy

The teaching process takes the learner along with himself in order to stimulate, promote and endorse learning. Learning occurs on the basis of some principles and laws (laws of readiness exercise and effect etc.); learning becomes more effective, if these are followed in teaching methods. Pedagogy targets teaching which prepares for future life as social skills and cultural norms and ethical beliefs.

Instruction is teaching to help procure knowledge and skill which is more well-organised, resourceful, effective and engaging.

Paulo Freire referred to his method of teaching as 'critical pedagogy' in correlation with instruction, the instructor's own philosophical beliefs of instructions are harboured and governed by student's background knowledge and experience, situation and environment; as well as learning goals set by the learner and teacher e.g.: Socrates school of thoughts.

The main focus of Robert Gagne's was instructional theory i.e. how to connect instruction and learning systematically.

Usually teaching and instructions used synonymously as there is very little but important difference between the two. Teaching begins its journey much before it comes into action in the classroom whereas instruction begins only when the teacher enters the classroom.

Learning is a sequential process which begins with teaching, progresses through instructions while obeying the pedagogy and results into behaviour change in the learner.

Q5. Analyse the different styles of teaching. Give suggestions for adopting effective teaching style.

Ans. According to Thornton, B. Paul, there are three basic teaching styles, which are as follow:

(1) **The directing style** promotes learning through listening and following directions. With this style, the teacher tells the students what to do, how to do it, and when it needs to be done. The teacher imparts information to the students via lectures, assigned readings, audio/visual presentations, demonstrations, role playing, and other means. Students gain information primarily by listening, taking notes, doing role plays, and practicing what they are told to do.

(2) **The discussing style** promotes learning through interaction. In this style, practiced by Socrates, the teacher encourages critical thinking and lively discussion by asking students to respond to challenging questions. The teacher is a facilitator guiding the discussion to a logical conclusion. Students learn to have opinions and to back them up with facts and data.

(3) **The delegating style** promotes learning through empowerment. With this style, the teacher assigns tasks that students work on independently, either individually or in groups.

Suggestions for adopting effective teaching style

- Teaching style must be such that both teacher and learners are clear about the content to be taught and its objectives.
- Clarity, Conciseness and Comprehensiveness that i.e. triple 'c' are the essence which should be included in any good teaching style.
- Any confusing, dicey or ambiguous contents are not acceptable by learners so they should be avoided.
- Confidence in a teacher regarding content knowledge is essential.
- Teacher should always be ready for any unexpected situations, too. This enhances his teaching style.
- Unbiased and non-partial teachers are always respected. During class activities, all learners must be given equal opportunities.

At the end, teaching style is an individualised talent which has to be developed by oneself.

Q6. Explain the concept, features, fundamental and types of teaching models.

Ans. Teacher model is to confirm in behaviour, action and to direct one's action according to some particular design or ideal. Hence, the meaning of a model is the process of bringing a change in the behaviour according to some objective.

According to Brace R. Joyce, "School Faculties and individual teachers create life in schools by models of teaching they choose and create".

- In teaching models, the following six activities are included:
- To give practical shape to the learning achievement.
- To select such stimulus so that the student may give expected response.
- To specify such situations in which the responses of the students may be seen.
- To determine such criterion behaviours so that the performance of the students may be seen.
- To specify the specific teaching strategies for achieving the desirable educational objectives by analysing the interaction in the class-room situations.
- To modify the teaching strategies and tactics if the expected changes in the behaviour do not occur.

Features of a good teaching model

(1) It should be interactive in nature.

(2) It should be helpful for better performance of both teacher and learners.

(3) It should have both philosophical and psychological background.

(4) It should complement the content which is to be taught.

(5) It should help in building interesting and motivating environment in the classroom.

(6) It should help in developing creativity and innovative ideas in teacher as well as learners.

(7) It should help in bringing out the expected behavioural changes in the learners.

(8) It must be viable in recognizing the strengths and weaknesses of the learners and assess them by their feedbacks.

Fundamental Elements of Teaching Model

(1) Focus: Every teaching model has one or the other objective the focus of a teaching model is that for which a teaching model is developed. The model has various phases. Hence, for this, some particular types of competencies are developed.

(2) Syntax: The syntax of teaching model means those points which produce activities focused on educational objectives at various phases.

(3) Principle of Sensation: The concept of action-reaction is to be maintained to create a bond between teacher and learner.

(4) Social system: It is related to the description of the following:

(i) Interactive roles and relationships between the teacher and the student.

(ii) The kinds of norms that are encouraged and the student behaviour that is rewarded.

(5) **Support system:** The model should be as a supplement to the regular teaching process which enhances the teaching effectiveness and learning experience.

(6) **Application:** It is an important element of a teaching model. It means the utility or usage of the learnt material in other situations. Several types of teaching modes are available. Each model attempts to desirable the feasibility of its use in varying contexts related with goal achievements in terms of cognitive and affective behaviour modification.

Types of Teaching Models

There are four types of teaching models which are as follow:

(1) Social Interaction Model

(i) Benjamin Cox and Byron defines **Social Inquiry model**. It deals with social and humanity related topics which are researched and proved with the help of data.

(ii) **Laboratory model** is based on the experiments to be undertaken in science or biology subjects.

(iii) **Group investigation model** defined by john Dewey and Herbart Thelim. It is a source of social interactivity which includes working in a group consisting of both pro- and anti- type of personalities.

(2) Behaviour Altering Model

(i) **Practice based:** Practice based involves teaching with the help of suitable methods; aids etc. and then after getting feedback arrange remedial classes to get mastery over the content.

(ii) **Direct model:** Direct model is almost like directive style of teaching. Teacher takes the main position of class and guides the learners through the class.

(iii) **Programmed:** It is programmed instruction style of teaching i.e. CAI (computer assisted instruction) Where computer and web technology is used for teaching. B.F. Skinner first gave it.

(3) Information Development Model

(i) **Schuman's model** is based on the strategies and assumptions used by scientists. It is basically scientific inquiry model. Both teacher and learners following scientific approach solve the problem.

(ii) **Bruner's model** is based on the fact that all the objects or events in this environment have relations with each other. Our surrounding has so many complexities that it can be understood by classifying them into smaller parts.

(iii) **Gagne's model** deals with sensory memory. It depends on memorisation and practice. There are various aspects like learners' readiness, motivation, perception, transfer of learning and retention.

(4) Personal Basis Model

(i) **Non-directive model** defined by Carl Rogers. He believed in concept of human relations and thus suggested instructions to be based on this model. This is similar to discussion style of teaching as discussed earlier.

(ii) **Creative model:** It was defined by William Gordon which states that projects can be assigned to the learners and they can learn by doing themselves. Teacher is just a supervisor and the learners either go in for field work or prepare a project on any activity. It is quite similar to delegate style of teaching.

(iii) **Self-Awareness:** Self-Awareness was given by Fritz Pauls and W. Schutz. Here, the development of self is emphasised where the innate strengths and creativity of learner is given freedom to grow. This gives them opportunity to know about themselves and their peers.

Q7. What are the methods and approaches of teaching?

Ans. During teaching of content, teaching methods and approaches play an important role. Teacher must be capable enough to decide which method will suit the learners. The teacher with correct approach of teaching is guided to impart education.

Teachers may use many methods depending on the level of class, curriculum, interest of learners, availability of resources etc. The methods used may be teacher-centered or learner-centered. When planning a lesson to be taught in the class, a teacher has to analyse many aspects of using approaches for teaching. This planning varies from person to person. Following are the some important and frequently methods used by teachers:

(1) Lecture method: The teacher plays a major role in lecture method whereas learners have minor or no role to play. This method is useful for higher class where syllabus is vast. This method is commonly and frequently used in the classroom. But many a times lecture becoming boring. Therefore, the teacher must try to plan her lecture with interesting tools like illustrations, experiences, anecdotes etc.

(2) Demonstrative method: Demonstrative method is a very common method used in science and mathematics teaching. The senses of sight and hearing make the learner more alert. The drawback is that learners are not allowed to handle the equipment used in demonstration. This can be seen in many schools where computer classes are run. The teacher demonstrates by using computer in front of learners but they are not allowed to touch the sets. It is very clear that this hinders in complete transfer to the content to the learner.

(3) Lecture-cum-Demonstration method: This is just the mixture of both the methods discussed above. The best of both methods can be used by the teachers for better results. This is almost teacher centered. For example, in science, when different types of lever are to be explained teacher can bring real objects for demonstration like scissors, pliers, tongs etc. By showing these objects, she can give explanation too.

(4) Heuristic/Discovery method: Learning by inquiry for making discoveries may be ascribed to the views of philosophers like Rousseau, Pestalozzi, Dewey and others who had advocated the need for experiential learning. Discovery method is also known as 'Heuristic method' and 'Inquiry method'.

Prof. Henry Edward Armstrong introduced this method for teaching science. According to him, "Heuristic method is a method of teaching which involves our placing of children as far as possible in the attitude of a discoverer". In this method, children discover and find things by themselves. They are placed in the position of discoverers or inventors. A teacher is required to involve students in finding out the solutions to a problem by themselves instead of telling or lecturing them. Problems are provided to the students. The students are expected to take observations and conduct experiments as per the instructions. Conclusions are drawn by the students, and hence, they are introduced to reasoning skill from their own observation and experiments.

(5) Problem solving method: According to Gagne, "Problem solving is a set of events in which Human being wants to achieve some goals."

A child cannot solve a problem unless and until he has a sense of familiarity with it. Thus, the problem should be such that it motivates and attracts the learner to try to solve it. The problem solver must be aware of the nature of the problem and whether it is practical for him or not. If the objectives are clear, the learner will involve himself wholeheartedly finding the solution.

This method is commonly used in mathematics, physics, chemistry etc. During this method, the learning process sometimes gets slowed down. This is because many learners are slow in this process and their problems are taken up by the teachers then.

Some features of problem-solving method are as follows:

(i) A felt difficulty/need to reach the goal;
(ii) A goal to be reached;
(iii) Reaching the goal or arriving at satisfactory solution to the problem at hand; and
(iv) Challenging the felt difficulty through conscious, planned purposeful attack.

(6) Project Method: According to Kilpatrick, "A project is a wholehearted purposeful activity proceeding in a social environment". This method is helpful in bringing out the creative and investigating aspect of the child. It requires lot of logical thinking. But again the same limitation occurs that in itself it is not a perfect method of teaching.

There are two types of project method.

(i) When some static or working model is made as in science or social science.

(ii) Second is the investigatory project where some research or survey is done and then a report is made based on the findings.

This method also comes under experimental method or laboratory method.

(7) Inductive and Deductive method: Inductive method is moving from specific to general and deductive method is from general to specific. Specific facts or examples are given and the learner reaches generalisation and vice versa for deductive approach.

For example, "Electricity consumption is increasing day by day. The electricity cost has increased. The petrol and diesel prices are rising. The coal deposits are depleting. Forests are reducing day by day."– all these statements can be generalised into one sentence and that is "Natural Energy Resources are decreasing with increasing population." –Inductive.

"Save Natural energy resources". Population is increasing and so is the consumption of natural resources. Forests should be protected and massive plantation should be done. Mining should be controlled. Country should now move towards generating electricity by nuclear energy instead of coal. People should move through public transport or opt for car-pooling, electricity at home should not be wasted unnecessarily.–Deductive.

(8) Analytic & Synthetic method Analysis refers to taking a big or complicated problem or concept and trying to understand by breaking into smaller units to understand better. In this method, we move from unknown to known or from conclusion to hypothesis.

For example, "Stomach is an organ up of group of different kinds of tissues". Now the analysis of the various tissues is done, i.e. the different kinds of tissues like epithelium, squamous, columnar, connective, blood tissues etc. are analysed.

Q8. Analyse Philip W. Jackson phases of teaching.

Ans. Philip W. Jackson divided teaching operation into three phases and they are:

(1) Pre-active phase: It is the phase of planning for teaching. All that a teacher plans before going to classroom to deal with students or to teach. In Pre-active phase of teaching the following operations or sub phases are involved:

(i) Formulation Goals: The teacher formulates in detail the instruction or teaching objectives in behavioural terms by using taxonomy of educational objectives. These objectives are of two types: Entering behaviour of learners and terminal behaviour of learners. These goals are based on psychology of the students as well as need of the society.

(ii) Decision Making About the Subject Matter: The teacher decides about the content to be taught to the students and structure of the content (Memory, Understanding and Reflective level). This decision is based on the following considerations:

(i) Demand of the curriculum prescribed for the students.
(ii) The entering behaviour and needs of the students.
(iii) Level of motivation of the learners.
(iv) Teacher's preference for assessment relation to the content.

(iii) Arrangement of the ideas and style of teaching: The teacher has to arrange sub-contents in a logical sequence, in such a way that it should function empirically. It means sub contents, should be so arranged that it should facilitate the transfer of learning.

(iv) Decision Making About the Strategies of Teaching: The teacher has to select appropriate strategies and tactics of teaching, keeping in view nature and structure of the content and objectives of teaching. This operation is very important in teacher-education programme. Such skills and abilities should be emphasised during the teacher-training course.

(v) Development of Teaching Strategies: The teacher has decide before hand or in advance about strategies the tactics which s/he has to use during the course of his classroom teaching. When will teacher use questioning, when lecturing, when will s/he show pictures, charts, models and when will s/he use blackboard, when recapitulation or evaluation, etc. These activities or sub-takes must be clearly decided by the teacher at pre-active-stage of teaching for successful teaching.

(2) Interactive phase: The interactive phase of teaching includes all those behaviour, activities which a teacher uses after entering the classroom. The interactive stage involves all activities in presenting the subject-matter. According to P.W. Jackson (1966), the interactive phase: "The teacher provides students verbal stimulation of various kinds, makes explanations, asks question, listens to students responses, and provides guidance."

The following are the activities at the interactive-phase of teaching:

(i) Sizing Up the Class: The teacher enters in the classroom, s/he perceives the size of the class and rolls his/her eyes upon the faces of the students. He locates or identifies spot which may be troublesome or helpful for him. He identifies which faces are discouraging, encouraging to him. Thus, s/he tries to size up the class group before teaching. Similarly, the students also size up the personality of a teacher within a few initial seconds. The phase requires that teacher must look like a teacher first. His/her dress is most important. He should look like a teacher.

(ii) **Diagnosis of the Learner:** The teacher tries to diagnose the levels of their achievements in his students in three areas:
   (a) Abilities
   (b) Attitude and interest and
   (c) Academic background

(iii) **Actions of Achievement**

   (a) Selection of Stimuli: The stimuli in the action or activity of teaching can be verbal as well as non-verbal (verbal praise, gestures, expressions through face, eyes) the way the teacher stands and moves around, etc. A good teacher must know which one is appropriate stimuli or which is irrelevant stimuli in that particular teaching situation. Teacher should be able to select desirable or functional stimuli in view of the present situation before him.

   (b) Presentation of the Stimuli: The teacher must know three things in presenting the stimuli:
   - Form
   - Context, and
   - Order or Sequence.

   (c) Reinforcement: It is a condition which will increase the probability that a particular response will be repeated in future. It may be of tow types:
   - Positive Reinforcers,
   - Negative Reinforcers.

(iv) **Development of Strategies:** The strategies of reinforcing the students, of controlling their verbal and non-verbal behaviour are used for imparting the subject-matter effectively while a teachers teaches in the classroom.

(3) Post-active phase: It is an evaluative phase of teaching. It includes the teacher tasks which evaluate student's performance based on classroom teaching. The behavioural change of students are assessed at the end of teaching. The oral of written questions are asked at the third phase of teaching. The following are the main operations at this phase of teaching.

(i) **Defining the Exact Dimensions of the Behavioural Change:** The teacher evaluation the expected behavioural change with their actual behavioural change during his teaching. Most of the students emit the expected behaviour.

(ii) **Selecting Appropriate Testing Devices:** The teacher chooses certain suitable testing techniques and tools to measure the various desired dimensions of behaviour. The test should be reliable, valid and objective in nature. Cognitive and non-cognitive outcomes require different type testing devices.

(iii) Changing or Improving Strategies of Teaching: The student's testing result is also used for evaluating the effectiveness of instructions and teaching strategies. It may provide a basis for improving his teaching by reorienting his teaching and changing strategies of teaching.

Q9. What is the content of maxims of teaching? Also explain levels of teaching.

Ans. Maxims of Teaching are the universally facts found out by the teacher on the basis of experience. They are of universal significance and are trustworthy. The knowledge of different maxims helps the teacher to proceed systematically. It also helps to find out his way of teaching, especially at the early stages of teaching, it make teaching interesting, creative and purposeful.

Content of maxims of teaching

Teacher can decide the activities in a classroom, which will help the learners to grasp the content. The different content of maxims of teaching are briefly explained below:

(1) **Simple to complex:** It means, teacher teach simple part to students and slowly gradually teach complicated problem.

(2) **Known to unknown:** It means that old knowledge serves as a hook, on which the new can be hanged. Teachers should consider all the small, simple information and knowledge which a child knows. Based on it, fresh knowledge could be started.

(3) **Concrete to abstract:** It is very important for the child to be able to abstract ideas. To achieve this purpose teacher should approach the child via concrete objects, activities and example. The imagination is greatly aided by concrete material. So, while teaching abstractions in any subject, teacher should take help of concrete things as far as possible and then lead to higher levels of thinking.

(4) **Direct to indirect:** Whatever is to be taught cannot be put straightaway before the learner? It should be connected to the facts already known to him. For example, if topic 'Acid' is to be taught then learners should asked about sourness, sour fruits, causes of sourness, citric acid and then teacher can teach them about mineral acids.

(5) **Particular to General:** While teaching, the teacher should first of all take particular statements and then on the basis of those particular cases, generalisation should be made. Suppose the teacher is teaching present continuous tense while teaching a English, he should first of all give a few examples and then on the basis of those make them generalise that this tense is used to denote an action that is going on at the time of speaking.

(6) **Analysis to Synthesis:** Analysis means breaking a problem into its convenient parts while synthesis means grouping of

these separated parts into one complete whole. A complex problem can be made simple and easy by dividing into units.

(7) **Empirical to rational:** Empirical know is based on observation and first hand experience; rational knowledge implies a bit of observation and argumentative approach. It is a general feeling that the child feels the rational basis for any knowledge much after he has experienced it in his day-to-day life.

(8) **Psychological to Logical:** While teaching, the teacher should first keep in mind the interest, aptitudes, capacities, development level etc. of the children during selection of subject matter and then on to its logical arrangement. In teaching English, the structures are selected as per needs and requirements of the students and then arranged in a logical way. The psychological appeal of the thing is more important at the early stages. Then the logic behind it should be seen.

(9) **Whole to Part:** In teaching, the teacher should try to acquaint the child with the whole lesson first and then the different portions of it may be analysed and studied intensively. This principle holds good while teaching a thing to the small children. At the early stages, the child loves to speak full sentences because in daily life situations, full sentences are used. The child should be given a full sentence. Then he may have full familiarity with the different words contained in that sentence. Later he may have the knowledge of words. Then he will have the knowledge of different letters forming the words.

(10) **Definite to Indefinite:** In teaching, definite things should be taught first because the learner can easily have faith in them. Gradually he should be given the knowledge of indefinite things. Definite things, definite rules of grammar help the learner to have good knowledge. Gradually he can be taught about indefinite things.

Levels of Teaching: There are five levels of teaching as defined by Hokanson and Hooper:

Table 3.1

Level 1	Reception	Receiving Information
Level 2	Application	Applying Ideas
Level 3	Extension	Extending Ideas
Level 4	Generation	Generating Solutions
Level 5	Challenge	The Learner's Challenge

Level 1: Reception: The simplest form of educational activity involves the transmission of information. At this level of instruction, answers are given to students, not questions to answer or problems to solve. All of the analysis, synthesis, and problem solving have been done by the instructor. Requirements for attendance, seat time, and/or contact hours are common expressions of this form of education.

The learner is considered an information receiver, and the challenge for instructional designers is to transmit the proper content in the proper sequence in the most efficient manner possible. Material is organized and presented to the learner through a generally linear procedure according to principles of instructional message design.

Level 2: Application: Interaction between the teacher and learner begins now. It may be in the form of question, inquiry, discussion etc. At this level, the class becomes more interesting and creative. The level of thinking and analysing the concepts increases.

Level 3: Extension: Instruction at the third level encourages learners to apply the principles of what they have learned to solve a new and different question. Learners at this level extend a lesson to a different or authentic context. This level of development can also be described as "far transfer".

Level 4: Generation: Learners must eventually learn to generate or create their own solutions to complex problems. At this level, the instructor poses a problem to be solved; learners must recognize, regulate, and marshal the resources needed for a successful solution

Level 5: Challenge: The highest level within our learning taxonomy is for learners to challenge others (and themselves) to learn. Those who seek, find, pose, and eventually resolve exploratory problems for themselves, challenge their own limits of learning. The most widely understood example, the dissertation, is a sophisticated problem posed by the learner.

Q10. Write a note on the following:

(a) Teaching as a complex activity

Ans. Teaching itself is always a highly complex activity. Teaching is an intelligent and purposeful activity intended to promote learning, focused on and relating to the learners themselves, adopting the best means to achieve that end and engaging the motivation of the learners to maximise their learning. Teaching involves numerous dimensions like:

- Being intelligent with good IQ, Knowledgeable enough to satisfy learners' quest
- Logical preparation and presentation with clear objectives and goals
- Rational and sensibilities to be shown and developed in learners
- Strength, both physical and mental, able to face stress and criticism
- Expressive with ideas and thoughts without fear and apprehensions
- Fervent and ardent i.e. enthusiastic and zealous towards his work
- Warmth and empathy in order to bond with class
- Sensitive towards learners who face problem
- Simultaneously upgrading and updating oneself with new discoveries
- Orienting oneself by continuous short term courses or workshops
- Evaluating oneself and learners
- Using innovative strategies in and out of class settings
- Other miscellaneous work other than class teaching

- Working directly or indirectly for the society etc. and much more; the teacher has to perform accordingly which is very tough.

In teaching, all the activities have to be performed keeping in mind the level of school (govt., private, public, convent, rural, urban etc) and children (their interest, ability, attitude, background etc). Usually the teachers who undergo teacher training are somewhat prepared for the real teaching job. During teaching, they are trained in many of the aspects discussed above but sometimes the real life situation takes a toll on the new teacher. The teacher has to face many challenges during the job period. Some learn gradually and some succumb and leave the job. Thus trained teacher must be made aware and oriented accordingly to face the practicality of the teaching job. It is better that trained teachers pass out confident enough to face the teaching job full with complexities. The future of many learners is in the hands of a teacher therefore keeping in view the individual difference among learners has to be tackled. Also the teacher has to strive for the holistic development of learners. Not only this, learners as well as teachers performance is evaluated which specifies their progress. Thus, teaching is multi-faceted activity. After evaluation step the feedback has to be collected so that the teaching can be modified into better activity. The weak learners should be tackled in such a manner that they do not feel inferior. Teacher in herself is a learner who adapts daily to the new situation. Teaching is surely a complex activity with so many roles to play.

(b) Teaching as a profession

Ans. In Vedic period, "Guru" and his teachings were deeply revered. The pure and unselfish bonding between Guru-shishya was prevalent at that time. His position was considered above the God because he showed the path to reach the divine power.

गुरु, गोबिंद दोऊ खड़े, काके लागूं पाय।

बलिहारी गुरु आपने, गोबिंद दियो बताय।।

However, today, situations have changed. Now it is the last opted profession. Those who go in for teacher training courses do so to get a government job. There are very few people who really want to do teaching with nobility. Besides, there has been mushrooming of coaching institutes around us. The teachers lure or force learners to join their coaching institutes as the salary packages in private institutions are less. They all are responsible for changing this noble profession into a money raising business. The various creative and innovative ways to teach learnt during training classes are rarely followed when actual teaching occurs. They don't want to take the pains or waste time and energy on these activities instead just try to wind up the course allotted. This is the reason respect for a teacher is at its minimum and empathy for learners is no more there. This is just cheating the small children who look up to their teachers as their role models or ideals.

Teaching must be given the same respect like any other profession. Engineers, Doctors, Architects, Officers etc get good salary package which private teachers do not get. The salary and working conditions in school need revamping. This profession will get its due when all of us work for its upliftment as a profession. Teaching is in need of its well-deserved position in society. Teaching should be given role to take part in professional decisions, diagnosing related needs, planning instructional programmes and evaluation policies.

Professional relationships should be adopted by school organizations and should recruit teachers on the basis of eligibility criteria. Inexperienced teachers should not be employed because inexperienced teacher causes more dents than no teacher. Therefore, a standard has to be maintained.

Q11. Discuss the role of teacher in providing dynamic curricular experiences.

Ans. According to Brown Douglas, "teachers can play many roles in the course of teaching and this might facilitate the learning. Their ability to carry these out effectively will depend on a large extend on the rapport they establish with their learners and on their own level of knowledge and skills." A good teacher is aware of the dynamics of a classroom. In the classroom teacher has to maintain a conducive environment and provide them with experiences through her experiences. The role of teachers is changing very fast. Now, they have become more of facilitators providing knowledge of content and the curricular experiences. For this the teacher has to play the role of a creator also as they has to develop the learners on the experiences of his own. This cooperative curriculum based experience in the classroom develops reflective level of thought process, operative skills and recent developments in the field of education.

Scenario interdisciplinary approach has become common is today's education. So a teacher can use her knowledge in different fields to give knowledge to the learners. In this way, good concepts and experiences of different disciplines can be incorporated during teaching. Today a teacher's role has become challenging when so many technological advances has taken place. And for this the teacher has to instill in them a sense of responsibility when using this source of information.

Ways of providing dynamic curricular experiences

- Learners must be made aware that curriculum covering is not at all theory driven but there are other aspects attached to it.
- In involves healthy communication and interaction within and outside the classroom.
- Whatever the curricular developments are there, the positive behavioural outcome should be the ultimate goal.
- Curriculum development should be according to the human development.
- Curriculum should not limit either a teacher or the learner. They should get opportunities to explore avenues related to the content.
- The teaching style, method, strategies, approaches etc, should be modified according to the curriculum changes.
- The teacher has to be clear of the objectives related to curriculum instruction and the learners also have the right to know about these objectives.

- The instructor of the class has to plan and engineer his role according to the curriculum with respect to the learners.
- The curriculum is not to be tackled superficially but rationally.
- At the end of curriculum transaction it is the child only who matters. It is upto him what he 'wants' to receive; but the teacher can help and guide him through this process which is in harmony with society, environment and himself. There should be minimum scope of conflict.
- Integrated curriculum is the new concept which helps teacher to perform effectively.
- Activities and aids to be used should be used flexibly and interdisciplinary approach has to be used.
- Curriculum is developed with psychological, philosophical, and social context but these have dynamic nature so does the curriculum. Here teacher has to be updated with these modifications.
- Curriculum gives a defined path to teachers and learners for smooth teaching learning process.
- The technological advancement has changed the role of teachers drastically.

A successful curriculum is one which engages both the teacher and learner to enhance the performance of both as well as institution so that a society benefits from it. Also the dynamics of curriculum must be known to the teachers as well as to the learners.

Q12. What does instructional planning mean? Elaborate the consideration for instructional planning in classroom.

Ans. Planning plays an important role in instruction. In general terms, planning means the "act or process of making or carrying out plans." Instructional planning is a process of the teacher using appropriate curricula, instructional strategies, and resources during the planning process to address the diverse needs of students. While considering the instructional planning, it is important to recognise that students in schools form enormously diverse groups. Formally and informally both teacher and taught constantly interact with the school environment during structured or unstructured time. Instructional planning depends upon several factors. Following are some considerations for instructional planning:

(1) School Environment: School environment in which students are imparted with different types of learning experiences. The term 'school environment' encompasses the terms 'school culture' and 'school climate' that affect the behaviour of teachers and students.

Every school environment should have conducive atmosphere which would make every student feel relaxed and secure. This is because the physical quality of every school can make negative or positive impacts on students, teachers as well as the learning process.

The school environment as a vital learning place to the educational system with a great impact on teaching and learning at any level that will contribute to great academic performances of learners.

School environments have significant influence on teacher as well learner outcome. A positive school environment influences the attendance and engagement of learners in school. Poor school environment is strongly linked to poor achievement, low attendance and low learner disengagement. Caring and supportive school environments contribute to learners' academic attitudes, motivation, engagement, and goal setting. It is the prime responsibility of the school to set positive and supportive environment. According to Schaps, school environment is shaped by many factors which are as follow:

- The faculty's teaching and discipline methods
- The school's espoused goals and values
- The inclusion or exclusion of learners and parents in the planning and decision-making processes
- The polices regarding grading and tracking
- The principal's leadership style

(2) Physical Environment: Physical environment of a school is composed of its physical surrounding and facilities, which a learner finds oneself while in school. The physical surroundings and facilities differ from school to school. In India, enough attention is not paid to the importance of physical environment for learning. Often classrooms are overcrowded, with no alternative spaces to learn, nor they are attractive, inviting or sensitive towards children's needs. Inappropriate school design may drastically affect the teacher's productive output and classroom management. In fact, the role of this all-encompassing, physical environment has been restricted merely to shelter the educational activity.

We should remember that the physical environment of school is key factor in the overall health and safely of learners and staff. It must be design and maintained to be free of health and safety hazards and promote learning. School policies must be practiced to ensure food protection, sanitation, safe water supply, healthy air quality, good lighting, safe playgrounds, violence prevention, and emergency response, among other issues that relate to the physical environment of schools.

(3) Psychological Environment: The psychological environment of a school refers to the stimuli that impinge upon the learner's psyche in the school. For example, the attitude of the principal and teachers towards a learner would act as a stimulus for the learner to do or not do certain things in the school.

Most teachers have their favourite students in the class and that they are usually the so-called good students of the class. Imagine the class where teachers have only one such favourite student and teachers give importance to that student on every occasion. Like a pampered child at home, this student would grow as an individual characterised by a tendency to be rather aggressive and dominant over others. By pampering, children are taught that they can take without giving. Their wishes are everyone else's commands. This may sound like a wonderful situation, until we realise that the pampered child fails in two ways. First, s/he doesn't learn to do things for himself/herself, and discovers later that s/he is truly behind. Secondly, s/he doesn't learn any other way to deal with others than giving the commands. And society responds to pampered people only in one way, i.e. hatred.

On the contrary, a class where the teachers are always suspicious of some children's ability and where they doubt or criticise the children, they need to defend themselves from such occurrences, and hence, may avoid expressing their true self. In such a psychological environment, a child grows into a sensitive person and has developed a shell around him, which protects him. We should note that the neglected children include not only orphans and the victims of abuse, but also the children whose parents are never there, and the ones raised in a rigid, authoritarian manner.

Thus, school has a role that is strategic as well as indispensable in the development of healthy personality. For example, much attention has been given to the conflict between the democratic tradition to which the school is dedicated and certain antidemocratic practices and attitudes to which it is often prone, like authoritarianism in human relations, competitiveness rather than co-operation in the classroom, caste and religion based segregation, and other less tangible forms of inter group discriminations.

(4) Learner: A classroom has a diverse group of learners. Diversity comes in many forms, including personality, race, gender, class, ethnic background, sexual orientation, religion, class etc. It is a challenge for teachers to cater to the needs of all in an inclusive classroom. In an inclusive classroom, both teacher and learner work together, and it is required that the learner is active rather than just being a passive listener. Together they create a safe and supported environment and are encouraged to express their views and concerns. It is the responsibility of teachers to make sure that all of them comprehend the concepts. All the learners must be actively engaged in what they learn to make teaching-learning interesting. Learners must be encouraged to take an active interest in learning. The focus must be on the learners experiencing the harmonious environment which would prove helpful in developing higher order thinking skills, effective communication skills and collaborative skills. Learners must be encouraged for self-direction because self-directed learners not only encourage each other, but also work with their teacher to achieve academic and behavioural goals. Teachers should employ a variety of strategies to promote responsible decision-making ability among learners and make them self-reliant learners.

(5) Content: Content plays a significant role in instructional planning. It refers to the information provided through the medium. In learner centered classroom, the way in which the information is presented is considered important. Content must be explicitly viewed from the multiple perspectives keeping in mind the diversity in group. It must be presented in a manner that reduces learners' experiences of marginalisation. It should cater to individuals' experiences, values, and perspectives. It must include multiple perspectives of topic rather than focusing only on a single perspective.

Q13. What is the planning for teaching? Discuss its classification.

Ans. Planning for teaching means teacher plans the content of instruction, selects teaching materials, designs the learning activities, plans the pacing and allocation of instruction time etc. Planning should be a cyclic process, incorporating decision of learning outcomes, strategies for teaching and evaluation. This includes planning on a whole- school, subject, year and class level. Planning must provide opportunities to all learners to-perform their best.

One of the most important units of teaching-learning process is a teacher. Researches reveal that the teacher is the single most important factor affecting learner achievement. According to Wong, there are several characteristics of an effective teacher:

- An effective teacher has positive expectations for learner's success; and lesson plan reflects such expectations,
- An effective teacher knows how to design lessons for learner's mastery; which is reflected in lesson plan, and
- An effective teacher is also an extremely good classroom manager; which is possible via good time management during class time and that is possible only by effective implementation of a good lesson plan.

Planning for teaching and learning affects not only teachers' instruction but classroom management as well. In a well managed classroom:

- learners are deeply engaged with their work; which would be possible if their roles are described and they have a goal as provided in a good lesson plan;
- learners know what is expected; which would be possible via routinely implemented good lesson plans;
- there is little wasted time, confusion; which would be possible via effective implementation of a good lesson plan; and
- the climate of such a classroom would be work-oriented, but relaxed and pleasant; which would be possible via good time management due to effective implementation of a good lesson plan.

Every planning of classroom can be classified in three major plans which are as follows:

(1) Annual Planning: The annual or yearly plan is formulated thinking about a year of a child's life in relation to the curriculum of a kindergarten. When formulating the plan, teachers firstly should know about the children. Thinking about the number of children, the ratio of boys and girls, and age difference in the class helps teachers to grasp their interests and curiosity. Secondly, they have to think deeply how to place annual events that mark the stages of their lives at kindergarten. It is important to formulate a yearly plan, which ensures that the children do not to feel overwhelmed. In addition, the changes of the seasons should be taken into consideration. A plan should encourage children to notice the changes of the seasons, and to develop their emotions through close contact with nature and the seasons.

While preparing the scheme of lessons for one academic session, a teacher should note the following:

(i) The total number of units prescribed in the syllabus for the session.

(ii) The total number of periods allotted separately for 'teaching' and 'learning activities' in the school time table (weekly).

(iii) The number of units identified to be taught month-wise keeping in view the quantity and quality of the course contents contained therein, and the available period for teaching of the same.

(iv) The actual number of working days available week-wise and month-wise in an academic session/year for teaching and learning activities relating to the subject concerned.

(v) The number of working days in a month to be actually devoted to teaching of the subject excluding the days for examination, holiday, field visit, etc.

(vi) Unit wise concept load (number of concepts within the unit) that determines the unit-wise total number of periods required for successful and effective teaching of the course contents of the units.

(vii) The total number of possible sub-units to be covered during the session.

(viii) The total number of required periods for the teaching of the prescribed course contents and facilitating learning of the subject.

(2) Unit Planning: Every student teacher should design at least one unit plan complete with a justification, objectives, materials and resources, daily and/or weekly outlines, activities, assignments, and assessments.

The unit consists of interrelated meaningful learning activities and not just chunks of subject matter or content to be learned that is memorised by students. Unit planning and teaching implies the use of principles of self-activity, motivation, individual difference, integration and many other principles of learning. A unit may be small covering only four hours of activity, or it may be large covering several weeks or even months of activities.

Unit plan is proper selection of learning activities, which present the absolute picture of particular unit. It is a systematic arrangement of subject matter. It is similar to lesson plan. Its format is almost same as a lesson plan, but covers and entire unit of work, which may span into several days or weeks. Even the unit plan also may include specific objectives and timeliness as lesson plan, but the difference is lesson plans are more fluid as they adapt to various needs of learners and their learning style. A unit plan has five sections, namely, introduction, objectives, contents, hints for teachers and evaluation.

Subject/Course: Unit: Class: • Previous Knowledge/Entry behaviour of Learners • Major objectives of the Unit • Overview of the theme of the unit;			
1	2	3	4
Sub-Units Teaching topics No. of Periods	Major Teaching points under each topic	Specific objectives of each teaching point	Methods/ media/ approach adopted by teachers' and pupils' activities Learning Resources
• References for Pupils • References for Teachers • Evaluation/Assignement			

Fig. 3.1: Format for a Unit Plan

There are some criteria for a good unit plan. If any unit plan is fulfilling these criteria it means that plan is meeting with the needs of learners. These criteria have been given below:

- Fit with yearly and term goal.
- Should be organised and in sequence.
- All round development of learners' personality.
- Needs, capabilities, interest, aptitude and involvement of the learners should be considered.
- Provide a new learning experience; systematic but should be flexible also.
- Prepared on the sound psychological knowledge of the learners.
- Maintain the attention of the learners till the end.
- Related to physical, social and emotional environment of the learners.

(3) Lesson Planning: Lesson plans specify the learning objectives, content, methods, materials/equipment, application, and evaluation for each lesson that is taught. Lesson plans serve several purposes. Such plans can be easily modified in subsequent years of teaching a program. Lesson plans can be evidence of good sound planning and preparation and provide detailed information about teaching performance and level of expertise. Even after the lesson is taught, administrators and teachers themselves can analyse and reflect on instructional methodology. They can also provide useful information for school administration. Ideally, instructors will use formal plans such as lesson plans, which usually include the four step method for teaching to a specific outcome or objective: preparation of the student, presentation (procedure), application and evaluation.

Before writing the lesson plans teacher should adopt several strategies. Before writing, teacher should be aware of the learning styles and level of learners. Teacher should try to answer these questions as; what do I want all learners to know and be able to do at the end of this lesson, what will I do to cause this learning to happen, what will learners do to facilitate this learning, how will I assess to find out if this learning happen and what will I do for those who show through assessment that the learning did not take place? Answers of these questions help teacher in writing-up an effective lesson plan.

As per answers, teacher should prepare her/his lesson plan. According to Richards (1998), a lesson plan should address the following:

- Concepts to be taught and objectives to be achieved.
- Time blocks, e.g., approximate time expected to be devoted to the lecture.
- Procedures to be used for instructional design.
- Materials needed both for the learner and for the teacher.
- Independent practices or learner time on task.
- Evaluation, applications, and learner understanding, e.g. main questions to be asked by the teacher to check learner understanding.

<table>
<tr><td colspan="5">Subject: Target Group:
Topic:
1. Entry behaviour
2. General objectives of the Topic
3. Methods and Media
4. Introduction
5. Presentation</td></tr>
<tr><td rowspan="2">Teaching points in sequence</td><td rowspan="2">Specific objectives in behavioural terms</td><td colspan="2">Learning Experience</td><td rowspan="2">Partial Evaluation</td></tr>
<tr><td>Teacher's Activities</td><td>Pupil's Activities</td></tr>
<tr><td colspan="5">6. Recapitulation/revision/evaluation
7. Home assignment
8. Blackboard work plan</td></tr>
</table>

Fig.3.2: Format for a Lesson/Topic Plan

Before preparation of any lesson plan, a teacher should keep these several important things in his mind.

- Each learner is different from other learners so her/his educational needs are also different. Because of this difference their interests, needs, and skills also differ from each other. So teacher should not expect the same learning performances and behaviour patterns from every learner.

- Instructional materials to be mentioned in the lesson plan must consist of reasonable items.
- Teacher should recognise the parents and neighborhood of the school and take advantage of such factors when preparing the lesson plan.
- Lesson plan must be prepared based on the intellectual level of learners.
- Lesson plan should not be too short or too long.
- Title of the course and units, allocated time for each activity, instructional methods, and instructional materials need to be mentioned in the daily lesson plans.
- Teacher should act as he/she is the leader of the class; however should listen to the learners as well.
- Lesson plan should also include a backup plan explaining how the parts of the lesson plan, which cannot be realised can be made up for.
- The plan for a field trip or for an experiment may be included in the daily lesson plan or attached as a supplemental document.
- Lesson plans serve as proofs that the teacher had implemented the activities mentioned within the daily lesson plan.
- Lesson plan should serve as guidelines for the teachers.
- Teacher should encourage the learners to work individually; but should not overload the learners with too much homework.
- Lesson plan must be flexible enough and not too strict.

Q14. Define behaviourist lesson planning. What are the steps and criticism of it?

Ans. Behaviourism assumes that all behaviors are either reflexes produced by a response to certain stimuli in the environment, or a consequence of that individual's history, including especially reinforcement and punishment, together with the individual's current motivational state and controlling stimuli. Although behaviorists generally accept the important role of inheritance in determining behavior, they focus primarily on environmental factors.

Conditioning is a key word of behaviouristic approach. This term for learning is based on what the individual does in response to a specific object, event, or stimulus. Pavlov, Skinner, Watson, Thorndike are pioneer psychologists of behaviourism. According to their theories, in behaviourism, learning of an individual is directed by some external stimulus and feedback. These are as follow:

- Indentify the desired behaviours: Explain exactly what is expected, what we want to see.
- Indentify the consequences, both negative and positive. This enables the learner to know what to expect from us.
- Establish the rules, the consequences, and the rewards for each behaviour.

There are eight steps for the development of behaviouristic lesson plan. These steps are as follow:

(1) **Purpose or Objective:** This step is related to particular chapter that learners are going to learn, why they are going to learn that particular chapter and which type of behavioural changes (cognitive, affective and psychomotor) are going to occur after the lesson. In simple language it can be called as learning outcomes.

(2) **Anticipatory Set (Focus):** Anticipatory set is related to how successfully a teacher is going to acquire the attention of learners for the lesson. It is a short activity or prompt that focuses the attention of learners before the lesson begins. In a simple language it can be called as introduction. A teacher may ask some questions related to lesson, can give some examples, can tell a story, or can write some problems on the blackboard.

(3) **Input:** The next step is input. In input teacher imparts vocabulary, skills, models, theories, concepts what learners should know in order to be successfully placed in the sequence of the lesson.

(4) **Modeling:** At this level, teacher shows a graphic form or demonstrates to his learners. It is related to the examples used by the teacher throughout the lesson and that behaviour what a teacher wishes learners to imitate.

(5) **Guided Practice:** Teacher leads his learners through the steps essential to perform/get the skill by hearing, looking and doing. Here learners do some activities. These activities may be individual or group; some class work or field work.

(6) **Checking for Understanding:** In this step, teacher tries to check the understanding of concepts, learners have acquired during the transaction of lesson. It is sequence of the lesson. Here to evaluate their level of acquisition, teacher uses variety of questions.

(7) **Independent Practice:** In this step, learners practice on their own. Learners work on own such as presentation, homework, etc. Teacher uses this to verify progress or justify remediation or enrichment.

(8) **Closure:** It is related to the lesson's review. Here, teacher asks some assessment questions and tells what they are going to learn next.

Criticism of Behaviourist Lesson Planning

Behavioural theories do not account for free will and internal influences such as moods, thoughts and feelings.

- There are many instances of learning that occurs without the use of reinforcements or punishments.
- Behavioursists focus on the target, desirable behaviour that is the product. They fail to explain how humans learn, the process through which the learning takes place.

- Language acquisition was one type of learning. Skinners learning theory cannot account for.
- For a behaviourist what occurs between the stimulus and the response is of little importance. The very meaning of the learning process is banned from any scientific analysis in the behaviouristic approach.
- It is appropriate for small classes, not for large classes.
- Behaviourism doesn't take into account important internal processes that take place in the mind.
- It is not appropriate for higher classes.
- People and animals are able to adapt their behaviour when new information is introduced, even if a previous behaviour pattern has been established through reinforcement.

Q15. Describe the concept mapping as a strategy for planning.

Or

What is concept mapping? Discuss with the help of an example.

Or

Define and explain concept map with example.

Ans. The graphic tools in the form of drawings or diagrams that can be used to visually describe relationships between and among concepts as well as show the mental connections students make between new concepts and prior knowledge is known as concept mapping. It requires critical thinking, knowledge and an understanding of the interrelationships between concepts. Furthermore, concept mapping reflects the inherent cognitive hierarchical processes between new learning and prior knowledge.

In the subject mathematics and others, students have learnt various concepts, but gradually, they are unable to interlink the relationships between these concepts. As no concept in mathematics is isolated; a particular concept of mathematics is interlinked with different branches of mathematics and with other subjects like science and social science in different ways and different manners. Thus, it is very important to use concept maps in the process of assessment. A concept map on quadrilateral is exemplified below:

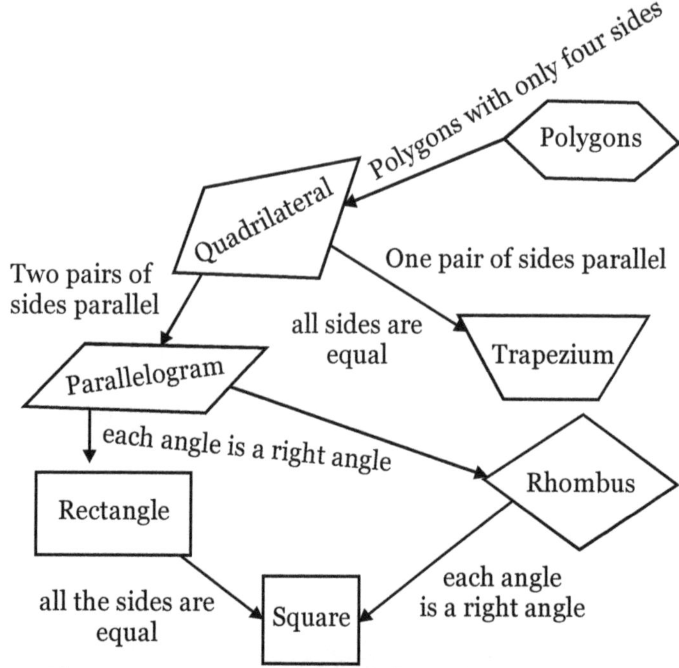

Fig. 3.3: Concept map of quadrilaterals (An Example)

Students, on their part, can form different ways/types of concept maps on a particular concept, depending upon the number of sub-concept and linking words they want to include. Therefore, the number of connections and depth of understanding can be assessed by the number of linking lines and used by the student's concept map. Hence, a concept map provides a concrete record of the connections perceived by the students, and thus, it indicates how the student's knowledge is organised and interconnected. More specifically, concept mapping can furnish valuable insight into the depth of students' understanding because it reflects the accuracy and strength of their connections. Even Venn Diagram of some concepts can play a role of concept mapping.

Therefore, in following ways concept map helps the teacher as well as taught:

- It provides opportunities for teachers to know how learners may see or organise knowledge differently.
- Concept map increase the potential of teacher to formulate the multiple ways of constructing meaning for diverse group of learners.
- Concept map helps in holistic style of learning.
- Concept mapping helps to reduce abstract knowledge to concrete diagrammatic representation.
- Concepts map help in selecting appropriate instructional materials.

- With the help of concepts map teacher can design the content of the study that is relevant, meaningful and interesting.
- Mapping help to develop well integrated, continuous and logically sequenced in content.

Concept maps are widely used instructional and teaching learning tools. It helps teachers and learner to indentify and visually represent their views and knowledge. Teachers can also use concept map to identify learner's previous knowledge or misconceptions as it provide a graphical summary of what learners have learned.

Concept maps can be used for the purpose of both formative and summative evaluation. Concept maps can facilitate teaching and learning in several ways. It can help both teachers and learners to identify the key points of concepts in propositions. It is an effective tool which makes structure of knowledge explicit and accessible.

Q16. Explain constructivist lesson planning (5-E approach) with example.

Or

Mention the steps of 5-E Approach of lesson planning.

[Dec-2017, Q.No.-3 (f)]

Ans. Constructivism is an approach which tries how learning is realised in a person's mind. According to this approach, each person comes to the learning environment with their prior knowledge and they construct their new learning on this knowledge. Constructivist approach is a learning process which helps learners to make their knowledge meaningful in their mind (Fardanesh, 2006). This approach is focused on learning environments which gives individuals a chance to construct knowledge by themselves or by discussing with other individuals.

The 5E's can be used with students of all ages, including adults. Each of the 5E's describes a phase of learning, and each phase begins with the letter "E": Engage, Explore, Explain, Elaborate, and Evaluate. The 5E's allows students and teachers to experience common activities, to use and build on prior knowledge and experience, to construct meaning, and to continually assess their understanding of a concept. According to ATES, "Learners are prevented to memorise the subject with this model. It is aimed that learners take active part in various activities such as brain-storming, question and answer, drama, painting, cooperative learning, teamwork, presentation skills, discussion." 5E Model not only implicates learners into activity at every stage in consideration of the information given to them but also encourages them to create their own concepts. The five phases of "Constructivist Learning Approach" are as follows:

Engage: This phase of the 5E's starts the process. The goals of the Engagement phase are to invite the learner's consideration, encourage their interest, spur them to unearth their prior experiences with the concepts about to be studied and pique their interest to know more. Teachers can ask a question, define a problem, show a surprising event and act out a problematic situation to engage the learners and focus them on the instructional tasks. This is a warm up phase in which learners become ready to learn. An "engage" activity should do the following tasks:

(i) Make connections between past and present learning experiences

(ii) Anticipate activities and focus students' thinking on the learning outcomes of current activities. Students should become mentally engaged in the concept, process, or skill to be learned.

Explore: This phase of the 5E's provides students with a common base of experiences. They identify and develop concepts, processes, and skills. During this phase, students actively explore their environment or manipulate materials. At this stage, the teacher acts as a facilitator, providing materials and guiding the learners' focus. Learners have the opportunity to get directly involved with phenomena and materials by actively exploring their environment and manipulating materials. Learners test their own knowledge by observing and gaining experiences about the phenomena.

Explain: Explanation means the act or process in which concepts, processes, or skills become plain, comprehensible, and clear. The process of explanation provides the students and teacher with a common use of terms relative to the learning experience. In this phase, the teacher directs student attention to specific aspects of the engagement and exploration experiences. First, the teacher asks the students to give their explanations. Second, the teacher introduces scientific or technological explanations in a direct and formal manner. Explanations are ways of ordering and giving a common language for the exploratory experiences. The teacher should base the initial part of this phase on the students' explanations and clearly connect the explanations to experiences in the engagement and exploration phases of the instructional model. The key to this phase is to present concepts, processes, or skills briefly, simply, clearly, and directly.

Elaborate: This phase of the 5E's extends student's conceptual understanding and allows them to practice skills and behaviors. Through new experiences, the learners develop deeper and broader understanding of major concepts, obtain more information about areas of interest, and refine their skills. Connections between knowledge formed at this stage, often, lead to further inquiry and new understandings.

Evaluate: The teacher supports students to continuously refine and improve their work using assessment criteria in preparation for a performance of understanding. They integrate evidence from each phase, formally recording students' progress against learning goals. The teacher provides feedback and assists students to evaluate their progress and achievements. They support students to reflect on their learning processes and the impact of effort on achievement. The teacher guides students to identify future learning goals.

Example of Lesson Plan using 5-E Approach

Table 3.2: Lesson Plan Using 5-E Approach

Subject: Social Science
Class: 9th
Topic: Population Policy
Objectives: **Cognitive:** 1. Learners will be able to define population. 2. Learners will be able to name and identify the problems caused by overpopulation. 3. Learners will be able to explain the population rate of the country. 4. Learners will be able to explain relationship between the population rate of a country by age group and the level of development. **Psychomotor:** 1. Learners will be able to construct a model depicting the social and economic problems caused by overpopulation. 2. Learners will be able to classify the countries according to population rate and present with diagrams with 90% accuracy. **Affective:** 1. Learners will demonstrate perseverance as they attempt to construct a model. 2. Learners will display open-mindedness as they work with their peers to work on population policy.
Material: Different types of charts
The activities about Population Policy (5 E Approach):
Engage: Lesson can be started with the following questions: Do you know the population of our country? What do you think about population in which you live? What kind of advantages or disadvantages are due to this population? Are there any crowded cities in India? What sort of problems are there? Do you have any experience about it? What kind of problems would there be if our country didn't have enough population? Various visuals will be used supporting the questions, learners are allowed to raise attention and their current knowledge is assessed.

Explore:

Learners will be divided into groups and each group is allowed to choose a topic of interest. Examples of the topics are as follows:

Topic 1: Should there be any low to limit the population growth of a country?

Topic 2: What social and economic problems do the countries have due to overpopulation?

Topic 3: What social and economic problems do the countries have due to under population?

Topic 4: What kind of relationship is there between the population rate of a country by age group and the level of development?

Topic 5: Dramatise one or more possible problems of a country with overpopulation.

Topic 6: Dramatise one or more possible problem of a country whose young population rate decreases fast.

Explanation:

One representative of each group will share the results one by one. Teacher facilitates, explains and completes the lack of knowledge of learners if it is necessary. Teacher give information about the concept of "Population Policy" after the activities. Therefore, learners are allowed to understand what "Population Policy" is.

Elaborate:

Learners are provided environment of discussion regarding Population Policy to use their new knowledge and explore its implications. Learners will be divided into two groups and ask question "Is it sensible to practice Population Policy in order to increase or decrease population in terms of human rights?" Ask yes or no. At the end of the discussion both teacher and learner will summarise the topic.

Evaluation:

Following questions will be used

What is Population Policy?

What is the purpose of population Policy?

What are the advantages and disadvantages of Population Policy?

What are the problems of overpopulation in a country?

What are the problems of underpopulation in a country?

Q17. What are the basic considerations for selection of an approach to instruction?

Ans. While selecting an instructional approach a teacher has to follow the basic considerations:

(1) **Learners:** Normally, in a classroom teacher knows that there are learners of diverse backgrounds. This diversity ranges from social, economical to intellectual level. To teach the group of learners of diverse backgrounds, it is necessary for teacher at least a method of instruction should be such that it offers learners to contribute in the teaching-learning process.

(2) **Grade Level of the Learners:** Next consideration for the teacher is the grade level of learners. If learners belong to the lower grade level, a method involving lots of activities may be chosen. But if the grade is higher than it, teacher would select a method wherein teacher would assign the work or distribute the work among learners and learners would be self-involved in the learning process.

(3) **Subject Matter:** In this consideration, the subjects like science and mathematics are scientific in nature, whose major emphasis is to verify the existing knowledge or discover the knowledge or solve the existing problem with rational scientific method. Therefore, appropriate approach to select an instructional method for teaching of science would be inquiry method or problem solving method. But in case of languages, problem solving or inquiry method is inappropriate, as in language teaching it is more often developing skills of language where drill and practice method would be an appropriate one.

(4) **Intended Learning outcomes:** The intended learning outcomes are generally the behavioural changes that take place within learners after the content is taught to them. Normally, intended learning outcomes are framed by teacher but it also depends upon the content to be taught. It is normally set before the teaching-learning process starts. For example, if teacher wants to teach learners about the reflection and its laws, the intended learning outcomes set by the teacher would be:

(i) learner will able to define the term reflection,

(ii) learner will be able to state the laws of reflection and

(iii) learner will be able to verify the laws of reflection.

(5) **Learning Environments:** Another key consideration while selecting the instructional method is the learning environment. It refers to the diverse physical, cultural, social environment in which learners learn. It is also called the ecosystem of school or classroom or any environment where teaching-learning process takes place. It includes physical, biological and psychological components and their continuous interactions among them will determine the learning environment. Thus, learning environment is an ecosystem wherein individual entities play a

key role in creating it. For example, teachers' beliefs and behaviours, learners' beliefs and behaviours, school policies, motivation among learners and teachers, learners need and interest appropriate ventilation and sunlight, etc., make learning environment. Learning environments have both a direct and indirect influence on learning, including their engagement in what is being taught, their motivation to learn, and their sense of well-being, belonging and personal safety. For example, learning environments filled with sunlight and stimulating educational materials would likely be considered more conducive to learning then learning environment with drab spaces without windows or decoration, incidents of misbehaviour, disorder, bullying and illegal activity. How adults interest with learners and how learners interact with one another may also be considered aspects of a learning environment and phrases such as "positive learning environment" or "negative learning environment" are commonly used in reference to social and emotional dimensions of a school or class.

(6) Available Resources: Available resource is one of the other basic considerations for selecting an approach. Normally, resources refer to the material resources but they also include human resources. Often teacher requires help from its co-teachers, learners, and others like community members, experts and learners to enhance their abilities and competencies. Also a lot of times the teacher requires material resources like audio-visual and technological aids to supplement or integrate or integrate with teaching. Resources help learners to make their knowledge more concrete, permanent and effective.

(7) Teacher ability: Another criterion that needs to be considered while selecting an instructional method is teacher ability. It is important that teacher must be equipped with the specific abilities i.e. pedagogical- technological- content knowledge.

Q18. What is lecture method under teacher centered method? What are its advantages and disadvantages?

Ans. The word lecture comes from the Latin word lectus, it means "that which is read." Lecture method is the most commonly used method of teaching chemistry. This method is most commonly followed in colleges and in schools in big classes. This method is not quite suitable to realise the real aim of teaching chemistry. In lecture method only the teacher talks and students are passive listeners. Since the students do not actively participate in this method of teaching so this method is a teacher controlled and information centred and in this method teacher works as a sole resource in class room instructions. Due to lack of participation students get bored and some of them sometimes may go to sleep. In this method students is provided with readymade knowledge by the teacher and due to this spoon feeding the students loses interest and his powers of reasoning and observation get no stimulus.

In this method, the teacher goes ahead with the subject matter at his own speed. The teacher may make use of black board at times and may also dictate notes. This teacher-oriented method in its extreme from does not expect any question or response from the students.

Advantages of the Lecture Method: The following are the basic advantages of the lecture method:

(1) The lecture method is the most economical way of getting a large amount of information across to a large class. A teacher can convey the information in minimum time, thus enabling the syllabus to be covered within the stipulated time. It is economical in terms of both money and time.

(2) The lecture is useful in imparting in an efficient manner factual information to convey facts to students who have difficulty reading their texts.

(3) The lecture helps to channelise the thinking of students in a given direction.

(4) Some abstract topics in science are best taught by the lecture method. The teacher, through tact, style and presentation, can get her message through.

Disadvantages of the Lecture Method: The disadvantages of the lecture method are as follows:

(1) The lecture method is apt to be misused. The 'pouring in' of information is psychologically unsound unless it can be done in a meaningful way.

(2) Science is best learnt by doing. There is no provision for activities in this method as the students are passive (listeners).

(3) The rate of imparting information by the teacher may seem too fast for the students who are restless by nature, preoccupied with their own immediate problems and often hadicapped by limitations of vocabulary and background of experience.

(4) A poorly planned, poorly delivered lecture fails to motivate the students.

(5) The lecture method is not very successful in imparting attitudes and skills, as it does not touch the affective and psychomotor faculties of the learner.

(6) As student interaction is minimum, social attitudes and values may not be fostered.

(7) The lecture method cannot cater to individual grasping capacities of the students.

Q19. Define demonstration method. Explain its aspects, merits and demerits.

Ans. Demonstrations involve doing/performing something to facilitate understanding and enable learning by observation. It requires verbal elaboration but not as much as a lecture. It adds to the value of a lecture/discussion as it makes an abstraction concrete and provides empirical evidence. Thus, demonstration is based on pragmatism, a philosophy according to which theory is based on practice and knowledge emerges from empirical evidences. Demonstration, though a teacher centered method is economic, especially when the school does not have enough equipments and materials for all the students and especially if the equipments are costly or there is risk involved in an experiment. It also saves time. During a demonstration, learning is not just by listening but also by watching, and hence, learners use more than one sense. For example, a teacher may demonstrate that oxygen is essential for combustion by covering a lighted candle, which gets extinguished. S/he may demonstrate, with the help of a microscope, structure of organisms like algae collected from a pond. Apart from live demonstrations, s/he may also use media like videos with recorded demonstrations, especially if there are complex operations that are difficult to carry out in classrooms or s/he does not have the necessary resources. For example, videos are available for dissection of earthworms, fish, etc., Newton's Laws, working of simple machines, etc.

Aspects of demonstration method: A good demonstration method has various aspects, which are as follow:

(1) **Demonstration should be planned and rehearsed:** It is necessary for a teacher to identify the concepts that need to be demonstrated through activity or experiment. Therefore, initial planning and rehearsal is must for a successful demonstration. During planning stage, it is necessary that all the materials required for demonstration should be arranged beforehand and they should be placed on the demonstration table in a sequential manner so that teacher while experimenting needs not to worry about acquiring material as well as searching for it, After that, teacher needs to practice that demonstration as many times as possible so that it leads to expected outcomes.

(2) **Purpose of demonstration:** Teacher should be clear about its purpose before demonstration and make the aim of the demonstration clear to learners beforehand. Teacher should clearly state what specific things need to be observed while demonstration, based on which inferences can be drawn or generalisation can be made.

(3) **Active participation of learners:** Teacher should ensure that learners not only observe but also actively participate during the demonstration. It could be in the form of setting up of instruments related to experiment or activity or it can be in the form of seeking answers from the learners. It can also be that learners can write their observations on the blackboard.

(4) **Training in scientific thinking:** To develop process skills, demonstration method provides learners with opportunity i.e. observe, explain, analyse, infer, verify and review.

Merits: Demonstration method has several merits:

(1) Demonstrations are very helpful in the teaching of skills.

(2) It does provide opportunity to learners to participate during demonstration.

(3) It is possible to instruct a reasonable number of people in basic skills of agriculture at one time.
(4) It is suitable for a multicultural and differential classroom.
(5) Theorisation of concepts through verbal mode by teacher is reduced and focus is on demonstration of concepts through experiment or activity.

Demerits: Demonstration method has several limitations also:

(1) Many people may not be able to practice the skill demonstrated adequately due to shortage of time or facilities.
(2) Since the teacher performs the experiment in his own pace, many students cannot comprehend the concept being clarified.
(3) Demonstration needs a great deal of time and energy for proper presentation.
(4) Demonstration requires an expert presenter.
(5) In a demonstration, a trainee can learn the characteristics of a skilled performance through observation but have no opportunity to practice the skill which is one of the basic requirements to develop skills.

Q20. What do you understand by the term team teaching? What are its characteristics, advantages and disadvantages?

Ans. Team teaching is one of the most interesting and potentially significant recent developments in education. It is an organisational structure to improve teaching learning process in the classroom. It is an innovation in school organistaion in which two or more teachers teach a group of students. The group is benefited by the expertise of different teachers.

According to David Warwick, "a team teaching is a form of organisation, in which individual teachers decide to pool resources, interest and expertise, in order to devise and implement scheme of work suitable to the needs of their learners and the facilities of their school."

Characteristics of team teaching

- Team-teaching is considered a teaching method.
- In this type of task, two or more teachers participate in the teaching.
- Team teaching is based on cooperation. All the teachers participating in the team teaching apply their resources, abilities and experiences.
- All the teachers involved in the team teaching plan teaching cooperatively and execute it cooperatively. Inspite of this, evaluation is also done on cooperative basis.
- In the team-teaching process, the needs of the pupils, and schools and existing resources are also considered.
- In team-teaching various aspects of any topic of one subject is taught by two or more teachers turn by turn.
- The main aim of team-teaching is to make the teaching-learning more effective.
- In team teaching, isolation among the teachers is removed.

- In team teaching, the entire responsibility does not fall on one teacher only but it is shared by others too. Hence, this method is based on collective responsibility.

Advantages: Team teaching has several basic advantages. They are:

- Team teaching contributes to flexibility in teachers. There is a lot of opportunity for free discussion.
- Team teaching can be organised in a number of different ways to meet the needs of the particular school and the course content and it is also helpful for the development of human relations.
- Team teaching can meet the aspect of individual differences better than the usual classroom system and helpful for the development of professional status of teachers.
- Larger group sessions enable more students to benefit from instruction by the most skilled and proficient teachers. It provides for a better untilisation of superior teacher.
- Team teaching relieves teachers of many non-teaching chores.
- The plan of group teaching facilitates a more effective use of space, materials and equipment.
- Student teachers too can gain valuable experience by observing the teaching of more than one teacher and by participating in cooperative planning. This also will help them in modifying their behaviour.
- The quality of team teaching is often better than conventional classroom teaching as the team members plan very carefully.

Disadvantages: Team teaching has following disadvantages also:

- It is very difficult to find people with special competencies and high qualifications necessary for working as team-teaching leaders and senior teachers.
- Members of the group have to spend a great deal of time working on plans for scheduling for team activities and for individual projects.
- The success of group teaching depends to a great extent on the ability of members of the group to work together harmoniously. The program suffers if friction develops in interpersonal relations.
- The problem of selecting supervisor teachers to serve as group leaders is a complex one. Teachers who are very successful at working with a group of students may experience frustration when they are faced with the semi-administrative tasks involved while serving as group leaders.
- Opportunities for student relationship may be lost because of the complexities of the program and size of the group.
- Teaching may tend to become lecture type and formal.
- Noise may become a problem in a large group or when several groups are working in a room.

- It is a costly affair. Team or Group teaching calls for the use of special physical facilities. If these facilities are not available, they must be provided at considerable expense.

Q21. What is learner centered approach what are its method of instruction? Also explain their characteristics.

Ans. Student-centered learning, also known as learner-centered education, broadly encompasses methods of teaching that shift the focus of instruction from the teacher to the student. In original usage, student-centered learning aims to develop learner autonomy and independence by putting responsibility for the learning path in the hands of students.

A learning-centered approach does not necessarily mean that student activity is the focus of the teaching strategy. This approach is mainly based on the tenants of constructivism whose basic belief is that the learner constructs his/her own knowledge. Following are the major characteristics of the learning-centered approach:

- The process, techniques and strategies of learning are emphasised. If the process of learning is better, then acquisition of knowledge and competencies would be easier.
- In a natural and contextual situation, learning takes place.
- Learner dominantly controls learning. Consequently, the learner learns at the pace s/he desires. In that sense, learning is quite flexible and democratic.
- Learner is active and the teacher facilitates for active learning. The major role of the teacher is facilitating and supporting learning.
- Activity-based methods activate the learner for learning.

Method of instruction: There are two important methods of instruction under learner-centered approach that are as follow:

(1) Inquiry Approach: Inquiry approach is a very effective technique of teaching science to fast learners in primary and upper primary levels, and even in higher classes. Inquiry is a multi-faceted activity that involves making observations, posing questions, examining books and other sources of information to see what is already known, planning investigations, reviewing what is already known in light of experimental evidence, using tools to gather, analyse and interpret data, proposing answers, explanations, predictions, and communicating the results. Inquiry requires identification of assumptions, use of critical and logical thinking, and consideration of alternative explanations.

The inquiry approach requires a skilled teacher who can develop a learning environment that stimulates learner curiosity and desire to investigate. Carefully planned questions can engage thinking and motivate learners to seek information while carefully guided investigative activates can lead learners to make discoveries that have personal meaning. The power of an inquiry-based approach to teaching and learning is its potential to increase intellectual engagement and foster deep understanding through the development of a hands-on, minds-on and 'research-based disposition' towards teaching and learning. Inquiry honours the complex, interconnected nature of knowledge construction, striving to provide opportunities for both teachers and learners to collaboratively build test and reflect on their learning. Inquiry approach requires a high level of interaction among the learner, the teacher, area of study, available resources and the learning environment. Learners become actively involved in the learning process as they:

- act upon their curiosity and interests;
- develop questions;
- think their way through controversies or dilemmas;
- look at problems analytically;
- inquire into their preconceptions and what they already know;
- develop, clarify, and test hypotheses and,
- draw inferences and generate possible solutions.

Characteristics

(i) The Inquiry approach is process rather than content oriented and emphasises process outcomes.

(ii) The content in the Inquiry approach, instead of providing narrative and descriptive account of events, highlights basic concepts and generalisations.

(iii) In Inquiry approach, the teacher plays only a facilitative role, data collecting and other related work is to be undertaken by the students. In the process, they learn to probe issues, to analyse and to make decisions on alternatives and thus become active and independent learners and also critical thinkers.

(iv) Because of active involvement of the students in the teaching-learning process, they develop a favourable attitude towards the subject matter and towards the teacher.

(2) Problem solving: Problem solving is not much different from a higher level inquiry as both seek solutions but the term 'problem solving' implies the adoption of scientific method. Problem solving includes higher order thinking skills such as visualisation, association, abstraction, comprehension, manipulation, reasoning, analysis, synthesis, generalisation etc. It provides learners with opportunities to use their newly acquired knowledge in meaningful, real-life activities and assists them in working at higher level of thinking.

In his learning theory, Gagne has placed problem solving at highest level of learning in hierarchy. He pointed out that the end result of problem solving is when the learner actually discovers a higher order rule or generalisation and constructs new relationship and meaning for a concept under investigation. Problem solving engages learners in investigations where they raise questions, plan, procedures, collect information and form conclusions.

Characteristics

(i) It is based on purposeful activity.

(ii) It is characherised by a learner-centered approach with teachers as "facilitators rather than disseminators".

(iii) It is based on scientific skills and abilities like reflective thinking and reasoning.

(iv) It begins with the assumption that learning is an active, integrated, and constructive process influenced by social and contextual factors.

Q22. Analyse the stages of inquiry-based instruction. What are its advantages and disadvantages?

Ans. There are generally five phases under inquiry based instruction, they are:

(1) Orientation phase: Inquiry begins with this phase. The main aim of this phase is to stimulate curiosity about a topic and provide pupils with opportunities for defining a problem statement. A teacher's main aim is to find issues and topics which are relevant to learners.

(2) Conceptualisation phase: This is the phase during which research questions and/or hypotheses are stated. A teacher needs to encourage his/her pupils to define research questions or hypotheses. This phase includes two sub-phases: Questioning or Hypothesis Generation. The difference relates to the familiarity of pupils with the theory that underlies the topic under study. If pupils have little to no background, then they should start with the Questioning sub-phase (which subsequently guides them to the Investigation phase via the Exploration and Data Interpretation sub-phases). After acquiring experience with the topic, pupils can return and select the Hypothesis Generation sub-phase. Alternatively, pupils who are familiar with a topic can move from the Questioning sub-phase to the Hypothesis Generation sub-phase if they have already collected enough background information to formulate a specific hypothesis. In any case, Hypothesis Generation is an important phase because it leads to the Experimentation sub-phase.

(3) Investigation phase: The Investigation phase is based mostly on hands-on activities. It is a process of gathering empirical evidence to answer the research question or verify hypotheses. For example, pupils work in groups in a science laboratory to find evidence for the problem statement defined in the Conceptualisation phase. The Investigation phase includes three sub-phases: Exploration, Experimentation, and Data Interpretation.

(4) Conclusion phase: In this phase, research findings from the Investigation phase are reported and justified by the results of the investigation. Here, a teacher's role is to encourage his/her pupils to communicate with their peers to present their findings and results of their investigation.

(5) Discussion phase: This phase of inquiry is directly connected to all the other phases. It consists of communicating partial or completed outcomes as well as reflective processes to regulate the learning process. The Discussion phase includes two sub-phases: Communication and Reflection. The Communication sub-phase generates support for scientific research or study, or serves the purpose of informing decision-making, including political and ethical thinking. The Reflection sub-phase aims to meaningfully raise pupils' skills in developing creative, scientific problem-solving and socio-scientific decision-making abilities.

Advantages of inquiry approach

- Inquiry approach increases reasoning and thinking skills of the learner. Since the learner uses higher order mental process, he grows intellectually.
- Inquiry approach creates motivation in the learner to discover and investigate. On achieving success he gets further motivation.
- By using this method, students learn to structure problems and focus on the key variables. They also learn to organise and conduct investigation.
- Since inquiry approach involves concrete activities, it helps in retention of concepts.
- It is learner-centred.
- It minimises cramming and leads to better understanding of concepts.
- It increases the efficiency of students in using scientific method.
- It develops scientific attitude.

Limitations of inquiry approach

- Science teachers are not well-versed in using this approach.
- Teachers need to have sound academic knowledge, as students may ask diverse questions.
- Science textbooks are not written on the lines of inquiry approach.
- Evaluation on the basis of written examination provides little scope for assessing the investigative skills of the students.
- Equipment and materials are not adequate for exploration and inquiry.
- It is more time consuming than traditional teaching.
- The whole syllabus cannot be covered through this approach. Certain topics may not be suitable for investigation.
- Many learners may not be competent to conduct investigation. They may move in the wrong direction without any fruitful learning.

Q23. State the steps of problem solving. Also explain its advantages and disadvantages.

Ans. Following are the various steps, which should be involved in problem-solving:

(1) **Identifying and defining the problem:** Problem arises out of felt need and out of existing students' activities and environmental activities. The students should be able to identify and clearly define the problem.

(2) **Analysis of the problem:** The problem should be properly analysed.

(3) **Stating clearly the relationships:** It should be done between different concepts.

(4) **Formulating hypotheses:** Possible solution may be formulated basing on the nature of the problem.

(5) **Testing the hypotheses:** Each hypothesis is to be tested to solve the problem.

(6) **Verification of the result:** The solution of the problem is to be verified number of times to test the validity of the hypotheses.

Advantages

- It encourages deep learning by replacing lectures with discussion forums, faculty mentoring, and collaborative research students become actively engaged in meaningful learning.
- Direct instruction is reduced; students are forced to take responsibilities in their own learning which often increase motivation.
- It activates prior knowledge.
- It encourages critical thinking.
- Learners tend to be more competent in information seeking skills than traditional learners.
- It is related to real-life situations, these skills are highly transferable.
- Learning is driven by challenging, open-ended problems.
- Social interaction is a very important skill. It promotes group dynamics, peer evaluation, and present opportunities for learners to develop confrontation and persuasive skills.
- It helps learners gain scientific view and thinking.
- It improves the ability of learners to identify problem and put forward hypotheses.

Disadvantages

- It is a very slow, long and time-consuming process which limits the coverage of adequate amounts of knowledge and information to be imparted to the students in the face of external examination. Therefore, the construction of an entirely different syllabus is necessary.
- There is too much stress on practical work which may, in fact, give students a wrong conception about the nature and philosophy of science in general.
- Teaching and learning science is a joyful process, but too much practical work may make it a more dull and routine work.
- Teachers who would use this approach are not available in abundance.
- It is also equally doubtful whether all students can equally benefit from this approach.

Q24. Explain strategies and techniques of conducting inquiry and problem solving.

Ans. Various strategies and techniques of conducting inquiry and problem solving are as follows:

(1) **Questioning:** Questions can stimulate thought and action. They are at the heart of the inquiry process. There is nothing

like a good question to get students thinking critically about the world in which they live. Skilled science teachers are good at asking questions that cause students to generate their own questions. When students formulate questions of personal interest, they are more likely to engage in activities they find meaningful. Questions can also be asked to direct learner thinking along the lines of the process skills such as observing, inferring, hypothesising and experimenting. Emphasis is placed upon the process of thinking as this applies to learner interaction with issues, data, topics, concepts, materials, and problems. Divergent thinking is encouraged and nurtured as learners recognise that questions often have more than one "good" or "correct" answer. Such thinking leads in many instances to elaboration of further questions.

(2) **Discrepant events:** Discrepant events can be used to promote inquiry. A discrepant event puzzles students, causing them to wonder why the event occurred as it did. Puzzlement can stimulate students to engage in reasoning and the desire to find out (Piaget, 1971). Some of the most provocative discrepant-event demonstrations pertain to the laws of motion, center of gravity, Bernoulli's principle, density, and vacuum, to mention a few.

Discrepant events can be used to stimulate inquiry about numerous concepts and principles. The discrepant event approach receives support from learning psychologists as valid instructional method. Discrepant events influence equilibration and the self-regulatory process, according to the Piagetian theory of intellectual development. Situations that are contrary to what a person expects cause him to wonder what is taking place. With proper guidance the learner figures out the discrepancy and attempts to find out the suitable and acceptable explanation, that rests temporarily at a new cognitive level.

(3) **Inductive activities:** The inductive approach provides students with learning situations in which they can discover a concept or principle. With this approach, the learner first encounters the attributes and instances of an idea, then names and discusses the idea. This empirical-inductive approach gives students a concrete experience whereby they obtain sensory impressions and data from real objects and events. As a result, the learner can perceive certain stimuli and may be in a better position to make sense of a situation than if he or she had received abstract information about the particular phenomenon solely from a classroom lecture. Empirically obtained information can be acted upon cognitively by the student and organised in the mind, where patterns may be discovered that are meaningful to the learner. This is how a concept is induced or discovered and how ideas are put forth to describe and explain a phenomenon. The teacher helps bring into the

discussion the appropriate terminology for naming the concept or principle and defining it. The inductive approach, which can be thought of as an experience-before-vocabulary approach to learning, has been researched and written about extensively as "the learning cycle".

(4) **Deductive Activities:** With the deductive strategy, a concept or principle is defined and discussed using appropriate labels and terms, followed by experiences to illustrate the idea under study. The deductive approach is a vocabulary-before-experience model of teaching in which lecture and discussion precede laboratory or field work. The deductive approach can be used to promote inquiry sessions and to construct knowledge. The first phase presents the generalisations and rules about the concept or principle at hand, and the second phase requires learners to find examples of the concept or principle. Some teachers claim that the deductive approach is useful when introducing complex ideas that do not have perceptible attributes.

Q25. What do you mean by brainstorming? Discuss its rule and procedure.

Ans. Brainstorming is an individual or group method for generating ideas, increasing creative efficacy, or finding solutions to problems. Group brainstorming participants generate ideas on a particular topic or problem in a non-judgmental environment following a set of ground rules about appropriate behaviours.

Rules of Brainstorming: There are four basic rules in brainstorming. These rules are intended to stimulate idea generation and increase overall creativity of the group while minimising the inhibitions people may have about working in groups.

(1) **Focus on Quantity:** This rule focuses on the maximisation of possible ideas, both good and bad. The assumption made is that the greater the number of ideas, the greater the chance of finding the optimal solution to a problem.

(2) **No criticism:** In brainstorming, criticism of ideas creates conflict and wastes valuable time needed to generate the maximum number of ideas. When people see ideas being criticised, they tend to withhold their own ideas to avoid being criticised. Criticism should take place, but after the brainstorming session is complete. Typical brainstorming sessions last about an hour or less.

(3) **Welcome Unusual Ideas:** All ideas should be encouraged, whether good or bad. People must be encouraged to think "out of the box", and this may generate new perspectives and a new way of thinking. Sometimes, what appears as a radical solution initially may be the best possible solution in the end.

(4) **Combine and Improve Ideas:** The best possible solution may be a combination of ideas. New ideas should be encouraged from the combination of ideas already presented.

Procedure of brainstorming: A teacher must prepare for the session as follow:

(1) **Set the problem:** The problem should be stated as clearly as possible, with specific questions, (e.g. "How can we streamline laboratory flow to improve turnaround time?"). Brainstorming sessions benefit from the specificity of the problem statement, since participants can focus on specific ideas that are germane to the issue.

(2) **Create a background memo:** A background memo is a form of invitation and information letter to the participants, containing the session name, problem, time, date, and place. The problem is described in the form of a question and some examples are given. The ideas are generally solutions to the problem, and used when the session slows down or goes off-track.

(3) **Select participants:** Participants must be selected for their expertise and understanding of the issue to be discussed, and the three types of participants are usually mangers, process owners, and customers of the process. In some cases, that group may include external customers, but usually the group consists of participants internal to the organisation.

Variation in the composition of team members is key to the brainstorming session. Some of them are as follow: Several core members of the project who have proved themselves, Several guests from outside the project, with affinity to the problem, One idea collector who records the suggested ideas.

(4) **Create a list of lead questions:** Normally, when leader go for brainstorming sessions, every member plunges deeply into it. These lead to sometimes decrease in divergent and convergent thinking. So, team leader must prepare some lead questions which should stimulate creativity by suggesting a lead question to answer, such as Can we combine these ideas? or How about a look from another perspective?

(5) **Conduct the session:** Leader must conduct the session according to the rules of the brainstorming process. Participants must feel empowered to express themselves freely in a nonthreatening environment, and they must feel that every opinion is valued by the team. Conducting the session is straightforward:

(i) Assemble the team for the session.

(ii) Briefly describe the problem and the process and then discuss any questions about either topic.

(iii) Indentify a timekeeper and a scribe to take down ideas as they occur.

(iv) The whole list is reviewed to ensure that everyone understands the ideas.

(v) Duplicate ideas and obviously infeasible solutions are removed.

(vi) The leader thanks all participants and gives each a token of appreciation.

Q26. Discuss the concept of cooperative learning.

Or

Define cooperative learning. What are its steps?

Or

Write any four key features of cooperative learning.

Ans. As a practising teacher, one might have observed children discussing their class work, home assignment and other school learning experiences. When a teacher gives them class test, they like to tally their answers; to compare their solutions and also to find out discrepancies. Children also like to express and communicate to other children (peers) their liking or disliking of a subject. They like to share their methods of learning, learning difficulties, supplementary reading book, etc. A teacher might have also experienced that if two or more children of the class live in the same locality or are neighbours, they like to study together at home. Children feel motivated and develop interest while working in groups. In a classroom, if teacher provides a child an opportunity to explain his/her correct solution to other children, s/he feels pride in doing so. Children feel responsible when they are asked to help or teach other children who have achieved less. Teacher would see from his/her own experiences that peer interaction and peer co-operation is the basic need of every child just like curiosity and desire to know new things.

Children enjoy working together and helping each other. At the same time, each child wants to do better than the other child. This 'peer group social psychology' of co-operation and competition can be used to facilitate learning and to achieve objectives, which cannot be achieved through individual and competitive methods (Deutch, 1949). Co-operative learning is based on peer co-operation. Co-operative learning methods make use of goal and reward interdependence. Children perceive that they reach their goal only if the other children also reach their goal. They sink and swim together. Based on these assumptions, more satisfaction and better academic performance are expected.

Key features of cooperative learning are as follows:

- Whenever possible teams include a mix of racial, cultural and gender of students.
- Students work in groups to master academic materials.
- Reward systems are group-oriented rather than individually oriented.
- Groups are heterogeneous consisting of high, average and low achievers.

Cooperative learning requires students to work together in small groups to support each other to improve their own learning and that of others. However, it is not quite so simple, because there are variations on cooperative learning and some fierce arguments amongst academics as to the value of each.

There are few important steps to be followed in cooperative learning that are as follows:

(1) Organise learners into groups, using criteria to make decisions regarding this process. Determine the desired outcomes for the investigation to be undertaken, then place the learners into groups accordingly.

(2) Identify topics or ideas that will motivate learner inquiry. Some teachers provide a preliminary list of ideas for their learners that relate to the course or unit under study, focusing their thinking process. However, this approach should encourage brainstorming in order to identify additional ideas for investigation by learners.

(3) Ask each group to provide a preliminary outline of their study or project. This step immediately places learners on a productive path. When teacher examine the outline, provide suggestions and guidance. It is the responsibility of the teacher to make sure that each learner in the group knows what exactly s/he has to do.

(4) Monitor the investigations. Teacher should have a good idea where each group is while the investigations are carried out. Some inquires and projects will be conducted during class time, making them easy to monitor. Other investigations will take place after school and on weekends. For this type of work, take some time during class to ask for information to determine how groups as well as individuals are progressing.

(5) Teacher should help learners to prepare their final reports so that they do well and feel good about their work. Help learners form an outline for these reports and designate who will do each part of the write-up. The report is an opportunity for learners to demonstrate their process skills, the questions and they attempt to answer, the inferences and graphs they construct to communicate their findings. This phase of work is ideal for helping learners represent knowledge, visualise models, give explanations and demonstrate various skills.

(6) Assist each group to identify learners to take part in presenting their report. This aspect of cooperative group work develops presentation skills and confidence in speaking before others.

(7) Evaluate the investigations and projects. This often takes the form of assigning points to groups and individuals learners and entering into the grade books.

Q27. Briefly explain role of the teacher in cooperative learning. Discuss its advantages or disadvantages.

Or

What are the roles of a teacher at different phases of the cooperative learning? Discuss.

Ans. The roles of a teacher at different phases of the cooperative learning are as follows:

***Phase 1* : Present goals and learning set:** Teacher goes over objectives for the lesson and establishes the learning set.

***Phase 2* : Present information:** Teacher presents information to students either verbally or with a text material.

***Phase 3* : Organise students into learning teams:** Teacher explains to students how to form learning teams and helps to groups make efficient transition.

***Phase 4* : Assist team work and study:** Teacher assists learning teams as to do their work.

***Phase 5* : Test on the materials:** Teacher lists knowledge of learning materials or groups present results of their work.

***Phase 6* : Provide recognition:** Teacher finds ways to recognise both individual and group effort and achievement.

Advantages: The advantages of co-operative learning are as follows:

(1) It helps in developing those complex abilities among learners, which cannot be developed through individualistic, competitive methods. These include contributing ideas, collecting and synthesising information and summarising.

(2) It has positive effect on academic achievement of students.

(3) It has positive effect on self-esteem of children. It helps children to develop good image about themselves.

(4) Co-operative learning methods are helpful in improving interpersonal behaviour and class environment. Students start liking their classmates, subject matter and school.

(5) Students learn to express support, acceptance, warmth and liking, thereby reducing fear of school and tensions.

(6) Students learn to coordinate activities.

(7) Students learn to express their feelings and also to understand others' feelings.

Disadvantages: Following are the disadvantages of cooperative learning:

(1) Cooperative learning is constantly changing, there is the possibility that teachers may become confused and lack complete understanding of the method.

(2) Teachers implementing cooperative learning may also be challenged with resistance and hostility from students who believe that they are being held back by their slower teammates or by students who are less confident and feel that they are being ignored or demeaned by their team.

Q28. What are the group activities of cooperative learning?

Ans. In the classroom learning process, both teacher and learner lose interest and eventually the entire process become boring after certain of time. To avoid reaching such situation, it is indeed necessary that a classroom leader should arrange such activities and engage all the learners in the classroom so that learners remain motivated and interested in classroom. It can happen only when a teacher arrange group centric activities. Group activities are the ones where involvement or participation of the maximum number of learners is ensured by the teacher. Learners not only participate in it but also enhance knowledge by gathering information and processing it by solving problems and articulating what they have discovered. Each activity provides learners with opportunities to deepen their learning by applying concepts and articulating new knowledge and many of these activities also provide the teacher feedback to the learners' learning. There are some common group activities a teacher can carry out in classroom:

(1) **Think-Pair-Share:** Think-pair-share is a type of group activity in which teachers ask their learners to think of a question of their own and then write it on the backboard. Thereafter, teacher provides an opportunity to learners to think and discuss it in pairs, and finally together with the whole class. The success of these activities depends on the nature of the questions posed. This activity works ideally with questions to encourage deeper thinking, problem-solving, and/or critical analysis. The group discussions are critical as they allow learners to articulate their through processes. Advantages of the think-pair-share include the engagement of all learners in the classroom quick feedback for the instructor encouragement and support for higher levels of thinking of learners.

(2) **Role-play:** Role-play in one of the most common method normally adopted by teachers for group centric activities. In role-play method teacher or learners selects the content to be played or dramatised, often picked up from the history, narrative tales, stories, etc. After that, it is either the teacher who assigns the role or character to learners or learners themselves select a character of their own and present in front of the class or audience. The learners who enact the characters from historical figures, authors, or other characters present the perspective of character. Advantages include motivation to solve a problem or to resolve a conflict for the character, providing a new perspective through which learners can explore or understand an issue and the development of skills, such as writing, leadership, coordination, collaboration and research.

(3) **Jigsaw:** This is a puzzle type activity (like rubrics) where learners are grouped into teams to solve a problem. Jigsaw strategy involves learners becoming "experts" on one aspect of a topic, and then sharing their expertise with others. These can be done in one of two ways-either each them works on completing a different portion of the assignment and then contributes their knowledge to the class as a whole, or within each group, one learner is assigned to portion of the assignment.

(4) **Circle of Voices:** In this type of group activity learners are given a topic and allowed a few minutes to orgainse their

thoughts about it. Then the discussion begins, with each leaner having up to three minutes (or choose a different length) of uninterrupted time to speak. During this time, no one else is allowed to say anything. After everyone has spoken once, open the floor within the subgroup for general discussion. Specify that learners should only build on what someone else has said, not on their own ides; also, at this point, they should not introduce new ideas.

(5) **Snowball groups/pyramids:** Snowball groups/pyramids involve progressive doubling: learners first work alone, then in pairs, then in fours, and so on. In most cases, after working in fours, learners come together for a plenary session in which their conclusions or solutions are pooled. Provide a sequence of increasingly complex tasks so that learners do not become bored with repeated discussion at multiple stages. For example, have learners record a few questions that relate to the class topic. In pairs, learners try to answer one another's questions. Pairs join together to make fours and identify, depending on the topic, either unanswered questions or areas of controversy or relevant principles based on their previous discussions. Back in the large class group, one representative from each group reports the group's conclusions.

(6) **Fishbowl:** This is the last method of group activity. It involves one group observing another group. The first group forms a circle and either discusses an issue or topic, does a role-play, or performs a brief drama. The second group forms a circle around the inner group. Depending on the inner group's task and the context of our course, the outer group can look for themes, patterns, soundness of argument, etc., in the inner group's discussion, analyse the inner group's functioning as a group, or simply watch and comment on the role-play. Debrief with both groups at the end in a plenary to capture their experiences. Be aware that the outer group members can become bored if their task is not challenging enough. Teacher could have groups switch places and roles to help with this. Also the inner group could feel inhibited because of the observers; mitigate this concern by asking for volunteers to participate in the inner circle or by specifying that each learner will have a chance to be both inner and outer group members. Although this method is easiest to implement in small classes, teacher could also expand it so that multiple "fishbowls" are occurring at once.

Q29. Define discussion method. Also discuss its characteristics and components.

Ans. Discussion method is one of the oldest methods of instruction. In this method, the teacher leads or guides the learners in expressing their opinions and ideas with a view to identifying and solving problems collectively. Discussion is a teaching strategy in which the teacher brings learners face to face as they engage in verbal interchange of ideas.

Discussion method is generally used for following purposes: laying plans for new work; making decisions for future action; sharing information; obtaining and gaining respect for various points of view; clarifying ideas; evaluating progress, etc. According to the James Lee, "the discussion is an educational group activity in which the teacher and the taught talk over the problem." Discussion is a kind of reflective thinking by two or more persons, who cooperatively exchange information and ideas in an effort to solve problems or to gain understanding of a problem. In discussion method, learners employ the skills of analysis, comparison, evaluation and conclusion to reach the solution of the problem.

Characteristics: Characteristics of discussion method of instruction are as follow:

- Discussion method is a systematic process of making a collective decision through competitive cooperation.
- It is group centered, therefore it stimulates metal activity of each of the members of the group.
- It is based on the exchange of ideas, concepts, and information among learners.
- In this method, there is a high probability that there is an agreement or disagreement among the group members related to acceptance of an idea.
- It trains the learners for reflective thinking.
- It provides learners opportunity to express freely their ideas.
- It is oral method of instruction.
- When shared among the group members, it develops clarity of ideas.

Components of discussion: There are four main components of discussion. They are:

(1) **Leader:** In this method, the teacher does planning, selection and organisaton of content. Therefore, in discussion, teacher normally acquires the role of leader. It is not that teacher alone can act as leader. But any senior person, by virtue of its experience and position, can also be the leader of the group discussion. The role of the leader should be democratic nature wherein s/he not only keeps an overall control of the discussion but also provides proper direction to the discussion. The role of the leader would be to give equal chances to all its members as far as possible to express their ideas or opinions freely by adopting the principle of equality. To facilitate the process of group thinking among the members is the main function of the leader.

(2) **Group:** A group in terms of specific abilities can be homogeneous and heterogeneous in nature. Normally, a class or a smaller entity of it comprises the group. Ideally, a group of heterogeneous social and intellectual backgrounds would serve a better purpose for discussion group as it provides diverse

thinking and thus contributes more to the discussion than the homogeneous group.

(3) **Problem:** The key for the discussion is the identification of the problem and working for its solution. In classroom based discussion, normally it is the responsibility of the teacher to define or state the problem in front of the learners, otherwise it is the senior person in the group who does it. It is important to remember here that the problem should be defined by the teacher or leader in exact manner. Leader or teacher should not impose the problem upon the group of learners. The problem should be in accordance with the abilities, need, interest, relevance and practical utility of the learners.

(4) **Content:** Johnson said that, the content of the discussion is the body of knowledge, facts and generalisation which must be drawn upon, if any problem is to be discussed and resolved. In many cases facts needs to be rediscovered or verified, and sometimes, we need to establish the relationships or verify the assumptions or hypotheses.

Q30. Illustrate the procedure for organising discussion. What are the advantages and disadvantages of discuss method?

Ans. Procedure for organising discussion: The following are the key points for organising a discussion:

(1) **Planning the discussion:** Discussion method can produce the desired results if the teacher and student representatives do considerable planning. Discussion, in fact, requires a good deal of planning and use of well-directed procedure.

(2) **Preparation:** Thorough preparation for the discussion is very necessary. The teacher should read wide and deep enough. He should read purposefully and critically and prepare the material conscientiously. Points to be discussed should be arranged logically. They should be written on the chalk board for guidance. The problem to be discussed should be a felt problem. If the students do not initially feel its need, they should be brought to do so.

(3) **Conduct of discussion:** While conducting the discussion, the teacher should see that it is disciplined. The arrangement of seats should ensure face-to-face talk, since the strength of the discussion is obtained from the information and viewpoint of all members of the group, it is essential which breaks down if one member of the group dominates it. The teacher must see that every member of the group participates. He should encourage sincere questions and comments. The discussion must be geared to the realisation of specific objectives and development of proper skills and methods.

(4) **Evaluation:** Discussion must result in certain achievements such as expanding information or lessening or removing prejudices, changing attitudes or ideals, increasing the range of

his interest, altering his ideas concerning national and international policies, or causing him to become a more active citizen.

Advantages of Discussion method

(1) It is useful for both the juniors and seniors.
(2) It helps in clarifying and sharpening the issues.
(3) It helps children crystallise their thinking and identify concepts needing further study.
(4) Discussion gives knowledge a round trip.
(5) Discussion activates thinking along the lines of self-evaluation.

Disadvantages of discussion method

(1) In this method, there is a chance that only a few students may dominate the whole discussion.
(2) It is possible that discussion is initiated on those aspects of the problem with which few prominent students of the class are concerned.
(3) This method is time consuming.
(4) This method is not adaptable to all teaching-learning situations.
(5) In this method, it is very difficult to assess all the students in terms of learning outcomes.
(6) Confusion may arise as a result of poor management.

Q31. Write a note on context specific approaches.

Ans. In the total teaching-learning process, the most important link is method of instruction. It is a link between the pre-determined to objectives and the change in the behaviour of the learner. Method of instruction determines the quality of result. It is always a matter of debate whether teacher follows a specific method to teach content or teacher should be eclectic in approach while selecting a method of instruction. Effective teaching is not a set of generic practices, but instead, is a set of context driven decisions about teaching. Effective teachers do not use the same set of practices for every lesson. A good teacher always constantly reflects about his/her work, observes whether learners are learning or not and adjusts his/her practices accordingly.

According to Saskatchewan Education (1991), effective instruction is guided by general pedagogical approaches and specific instructional practices. The approaches and instructional practices espoused in their study are based upon the following about what constitutes effective instruction:

(1) **Instruction is eclectic:** Professional teaching practices is not constrained by a belief that there is one best way. Teachers should be invited to extend their range of instructional approaches in a secure, risk-taking environment.
(2) **Instruction is tied directly to the success of the learning experience:** Effective instruction take place when the teacher links sound curriculum development and excellent instructional practice in a successful learning experience. Reciprocal, positive relationships between teacher and learners

are also necessary for instruction to be truly effective. This means in the teaching-learning process, learner must be viewed as an active participant.

(3) **Instruction is empowered professional practice in action:** Instructional judgment must be encouraged and nurtured in classroom professionals so that they acquire the flexibility needed to adapt to instructional practice to meet a wide variety of leaner needs.

(4) **Instruction integrates the components of the Core Curriculum:** When making instructional decisions, teachers should consider the content, perspectives and processes specified in the curriculum for a Required Area of Study or a Locally Determined Option, and the appropriate Common Essential Learning. To meet individual learning needs teachers need to make decisions regarding adaptation of instructions.

(5) **Instruction is generative and dynamic:** Instructional decision-making is affected by ever changing variables. Educators are encouraged to extend their range of practical and theoretical knowledge, and a regard for learners as active participants in the learning process.

(6) **Instruction recognizes there is an art as well as a science to teaching:** Instruction results from a blend of the art and the science of teaching. The science of instruction, which has predominated in the past, needs to achieve a balance with the artistry involved in the successful teaching act.

(7) **Instruction acknowledges a comprehensive understanding of the instructional cycle:** Teachers begin the instructional cycle by assessing individual student learning needs, interests, and strength through observation and consultation with learner's s. They then determine the instructional approaches required, deliver instruction in a manner appropriate to learners' learning abilities and styles, and evaluate learners' growth-and understanding. The cycle concludes with teachers' self-reflection and further teacher learner consultation,

(8) **Instruction finds best expression when educators collaborate to develop, implement, and refine their professional practices:** To professional development instructional practice can be improved through sustained and systematic attention. Teachers can improve their own instructional practices by participating in professional development programs or working with peers and supervisors. These programs must include elements of the individual reflection.

Q32. Describe the term "teaching-learning resources". What are its various types?

Ans. Teaching-learning resources refer to those resources what teacher use to assist learners to meet the expectations for learning defined by curriculum. These resources as materials used by a teacher to supplement classroom instruction or to stimulate the interest of learners. Obviously, teaching-learning resources aid to retain more concepts permanently. Also, learners can learn better when they are motivated properly through different teaching-learning resources.

According to Klaus, teaching-learning resources are tools that classroom teachers use to help their learners learn quickly and thoroughly. A teaching aid can be as simple as a chalkboard or as complex as a computer program.

Tamakloe, Amedahe and Atta (2005) explained that the teaching learning resource is a material, which the teacher uses to facilitate the learning, understanding and acquisition of knowledge, concept, principles or skills by his learners.

These learning resources are very important for effective learning because they stimulate learning and foster development at desirable changes in the behaviour of a learner. The basic purpose of teaching is to enable learning. The most effective teaching is that which results in the most effective learning.

There are so many resources available to make the teaching-learning process effectual. These resources are also known as teaching aids. Type of these resources is as follows:

(1) Audio Teaching-Leering Resources: These resources primarily stimulate the hearing sense of learner. It includes – human voice, telephonic conversation, audio discs/tapes, gramophone records, Radio broadcast.

(2) Visual Teaching-Learning Resources: These types of TLMs involve the sense of vision. They stimulate the visual impulses. These can be of various types as given below:

(i) Visual (Verbal) Print (the text is the main instructional or teaching learning aid)

(ii) Textbook, Supplementary book.

(iii) Reference books, encyclopedia, etc.

(iv) Magazine, Newspaper

(v) Documents and Clippings

(vi) Duplicated written material

(vii) Programmed material

(viii) Case Studies/Reports etc.

(ix) Visual (Pictorial- Non Projected):

(a) Non-projected two dimensional: Here the resource is in form of an image or picture explaining the concept. Examples of such type of resources are blackboard writing and drawing Charts, Posters, Maps, Diagrams, Graphs, Photographs, Cartoons, Comic strips.

(b) **Non-Projected three-dimensional:** This category includes three-dimensional representation of the real object or phenomenon. It helps learners in conceptualization. It includes – Models, Mock-up, Diorama, Globe, Relief Map, Specimen, Puppet, and Hologram.

(x) Visual (Projected but still) – Here the images are projected or displayed on a screen and thus are nearer reality than visual non-projected ones. It includes – Slide, Filmstrips, Over Head Projector (OHP), Microfilm, Micro card, etc.

(3) **Audio-Visual Teaching-Learning Resources:** These are the projected aids, which use both auditory and visual senses to enhance learning. The greatest advantage of these is they are the closest representation of reality. These include – Motion Picture Film, Television, Video discs/cassettes, slide – tape presentations, Multimedia Computer.

Q33. Analyse the importance of resources for teaching and learning process.

Ans. The importance of resources for teaching and learning process can be understood from the following:

(1) **Motivate learners:** Capturing attention is the first step to any learning and resources help in capturing the attention of learner in classroom. Once motivated to look at resources, the children are curious to learn new things. Resources provide a variety of stimuli, which helps in students to learn language effectively.

(2) **Help in longer retention of information:** The more the number of sensory channels involved in interacting with resources, the longer will be the retention of information. Therefore, the learning will be effective and will last long.

(3) **Facilitate holistic learning:** Learning objectives to be achieved through classroom teaching are in all domains-cognitive, affective and psychomotor. Therefore, to achieve varied objectives, varied learning experiences need to be provided, which can be done through the use of resources.

(4) **Help in organising classroom teaching:** A teacher need to organise learning experiences, making them as realistic as possible. S/he can use visual or verbal resources to present accurate data in sequentially organised manner. This helps teacher to verbal and visual communication in classroom. Thus, s/he may use resources to overcome shortcomings in verbal or visual communication.

(5) **Facilitate change in attitude:** Resources also help in changing attitude of learners towards learning in general and subject content in particular. Pictures, models and other resources help in inculcation of positive attitude of learners.

Learner can discuss pictures which help him acquire new language.

(6) Practical applications: Resources show application of theoretical knowledge into practical applications. The theoretical knowledge studied in class is shown in concrete form through resources for effective learning.

(7) Making learning fun: Resources help in making learning fun in the classroom. Students enjoy the novelty of handling new objects and learn new concepts through them.

(8) Concept formation: Resources facilitate the formation and attainment of concepts among children. They concretise the abstract concepts; thus, children are able to understand them and not resort to rote learning.

Q34. What steps should be followed by teacher to make the environment leaner oriented?

Ans. To make the environment learner oriented, the teachers should follow the following steps:

- Feedback is related to reaction on learner's performance of activities such as given responses by the learners during the class, creative activities, assignments, project work, discussion, etc. Here the role of teacher is to provide more individualisation of feedback to deal with more qualitatively assed learner activities to make classroom environment resource full. It has been found in researches that feedback, given by the teacher makes environment as resource for the learners.
- During the time of learning experiences gained are also helpful in making learning environment. When learners get good experiences while learning, a constant positivity affects their understanding.
- In the classroom use of new technological tools converts learning environment into a resource. These tools give opportunity to learners to be more creative.
- Teacher should know the name and background of each and every learner. It makes class more alive. A brilliant way to know the learners, establish a good relationship with learners. If a teacher calls his learners by their name, learners feel more attached to that teacher. Most learners enjoy this recognition and it empowers their engagement to learning.
- To make the classroom environment learner friendly, teaching style of teacher should be according to the learner. Teachers should try to keep their class interactive. To make the class learner oriented, teacher should provide the chance to the learners to teach their peer group. This also facilitates the learning process of the learners by making them aware of their responsibilities to attaining class objectives.
- The teaching content should be relevant to make the environment as resource. Learners should know clearly that why they are going

to study any particular topic. The learning goals of the class need to be perceived as relevant to the learner's aspirations or experience. In some classes, this can mean the use of socially relevant topics or case studies extended to problem-based learning.

- Every learner is different in his/her own way. Some learners learn best by listening, some learners do well with lecture, class discussions, etc. Lecture is considered the least effective teaching method, although some learners learn best by simply listening. Some learners really increase their learning potential when they get opportunity to do something by themselves, they learn by doing. Therefore, in teaching and learning teacher should try to use all these things.
- It is a proverb "during the class when a teacher stands his learners sit, when a teacher sits his learners lie down and when a teacher lies down his learners are just like inactive beings". Therefore, not only learners but also a teacher should play a very active role in the classroom. Active teaching helps teacher to make environment resourceful. For this teacher can use soft skills as humour or storytelling. Also teacher should be like a role model for the class.
- To convert learning environment in resource, teachers are encouraged to share their passion regarding the subject and to feel free to get personal by offering their own examples. The use of eye contact, voice modulation, provocative questions and the long entrusted pause to wait for answers continue to be important methods for drawing learners into the learning process. In a large classroom, teacher can walk the passageways to further involve learners in the new learning mode.
- Provide situations that give learners an acceptable challenge. Activities those are slightly difficult for the child will be more motivating and provide for stronger feelings of success when accomplished.
- Give opportunities to learners to evaluate their own accomplishments. Rather than stating that we think they have done a good job, ask what they think of their work.
- For the learners make the learning environment friendly, learner support is a critical component. Learner support describes about what a teacher should do to help his/her learners beyond the formal delivery of content or skills development. Learner support covers a wide range of functions and is a topic that will be dealt with more depth elsewhere.
- Mostly learners learn best when there is a logical sequence, delineated lesson that provides the objective and systematic steps to do the assignment. These type of learners benefit from the use of rubrics so that they can follow lectures and assignments in a better way.

- There are some other software tools which convert environment into resource they are: do-it-yourself, peer-instruction exercise, debate, discussion, project-based learning, and learner-centered learning environments.
- For making classroom environment, learner friendly temperature of classroom plays an important role. If the classroom atmosphere is too cold or hot, learners will have more of a hard time concentrating on what their learning task is. So the classroom temperature should be according to weather.
- Sitting arrangement should be comfortable for learners.
- The study area should be calm and quiet. The availability of light should be good with proper ventilation.
- Teachers should give break on regular time interval to learners.

Q35. Write a note on classroom as a resource.

Ans. *Classroom resources* area includes anything a teacher would use with students in the classroom. A classroom is also a resource for teaching and learning and a teacher can use his classroom like a resource. Teacher has to carry extra effort to make his/her class learner friendly and convert it as a resource room and this depends on the competency of the teacher that how is s/he going to convert his/her traditional classroom into resourceful classroom. There are four categories of classroom resources as follow:

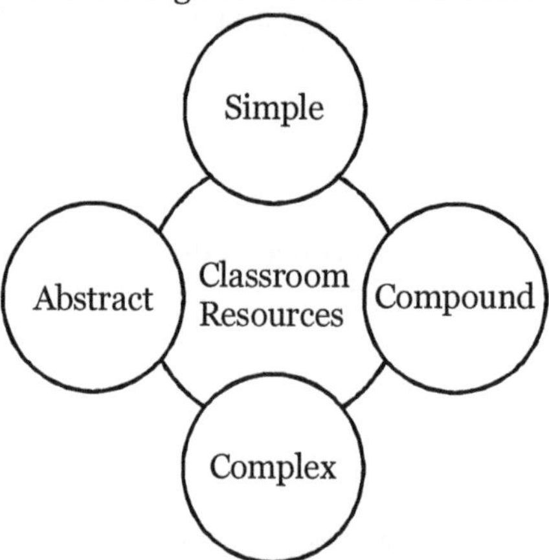

Fig 3.4: Classroom Resources (Grubb, 2008)

(1) **Simple Resources:** Resources that are physical objects (e.g. textbooks, blackboard and chalk) or classroom factors (e.g. teacher experience and expertise, teacher and learner ratio) that can be directly bought, adjusted, and measured.

(2) **Compound Resources:** Two or more resources that are jointly necessary for success (e.g. class size reduction and adequate teacher preparation).

(3) **Complex Resources:** Resources that are not easily bought, measured, or adjusted (e.g. instructional approaches and teaching philosophies).

(4) Abstract Resources: Resources that are difficult to discern and measure, and often embedded in a web of relationships and practices within a given.

Developing classroom as a resource room: A teacher should follow some steps to create the classroom as resource room:

- According to Judson (2006), teacher is the key determinant of implementation in establishment of any classroom innovation. If the teacher is not handling these resources and dealing with learners properly, all things are useless. Therefore, for the classroom as resource of teaching-learning process, a teacher should be knowledgeable and expert. With respect to educational technologies, teachers' beliefs in self-efficacy and the school context can affect their implementation use of technology.
- The best materials to make a class resource room are the traditional resources (chalk and blackboard). If a teacher has expertise in use of blackboard, other resources are secondary. Although using blackboard is basic skill of teaching but so many teachers are not very skilled in use of blackboard. Teacher can use chalk and blackboard in variety of way as – writing of important points of content, for lower classes writing full answers, draw diagrams, flowcharts, tree-charts, figures, to solve mathematical problems by him/her and learners also, use of colour chalks for diagram and figures, etc.
- Teaching technique and attribute of teachers also influence the classroom and learning outcome of the learners. An expert teacher can handle the all complexity of the classroom and can covert a normal classroom into a resource, which is learner friendly but for this a teacher should has bundles of techniques and ability to apply these techniques appropriately.
- To make the classroom as resource, a teacher can use various innovative learning and teaching methods, techniques and strategies as per the content and level of learners. Teacher should use schemes of work, phonics, different letters and sounds, spelling and story writing ideas for lower classes.
- To make the classroom as resource, instruction which is the main function of the class, should be on optimum level. The determinants of the good classroom instruction are the relationships and interactions between teachers, learners, materials, and their environment.

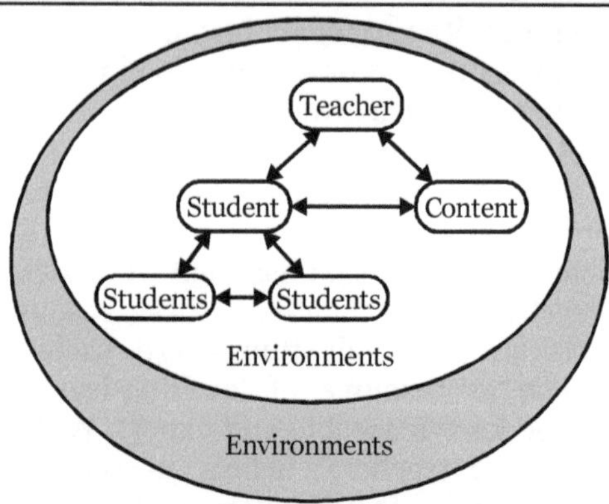

Fig 3.5: Instruction (Cohen, Raudenbush and Ball, 2002)

- Layout of physical classroom space also influences the environment of classroom. According to Marx *et al.*, the layout of physical classroom space influences the relationships among the learners, their peers, the teacher and the content being taught. The seating arrangement of the class affects the interaction and interrelationship of teacher and learners and also between the learner and learner. The semicircle seating formation makes classroom more interactive and every learner take participation in the teaching-learning process. At the same time, traditional rows and columns seating style affect classroom interaction and relationship negatively. Those learners who sit in 'T-zone' or central and front areas get more attention from the teacher side and be more interactive with teachers.
- Interaction among learner-learner will increase learning. So the interaction should not be only between teacher and learners but sometimes teacher should enforce interaction among learners. For this, s/he can give any brainstorming topic to learners to express their perception and ideas. And teacher should play a role of facilitator during discussion.
- In meeting with new challenges and developing learners' abilities and performance, smart class is a solution designed to help teachers. The Smart Class is a system designed to bring the teacher and learners at different physical locations together in an interactive environment, using videoconferencing and live broadcasting techniques.
- Indian classrooms are being move technical with the development of technology. Smart boards in the classroom make class as a resource. These smart boards are interactive whiteboards that uses touch detection for user input in the same way as normal PC input devices as scrolling and right mouse-click. A projector is used to display a computer's video output onto the whiteboard, which then acts as a huge touch screen.

To make classroom as resource, other factors related to teacher like prepared lesson-plans, credentials of teacher, years of teaching experience, behaviour of teacher with learners, instructional quality, emotional climate of classroom are important. If a teacher is able to hold the attention of learners, amount of social interaction, amount of task involvement, and group glee make classroom more alive. Before using these materials in the classroom a close assessment of the resources is required. A teacher should ensure that the materials are able to satisfying those purposes for which the materials are being used.

Q36. Analyse the role of community as learning resource.

Ans. Community-based learning refers to a wide variety of instructional methods and programmes that educators use to connect what is being taught in schools to their surrounding communities, including local institutions, history, literature, cultural heritage, and natural environments. Community-based learning is also motivated by the belief that all communities have intrinsic educational assets and resources that educators can use to enhance learning experiences for students. In formal education, community or society can also play an important role. Community is a school in itself for history, literature, cultural heritage, and natural environments.

As learning resource, use of community is also promoted as a way to develop stronger relationships between school and community, while also increasing the community's investment in, understanding of and support for the school and the learning experiences it provides. Community is not just an agency of informal education but it also works as learning resource for a learner. This resource is free and inexpensive. But sometime teachers ignore this resource due to various reasons/prejudices. It is also true that using community as resource is a very challenging task but a skilled teacher can do this. A teacher can utilize community as a learning resource in following manner:

(1) **Guidance Services:** Members of community can give guidance services to learners. Older members of community, expert of different area can help learners by their valuable guidance. In the schools, always ignore guidance part. Though as per guidelines of a professional person, guidance cell is essential in every educational institution but it is the ground reality that most of the schools are not fulfilling this norm. In such condition guidance, the community members may give service.

(2) **Lecture of Guests:** Experts of different area can be invited in the schools for delivering lectures and presentation. These guests may be expert of any area as social worker, mathematician, doctor, scientist, social scientist, sport person etc. With the collaboration of a local orgaiansation or group, an educational institution may provide additional learning experiences in the school premises such as a scientific institution can help the school develop a robotics program or in making of low budget household equipments. Like this, learners are getting information within the school, and community

resources and authorities are being used to enhance the learning experiences of learners.

(3) Community Participation: In community participation, learners would learn, at least in part, by actively participating in their community. For example, learners may undertake a research project on any local problems with NGO; participate in an internship program at a local level and can get some experience and recognition, write an article, or produce a documentary on particular topic. As such learners are learning within as well as outside of school premises, and such participatory community-based-learning experiences would be connected in some way to the school's academic programme.

(4) Citizen Action: This approach would be considered by some experts and educators to be the fullest or more "authentic" realistation of community-based-learning. Learners not only learn from and in their community, but they also apply what they are learning from this resource. Learners can influence, change, or return to the community in some meaningful way. For example, learners may volunteer for a local NGO and can create a multimedia presentation, citizen-action campaign or short documentary intended to raise awareness in their community about any social event/cause. In this scenario, the audience and potential beneficiaries of a learner's learning products would extend beyond teachers, mentors and other learners to include community organisations and the general public.

(5) Instructional Connections: In this form of community-based learning and teaching, a teacher makes clear and purposeful relationship between the content which has been taught in the classroom and local issues and contexts. For example, the workings of a democratic political system may be described in terms of a local political process. Also in this scenario, learners may be educated within the school campus, but community-related connections are being used to enhance learner understanding or engagement in the learning process.

(6) Libraries: The learners may use public, private or community library. In this condition, those reading material which are not available in school library can be utilised by the learners in community or public library.

(7) Nature Centers: Many nature centers offer homeschooling classes and resources, as well as apprenticeship opportunities. Nature centers can be utilised like learning resource.

(8) Museums & Historical Sites: For some content, learners can visit a local museum. Some museums also offer online resources and materials for curious learners. Learners also may be benefitted by this. For example, a small group of learners experiments with an interactive museum exhibit. They talk about what they see and what they know, to relate it their classroom experience. Any historical site represents a living history for the learners. These sites provide living history experiences and volunteer opportunities through a range of national, state and local resources, including historic palaces, homes, religious places, historical sculptures and battlefields.

(9) **Art Centers:** Many of art centers offer classes for young ones, youth and adults in handicrafts, drawing, art history and visual and performing arts etc., and are often accommodate homeschooling groups also, which is beneficial for learners.

(10) **Volunteering:** Community can play a significant role as a resource centre through volunteering. Learners can learn so many things by volunteering in community celebrations. They can learn basic human values like, tolerance, fraternity, healthy competition, cooperation, sympathy, empathy, helping others, etc. Learners can also participate in real world activities, skill and knowledge building.

(11) **Science centres:** Learners can also visit science centres, aquaria, botanical gardens and zoos and can use these things as resource.

Q37. Define improvised resources. What is the role of teacher in it? Also discuss its advantages.

Ans. *Improvisation* is the the ability to take existing pieces and put them together in a new combination for a purpose. The pieces could be bits of information about a problem or they could be parts of a melody. Teachers or students apply tools or methods to these pieces in a very flexible manner.

Every teacher should be equipped with improvised resources and it is very important. Often, language teachers complain, what they can use in the classroom as resources. There is a very limited scope of using the resource in classroom teaching. In such condition they can use improvised during their class.

In improvisation, we use local resources in our immediate environment to build, construct, mould or make instructional teaching-learning materials that can assist in the smooth dissemination and transfer of knowledge from teachers to learners.

In present scenario, improvisation in teaching-learning process has become crucial because the economic situation makes the cost of facilities and equipment very high amidst decreasing or near lack of purchasing power. Improvisation reveals that there are possibilities of alternatives to teaching and learning aids. It should therefore meet specific teaching and learning situation. Tikon has defined it as "an act of using alternative resources to facilitate instructions for teaching wherever there is lack or specific first-hand teaching aids".

Improvisation can be thought of as an "on the spot" or "off the cuff" spontaneous activity. The skills of improvisation can apply to many different abilities or forms of communication and expression across all artistic, scientific, physical, cognitive, academic and non-academic disciplines.

Role of a Teacher: In classroom, a teacher can use following skills and things as resource material:

- Different writing style (pen lettering skill, Calligraphy, Free-hand writing)
- Modelling technique
- Blank World & India map
- Lettering and painting
- Craft work
- Cardboards
- Cell phones
- Mathematical Tables/log book
- Use of different colours in graphics
- Newspaper
- Textbooks (Course book and secondary books)
- Blackboard and chalk

In the school, teachers should make more effort for acquiring knowledge, expertise on various ways by which they can develop improvised resources where the readymade resources are not available.

In preparing these resources, a teacher can get expertise by seminars, workshops and other training programmes. Such type of programmes should be attended by teachers on a regular time interval and they should also practice this acquired knowledge and should try to get mastery in that. For example, a teacher can use plastic bottles as breakers and funnel or a used light bulb can be improvised for a round bottom flask.

Advantages of Improvised Resources

- Improvised resources motivate learners through the participatory activities during construction.
- Improvised resources also raise the interests of the learners because they are made from raw materials they see daily in their immediate environment.
- Very low cost improvised resources make teaching and learning process easier for the teacher and learners both.
- Improvised resources can be used to teach large classes.
- Improvised resources are cheaper to produce or buy because the raw materials are locally sourced.
- Improvised resources encourage class participation since majority of the raw materials can be sourced by the learners themselves.

Q38. Illustrate the ICT and multimedia as learning resources. What are the factors affecting the use of ICT and multimedia?

Or

What are the various uses of ICT tools in a teaching-learning classroom? Discuss in detail.

Ans. Following are the various uses of ICT tools in a teaching-learning classroom:

(1) In the context of learning process: ICT enables the classroom by encompassing a variety of techniques, tools, content and resources. Ranging from projecting media to support a lesson, multimedia self-learning modules, simulations to virtual learning environments, there are a variety of options available to teachers and students for utilising various modes/ICT tools in the teaching-learning process. Each of these device or strategy involves changes in the classroom environment and understanding of its effectiveness. ICT plays a significant role in different forms of teaching learning process, viz. individual learning and teaching, group learning and teaching, collaborative learning activities, etc.

- **(i) Group learning and teaching:** In group work strategy, a teacher can take the help of different tools of ICT that are suitable for group learning. For example, a particular group of students can have access to online lecture and facilities for interaction with the presenter as well as with other members in the same group. Today various kinds of course based teaching materials are available on World Wide Web (WWW) which makes it possible for fast delivery of course materials as well as problem solving activities. In group learning strategy, students can access such material from the web and undergo group interactions.
- **(ii) Individual learning:** Searching alternative sources of learning, reading a text, making queries and communication directly with experts, solving problems, taking assignments, assessing own progress and getting feedbacks are some of the activities involved in individualised learning. Networking of computer and use of internet promotes such activities in individual learning. In such an approach of learning, students completely take the help of ICT and then task of a teacher is to monitor their learning and to regulate the learning process. This approach of learning is often called as Self-Regulatory Learning (SRL) in which ICT plays a vital role to make the learner as a self-regulatory learner.

(2) In collaboration: An important component in learning-centered approach of teaching, is sharing/interaction among the students and between the student and teacher There are some tools of ICT that can be used for the purpose of collaboration inside and outside the classroom. Teachers can share their views/ideas/knowledge with students by using such tools and in the same time, students also share their ideas, suggest different views, and also clarify their doubts. These tools of ICT particularly used for the purpose of sharing are called as Social Communicating Tools. Examples of such social networking tools are wiki, yahoo group, Google group, blog, Facebook, twitter, my space, etc.

(3) **Collaborative learning:** It is illustrated when groups of students work together to search for understanding, meaning or solutions or to create an art fact or product of their learning. It is a situation in which two or more students learn or attempt to learn something together. Unlike individual learning, students engaged in collaborative learning capitalize on one another's resources and skills (asking one another for information, evaluating one another's ideas, monitoring one another's work, etc.). Put differently, collaborative learning refers to methodologies and environments in which students engage in a common task where each individual depends on and is accountable to each other. These include both face-to-face conversations and computer discussions (online forums, chat rooms, etc.).

(4) **In Pedagogies:** ICT can provide the supportive or facilitative approaches in the classroom. By using tools of ICT, particularly the situating and communicative tools, teachers can guide the students learning and, at the same time, students also get the supportive service from the ICTs. Besides, teachers can also use the tools of ICT in different phases of pedagogical process, i.e. during the introduction, presentation as well as in the assessment phase. In the classroom during instructional process, the tools of ICT will motivate the students and encourage interaction among the peers. However, the ICTs by themselves will not improve pedagogy. Teachers who shift their pedagogies to be more student-centred, project-based and collaborative learning based teaching, ICT will support and assist. In a conventional education system, ICT may be used to support teacher-centered pedagogical approaches or in the combination of the two approaches. The aim is to make sound choices about what is best in different circumstances, selecting and using appropriate ICT tools for improving pedagogy.

The roles of ICTs in the different types of pedagogies/ classroom processes and how different tools of ICT can help such pedagogy is illustrated in the following Table 3.3:

Table 3.3: Use of ICTs in teaching styles

Teaching Style	**Main Characteristics**	**Use of ICT Tools**
Teacher-centred Approach	• Teacher as the source of knowledge. • Teacher tends to be more active and students receive the	A wide range of ICT tools can be used to aid the teacher's presentation and performance. Hand-outs, overhead projector

	information passively.	(OHP) slides, models, etc. can be used to capture and retain the learner's attention.
Learner-centered Approach	• Learner as knowledge seeker, with teacher as facilitator and guide. • The learner tends to be active, talking and doing things in the process of learning. • The teacher designs and manages the setting as well as the process of learning.	ICT can be used extensively to help the learner make the sense of the tasks assigned and learn what is required. Work sheets, informative and communicative tools of ICT need to be available to the learners on an individual basis or in small group.
Combination of the two approaches	• In some cases, the teacher dispenses knowledge and the learner has to take things on trust. At other times, the teacher simply creates the conditions for the learner to explore and discover knowledge.	ICT can be used to aid the teacher's presentation as well as to assist learners in their exploration

(5) **In Assessment:** Today, ICT tools can also be used to assess students' performance during teaching-learning process as well as after completion of the course. These tools enable both the process-based assessment as well as the product-based assessment. Suppose a teacher wants to assess the students' best work in his/her subject throughout the year. S/he can take the help of one of the tools of ICT called e-portfolio, through which s/he can easily and quickly assess students' performance. Similarly, other tools of ICT that can be used for assessment are online rubric, online peer-ssessment, digital concept mapping, etc. The advantages of using ICT tools in the assessment process are time management and it encourages reflection among the students.

Factors Affecting the Use of ICT and multimedia

Although for learning ICT and multimedia are very good resources but most of schools and teachers are not using tools to enhance the learning. These causes are as follow:

- Lack of time to spend on technology
- Cost of technology
- Unavailability of infrastructural facilities
- Negative perception of older people for multimedia and ICT

- Lack of perceived economic or other benefits
- Inadequate capital on the part of the individual
- Inadequate training or Lack of training
- Wrong choice of software or software inadequacy
- Lack of understanding of the value or possible benefits of multimedia facilities.
- Lack of power supply.

Q39. Discuss the advantages of ICT and multimedia as learning resources.

Ans. ICT plays an important role in the classroom by providing the opportunities to teachers and learners in operating, manipulating, storing, distributing and retrieving the information. Also ICT and multimedia are also very useful for open and distance learning. They promote learners towards independent and active learning. The most important feature of ICT is its flexibility. With the help of ICT and multimedia teachers and learners can learn after/outside school hours. There is a growing body of evidence that use of ICT in the classroom can enhance learning. Computer-based multimedia learning environments - consisting of images, text and sound - offer a potentially powerful setting for improving learner understanding. There is certainly no lack of vision within educational communities concerning the central role and importance of ICT in the educational context of the future.

- ICT extends the child's immediate learning environment, offering opportunities to push learning beyond the confines of the classroom.
- By enabling the learner, ICT tools can promote active learning to find, manage, evaluate and use information retrieved from CD-ROMs and websites. Even learner can also discuss his/her result and share them with others using presentation and authoring software.
- By using digital cameras, learners can capture images on field trips of events for project work and for active engagement in the wider environment.
- Content-rich software that offers tutorials, simulations and practice problems can be used effectively for the reinforcement or the revision of concepts.
- Internet provides to teachers and learners a number of authentic learning resources. It helps learners in questioning, analysing, to investigating and in thinking critically. Critical use of the Internet facility as an information resource is helpful in development of learners' capability to search for, manage, evaluate, use apply and create information.
- Multimedia tools enable children to record and chart their own learning progression.
- The combined range of ICT tools enables the teacher to maintain a useful electronic anecdotal record of each learner.

- ICT offer children opportunities to exchange information with other about their own local environment. It also facilitates authentic learning by offering opportunities for children to experience the outside world within their own classroom.
- For publishing learners' internet may offer a suitable site work on the school website, for viewing by portents and collaborating schools.
- ICT offers to learners the opportunities to develop social skills through turn taking, sharing resources, and helping other children in combined project work. Combined classroom-based projects which use technology as e-mail, chat, video-conferencing etc. can be used to support each other by the learners.
- ICT can support the learners' appropriation of new knowledge by offering him/her a range of tools related to knowledge representation like concept mapping software, presentation software and database software, which support learners in structuring their learning for later retrieval add application. Content-free software like databases, spreadsheets, and micro worlds offer children opportunities to interpret and manipulate data representations.

ICT and multimedia is not only beneficial for learners but also for teachers too.

- ICTs and multimedia can increase teachers' initial preparation by providing good training materials, facilitating simulations, capturing and analysing practice teaching, bringing into training institution world experience, familarising trainees with sources of materials and support, and training potential teachers in the use of technologies for teaching/learning.
- For teachers, ICTs open a world of lifelong upgrading and professional development by providing courses at a distance, asynchronous learning, and training on demand. ICTs advantages in response to emerging demands include ease of revision and introduction of new courses.
- ICTs break the professional isolation from which many teachers suffer. With ICTs, they can connect easily with headquarters, with colleagues and mentors, with universities and centers of expertise, and with sources of teaching materials.

Q40. Discuss the various criteria of selection and integration of resources in teaching-learning.

Ans. A teacher should ensure the objective of the curriculum/content and expected outcomes before the selection and integration of teaching-learning resources. There are certain criteria according to which the teaching-learning material should be selected:

- Teaching-learning resources should directly focus on ideas and essentials questions of the content/curriculum. Teacher should make it sure that the selected resources are presenting correct concept and picture of the curriculum.

- Today, fostering creativity amongst the learners is lacking on part of teaching-learning process. The teaching-learning materials should make the learners thoughtful, reflective and it should build high level of skills among them.
- Resources should be related to knowledge and need of learners.
- Teaching-learning resources should gear as per the different abilities, requirement and area of the interest of the learners. It should support the inclusive curriculum.
- Materials should incorporate outside experiences in which family and society involvement must be reflected.
- User friendliness is also required. These resources should be well orgainsed and teacher friendly, so teachers can use these materials and handle these materials very easily.
- These materials should encourage interdisciplinary connection. In this condition, learners can correlate it with other subjects and in broader sense, learners will be able to apply it not only in the class room condition but also in real world.
- If it is possible, teaching-learning resources should be related to all learning domains of the learner (cognitive, affective and psychomotor). It should be also related to different levels of these domains.
- Another important characteristic of good teaching-learning resource is flexibility. So during the selection procedure, it is important that choice of resource by the teacher should be flexible.
- During the selection of teaching-learning material teachers should keep in mind the family background and living environment of the learners.
- According to demand of the time, multimedia materials should be selected such television, computer, games, internet, audio etc.
- These resources must motivate the learners and teachers to inspect their own attitudes and bahaviour and to understand their responsibilities and rights.
- Resources should be according to the age of the learners for whom they are selected. If it will be as per their age, it can directly affect their physical, cognitive, social, emotional and cultural development.
- Teaching-learning resources can provide the way to find present, use, evaluate the information, and develop the critical capacities to make discerning choices.
- Teaching-learning materials should include valid and mixed assessments as conventional and performance based.
- Physical quality of the resources should be good.
- Teaching-learning resources should be grammatically correct. Language clearness is also one essential aspect of resources.
- Teaching-learning resources should not be offensive.

- It should not be controversial as related to race, religion, drug misuse, violence, crime, sexual activity, nudity, cruelty, suicide and objectionable phenomena.

Integration means combination, so according to learning activity combining the selected resources is integration. In teaching-learning activity, integration of resources is as important as selection is. The successful integration of resources in the teaching-learning process will depend on effective planning of teacher. For the integration of resources these points are important:

- First teacher should do the lesson planning and fix the place for certain resource. In the absence of planning, the resources can't be meaningful.
- Teacher should have expertise on the particular teaching-learning resources, which s/he is going to use during teaching-learning activity.
- Teacher should remove the illegibility from the resources.
- If any online method is being used as resource, there should be filtration for few sites. Teacher should try to block access of inappropriate sites. Even s/he should also use such type of tools by which s/he can track individual usage.
- There should not be any boredom to make learners enactive in the classroom. So teacher should integrate/arrange resources in such manner that the class is not dull.
- If it is necessary, the documenting, editing should be done by the teacher before using the particular resource. The teacher should do manipulation.
- If there is any lack of any resource, teacher should try to fill it by his/her efficiency.

Q41. Explain the concept of classroom management. Why it is important to understand learners' needs?

Ans. Classroom management is an important aspect of successful teaching. Classroom management means how the teacher works, how the class works, how the teacher and learners work together, and how teaching and learning happen. For learners, classroom management means having some control in how the class operates and understanding clearly the way the teacher and students are to interact with each other. For both teachers and learners, classroom management is not a condition but a process.

Heide discussed about classroom management as "those skills needed by a teacher to establish and maintain a learning environment in which students are taught to be independent and accountable as they assume increasing responsibility for their own learning and conduct." Shreve said, "Classroom management isn't how quiet your room is or how frightened your learners are into behaving, but rather how motivated and interdependent your learners are in their work. Classroom management is teamwork."

Like teaching and learning, classroom management is a complex activity. So there is no single clear-cut management procedure accepted by all. Shaping of environment takes place gradually in response to the teacher's beahviour. One might have observed that a class that is active and attentive with one teacher can be noisy or even difficult to control for another. The skillful teacher keeps his class attentive to what is being taught and involves the learners in productive activities.

Researchers have found that classroom management is correlated with learner's achievement in elementary as well as secondary schools. They have provided evidence that the teachers who are effective in promoting learner's achievement generally have a better classroom and fewer learner behaviour problems.

Classroom management depends upon establishing positive teacher-learner and peer relationships that help meet learners' psychological needs. Learners learn more effectively in an environment that meets their basic personal and psychological needs.

Understanding learners' Needs

Understanding learner needs is essential for providing quality education. In planning teaching and training tasks, the needs of learners are considered as basic inputs. The needs of the learners are an important factor in managing a classroom. Every learner attends a class with certain expectations in mind. If his expectations are not taken care of by the teacher, s/he, consciously or unconsciously, becomes inattentive and hence either disturbs other learners or misbehaves with the teacher. An effective teacher, therefore, manages his/her instructions in such a way that every learner gets the teacher's personal attention. In other words, in order to manage classroom instruction the teacher should cater to the learners' need (both academic and personal) which have an impact on learner learning.

In the classroom, the needs that influence the learner's behaviour by and large are psychological in nature. Teacher should remember that the needs of the learners reveal themselves in some form or the other. For example, one learner, say Pooja, does not take part in any conversation or discussions in the classroom. She does not ask question or seek clarifications for her doubts. The teacher has to make attempts to satisfy her needs through appropriate motivation and reinforcement. The teacher should involve her in instructional tasks and assess her understanding. Teacher should realise that the learners want freedom from discrimination in the class. The learner should not be discriminated on the basic of caste, colour, sex and economic status. In order to know their learners better, teachers can conduct a quick assessment by reviewing information available in the school's office. This is important so teacher can contact parents if need be and orgainse out of class activities. Teacher may collect information about the learners' pervious knowledge or performance through various tests that can be used for this purpose. Teacher may determine the range of ability of their learners so that the homework, teachers give them is according to their ability levels.

In addition, teacher may like to extract rather some personal information about their learners. For example, learner's attitude towards school and career, need for achievement, ability to make decisions, will for self-improvement, etc., make it necessary for teacher to adopt specific strategies to manage instruction. Such information may also help teachers to discover their learners' interests, which can enable to teach their subject more effectively.

Q42. Analyse the principles of classroom management.

Ans. The principles of classroom management reflect the concern of the teacher for his/her teaching task. According to Jyoti A. Christian (1991), the important principles of classroom management are:

(1) **Principle of clarity and mastery over content:** The teacher imparts knowledge of his subject with utilizing proper resources. The ideas, knowledge and thoughts are cleared out by him referring reference books and knowledge gathered from mass communication. If he studies his subject in depth and analyses content it becomes better for himself to maintain integrity of thoughts for his teaching. Ultimately it shows his grip and gird over the knowledge of his subject. Therefore, a teacher should arrange all the instructional tasks into proper learning sequences so that pupils accomplish each and every task eventually and master a particular unit.

(2) **Principle of participation and involvement:** In the era of explosion of knowledge, teacher and pupils in the class get wider opportunities to interact with one another. The background of knowledge is the base for teacher pupil interactions and communicating one's thought to another. In the instructional process the teacher should use and develop a skill of questioning i.e. simple, thought provoking, directive and informative questions to the group of pupils so that he can involve them to respond to the questions raised in classrooms. This way he will be able to generate a system of participation in the instructional process in the class.

(3) **Principle of fostering democratic behaviour:** The teacher and pupil growth flourishes in classroom through teaching learning process. The group of pupils also learns to observe and maintain their own rights and abide by the duties of classrooms distributed to them. Therefore the teacher should organize open discussions, provide opportunities for them to take leadership and allow them to raise questions to the teacher which would give them equality of opportunities following democratic ideals, ways and behaviour in teaching-learning situations.

(4) **Principle of action:** The teacher manifests his ideas with imparting the knowledge of the subject. For this he should develop objectivity, strong will power, confidence, determination, judgment and "self-knowledge" for his teaching behaviour and also take responsibility to lead and activate the classroom group better work and performance which ultimately show better output of the instructional process. It is also to be action oriented i.e., managing with desired and expected learning behaviour within the classroom situations.

(5) **Principle of firmness:** The teacher has to remain firm and definite with his ideas and actions in the instructional process. If he is clear, sure and strong with his conviction and commitments to the task then no other unfavourable environmental conditions can move him from his right path of work. The firmness of a teacher will be able to control his own behaviour from within and on the other hand develop the ideology of self-control in pupils. This will lead the teacher toward the growth and development of pupil's internal-control, positive personalities, attitudes, action and work through various learning activities in classroom.

(6) **Principle of flexibility:** Firmness and flexibility are the relative terms. In these days, too much firmness doesn't help get the expected outcome and lead a teacher toward exerting direct influence on the group of pupils. Therefore, he should learn to adopt some situations to bring change in work, plans and interactions. In the interactive situations the teacher should apply, Flanders Interaction Category System (FICS) i.e., accepting feelings, praising and rewarding, questioning and responding, teaching and clarifying, initiating and directing in the pupils learning situations.

(7) **Principle of warmth and enthusiasm:** The teaching-learning process is a pleasurable, joyful and enjoying task. The teacher-pupil should feel happy and show enthusiasm and life in teaching-learning situations. This indicates their lively and active tempo to transact with one another. The teacher's warm, sympathetic and empathetic natures impress most to the group of pupils in classroom.

Q43. What are the factors affecting of classroom management

Ans. The following factors affecting classroom management are described given below:

(1) **Effective instruction:** Well-planned instruction, which should include appropriate instructional activities like guided practice, attention to individual students, providing immediate feedback, and similar tasks tend to enhance order and effective learning. On the contrary, chaotic instructional activities lead to disorder in the classroom.

(2) **Setting and implementing rules:** Classroom instruction should be undertaken in a business-like manner, such as trying to achieve maximum amount of learning within minimum time without disruption of other classroom activities. Teachers, who set clear-cut goals for instructions and show a degree of commitment to achieve those goals, can manage their instructional activities more effectively. The teacher, therefore, must demonstrate the willingness and an ability to act when the rules are broken. The processing of setting and implementation rules has instructional as well as management value. The

learners learn procedure for ensuring that their participation is effective and they accept the social setting. The rules should be introduced in the manner in which any academic concept is introduced. The rationale for implementing the rules should be made clear of and respect for the rules. The learners need to know what will occur if they choose not to follow classroom rules and procedures.

(3) **Managing intervention:** The need for intervention increases when rules and instructional activities are not properly implemented, and when varied forms of misbehaviour such as mild verbal and physical aggression are demonstrated in the classroom. These have to be dealt with appropriately and immediately by the teacher. Based on experience, one who frequently observes from the back of the classroom would encounter less classrooms misbehavior than one who is clearly standing still in front of the room. It must be pointed out, however, that many classroom interventions do not always lead to improved learning. Some are counter-productive. Any intervention that tends to interrupt the flow of the lesson, for example, must be terminated right away.

(4) **Feedback on appropriate behavior:** The learner expects feedback, whether or not his behavior is acceptable. It is good point to remember that praise of behavior would be more effective if done sparingly and linked with good performance.

(5) **Classroom environment:** Learners normally would not want to learn in very chaotic environment. Poorly managed classes do not provide a pleasant supportive environment to teach or learn. A certain degree of calm, quiet and comfort are necessary for the teacher's as well as the learners' mental health.

Q44. Illustrate the techniques of classroom management.

Ans. In the classroom, teachers use various management techniques. They are:

(1) **Behaviour modification technique:** Behavior modification techniques include a series of teacher-implemented activities and actions aimed at improving classroom behavior. It is an effective way of correcting various behavior problems and is often used to modify the behavior of children one step at a time.

It is the job of the teacher to identify desirable and undesirable classroom behaviours. The teacher has to ignore inappropriate/undesirable classroom behaviour. According to the Skinner, the teacher can use reinforcement to shape the desired behaviour. For example, if the learner demonstrates (verbal or non-verbal) desirable bheaviour, it should be appropriately acknowledged and rewarded. In behaviour modification technique a more popular activity (such as playing or viewing of a TV programme) can be used to reinforce a less popular activity (Such as learning mathematical concepts and procedures). In other words, popular activates can be used to bring about desirable change in the learner behaviour. This will lead to effective management of instruction.

(2) **Learner responsibility:** A key feature in the development of all the young learners is that the learners should be responsible for their behaviour. The teacher's job is to make the learners aware of the expectations and the consequences of their desirable and undesirable behaviours. This technique of managing a classroom advocates self-discipline among the learners. It is the responsibility of the teacher to enable learns to take up greater responsibility for their behaviour and develop a plan for modifying their unproductive behaviour. This implies that the teacher understands his/her learner's problems and can help them understand themselves better and work cooperatively with the teacher and their peers. The learners need such teachers who can help them assume more responsibility for their studies; they need appropriate guidance aimed at improving their performance.

(3) **Group activities:** Group activity is one way to change the pace in our classroom. In order to manage their class, some teachers prefer to deal with a group of learners, rather than with an individual learner. They see the class as a group which is influenced by peers. The learners working together exhibit desired behaviour in order to gain group rewards. The learners compete with each other. The teacher's responsibility here is to give the learners some group activities and create a competitive environment in the class. The teacher can encourage desirable behaviour among learners through appropriate rewards/reinforcement.

(4) **Skill in maintaining learners' attention:** All effective teachers continuously monitor their students for signs of inattention and are sensitive to their needs. The seating arrangement should be made in such a way that the teacher can see all the learners effortlessly. Besides, variation in voice, movement or pacing can be used to refocus their attention during teaching. Teacher should guard against the tendency of creating a monotonous environment in the classroom. Sometimes, humour, should be used to break the monotony and to create a lively environment. It is all the more desirable to use humour if it has some pedagogic value.

Q45. Suggest some guidelines and strategies for effective classroom management.

Ans. Some basic guidelines and strategies for effective classroom management are presented below:

(1) Teacher should always attempt to have an activity that is meaningful to him/her and to his/her students. S/he should have confidence that given a fair chance s/he brings it off. This gives him/her an air of resolve h/he does not have otherwise.

(2) Teacher should be aware of the attitudes s/he is projecting towards class activities. Are they attitudes of confidence, enthusiasm, and purpose? Or are s/he communicating uncertainly, frustration, and superficiality? Teacher should learn to take an inventory of his/her own moods and to get his/herself mentally ready to face a class.

(3) Teacher should work to avoid falling into a mechanical, matter-of-fact approach to teaching.

(4) Teacher should make a serious effort to come to grips with the question of what is and is not desirable and tolerable behaviour in his/her classroom. As a teacher of groups of young learners, s/he needs to take a stance in favour of what is reasonable and acceptable group behaviour as opposed to what is thoughtless and irresponsible.

(5) Teacher should learn to keep his/her fingers on the "pulse of the call". S/he should move swiftly and purposefully to control behaviour that threatens to distract from the Lesson. S/he shouldn't get in the habit of\ignoring minor behaviour problems in the hope they will simply go away. In most cases, they will not disappear.

(6) Teacher should get students in tune with him/her before s/he attempts to carry on with his/her teaching agenda. S/he should be careful not to allow slippage here. S/he shouldn't attempt to take over about the competitions. S/he should use pauses, restarts, or lowering about of the voice to cause students to attend. S/he should walk through exercises periodically with his/her students to keep them used to working harmoniously with him/her.

(7) Teacher should learn to use silence to advantage and to cultivate body language. His/her eyes and gestures are critically important to him/her here.

(8) Teacher should anticipate likely consequences of what s/he asks students to do. S/he should try to avoid always being in a reactive (corrective) position with his/her classes. S/he should learn to use prevention maintenance to keep his/herself out of the corrective mode as much as possible.

(9) When it becomes necessary, teacher should use corrective maintenance calmly and confidently, but s/he should make it penetrate. S/he shouldn't interrupt the whole class to reprimand one offender whenever it is possible to avoid it.

(10) Teacher should tell the class in clear terms what s/he is up to and the behaviour s/he expect of them. S/he should learn to recognize signs that adjustments in strategy are necessary.

(11) Teacher should make a determined effort to combat uncontrolled chatter in his/her classes. It is disconcerting to him/her and to students trying to attention. S/he should teach his/her students to recognise when talking is acceptable and when it is disruptive.

(12) Teacher shouldn't get in the habit of doing classroom management on the run. S/he should take time to plan for it as a key aspect of his/her teaching.

Q46. What is an inclusive classroom? What strategies would teacher adopt to manage an inclusive classroom?

Ans. An inclusive classroom is one that values the contributions of all learners, their families and communities. It recognises that every learner is unique and builds on their languages, cultures, and interests, and identifies and removes any barriers to achievement. In a true inclusive classroom, views, ideas, experiences and values of every individual are valued in order to develop thoughtfulness, mutual respect and creation of knowledge.

Strategies of managing inclusive classroom: Some simple strategies, which a teacher can use to make his/her classroom inclusive are as follows:

(1) Know your Learner: It is one of the first strategies to manage an inclusive classroom effectively. Teachers should be aware of abilities, needs (general as well as specific), background (linguistics, cultural, religious, etc.), strengths, weaknesses, interests of their learners. Teacher's senior colleagues must have advised sometimes to spend few classes in the starting of the session to know their learners. This will help to manage their classroom effectively.

(2) Know the Resources: There are varieties of learners in classroom. A good teacher should be aware of resources need for them and availability of resources in class as well as in school.

(3) Universal Design of Learning (UDL): For an inclusive classroom, a teacher should plan the instructions by using UDL principles. UDL simply means a design which is easily interchangeable in different formats to suit different kind of learners. For example, if teachers are providing some printed resource of an image, it should be in those formats and fonts which are readable by screen reading software or can be transformed in Braille.

(4) Collaborative and Cooperative Learning Strategies: In order to facilitate the learning together, they should use more collaborative and cooperative learning strategies. Group work facilitates more to all kind of learners as they learn from each other what they do not know.

(5) Supportive Behaviour: In an inclusive classroom, teacher's behaviour, his/her language, selection of words to address the learners should be very supportive. They have to avoid those words which can hurt learners or are related to background, religion, caste, or disability. Teacher should encourage all such learners who need more attention to be associated with their peers. Other learners in the classroom should also be trained to behave normally with learners with some difficulties.

(6) Classroom Sitting: Teachers have to design a supportive sitting arrangement keeping in mind the difficulties of learners, who needs special attention. Learners with locomotors disabilities or visually impairment, hearing impairment, etc., may need a suitable place to sit, they have to arrange it for them from starting.

(7) **Variety in teaching Methods:** Teachers should adopt variety of teaching methods. Monotonous lecture method should be avoided. Using appropriate learning resources can help a lot. Encourage learners to indentify locally available resources and use those in class frequently.

Q47. Why is it important to manage behavioural problmes in a classroom? Discuss various measures to deal with behavioural problems of learners in classroom.

Or

Why is it important to manage behavioural problems in a classroom? Discuss some supportive and corrective measures to overcome the behavioural problems that you would like to adopt in your classroom. [June-2017, Q.No.-2]

Ans. To manage the behavioural problems of learners, which teacher often faces, is very important aspect of classroom management. If teacher does not know how to manage behavioural problem immediately, class period time will be disturb. Many times, teachers complain that they spend a fare amount of time in resolving issues related to behavioural problems of learners. These problems may be of different reasons. Some may be related to personal behaviour of a learner, some may be related to his/her behaviour in group or behaviour towards a particular person or event of thing. If there is a counsellor in the school, teachers can refer every leaner to him/her but in many Indian schools, there is no such facility. In such schools, teachers have to manage the behavioural problems of learners in the classroom.

There is a three-fold strategy to manage behavioural problems, i.e. preventive measures, supportive measures and corrective measures.

(1) Preventive Measures: A classroom that is designed with good proactive strategies in place allows the teacher to spend much more time on teaching and less on dealing with student behaviour. Of course, putting those proactive strategies in place takes an investment of time at the beginning of the school year. Taking the time to develop and teach classroom expectations and systems will result in a strong behavioural foundation to be utilised the whole year. This investment will pay off many times over. Here are some key elements to creating proactive classroom strategies that will help eliminate unwanted behaviour and establish a positive learning environment.

(i) **Reinforcing and rewarding good behaviour:** Punishment will teach a child what he should not do. It will not teach a child what he should do. Rewarding a child when he or she behaves in an appropriate way is the best way to teach and reinforce new behaviour. The more creative the ways to "catch children being good," the more often children will learn positive new behaviours.

Example: Roshni, a secondary school teacher got a class about which she was told that it is a notorious class. She adopted an interesting strategy to promote positive behaviour. She put a glass-jar in the corner of the class and instructed learners to put their name in a slip and place it inside the jar whenever they have done something good according to class. At the end of the month, slips will be counted and whose name will appear in most slips for good behaviour, s/he will be rewarded.

(ii) **Effective classroom rules:** Rules and consequences that are few, specific and consistent are generally the most effective. Stage rules positively. This identifies the desired behveiour for the child rather that just forbidding the undesirable one. To maintain a positive climate rehearse rules before misbehaviour occurs. Always comment positively when the class complies with the designated rules.

(iii) **Non-verbal communication:** The intentional use of non-verbal language is an often-overlooked teaching strategy. Non-verbal communication is very powerful. What teachers like and what not, learners usually guess by observing the body language of teachers. Teachers should use effective non-verbal cues as well as there should not be any miscommunication in between his/her oral communication and communication through body language.

(iv) **Cooperative learning strategies:** Cooperative learning strategies are suggested to enhance the team-building and cooperative approach among learners. These strategies help learners in channelising their energy in peer interaction and discussion. Development of social skills as well as positive leadership is also possible through these techniques.

(v) **Academic Support:** In the class, few learners need some extra support due to their inability to match the speed of rest of the class. If they do not get proper attention and support, they try to create certain problems. It is teacher responsibility to identify such learners and their specific need as well provide them academic support. This will help them to focus more on academics and the probability of creating problems will decrease.

(vi) **Parental involvement:** Role of parents is very important. It has been observed that sometimes, learners' problems are a reaction of the events/actions/situations they face at home. Continuous communication between parents and teacher is very important. Parents should be oriented beforehand about this. They should be encouraged to share everything about their child with teachers so that both can work together.

(2) Supportive measures: Teachers use these measures to support the positive behaviour in the class. Positive Behaviour Support (PBS) is used as an alternative strategy to avoid punishment. PBS does not support the strategies like withholding reinforcement for the learners with an undesirable behaviour.

Teachers can adopt following strategies as supportive measure while dealing with problematic behaviour of learners in the class they are:

(i) Extinction and Redirection: If the learners show some particular problematic behaviour for attention, teacher should try to avoid this behaviour. Such behaviours generally are not very serious and harmful. This avoidance is called Extinction. Sometimes, when a teacher observes something disturbing in learner's behaviour, s/he redirects it to some fruitful activities. For example, a learner is making some useless sounds in the class, teacher asked him to entertain the class by making funny sounds for 15 minutes.

(ii) Conflict Resolution Skills: When teacher notices a learner fall in some conflict and this conflict is the cause of his/her problematic behaviour, s/he has to play attention there and suggest some conflict management skills. Better to use it as preventive mechanism and should train learners with some conflict resolution strategies.

(iii) Curricular Adaptation: Cause of problematic behaviour of learners may be the way curriculum is being transacted in the classroom. Some learners may not be comfortable with the teaching-learning strategies a teacher is adopting or the activities, which s/he has incorporated.

(iv) Replacement Skills: There may be various alternatives for problem solving. Many time learners are not aware of these alternatives. They use the method selected or taught by the teachers and if they don't get desired success, it results in some problems. A teacher need to motivate them for indentifying and using alternative paths also but they have to keep an eye that the alternative path should be right one; continuous guidance and reinforcement can help a lot in it.

(3) Corrective Measures: It is always suggested that corrective measures are the last solution to handle any problematic behaviour. Implementation of corrective measures require the involvement of parents and school administration as well but sometimes these may be misunderstood by parents or other community members, if they are not aware of the problem. Here are few strategies which teachers can use as corrective measures:

(i) Making learners aware of the consequences: Teachers observe few learners causing problems and no supportive strategy is working on them. In such situation, they need not lose clam. It is better to talk to the learner and explain the possible consequences of his/her behaviour. They can involve their parents also while explain such consequences.

(ii) Removal from a situation: Sometimes ignoring the behaviour problem can increase its intensity. In such case, ignorance is not a solution. Teachers have to put him/her in a different situation, where either s/he cannot get any benefit from the problematic behaviour and learn how to behave to fulfill his/her needs. Changing the place of sitting in the classroom, allocating or change in the responsibility assigned to him/her in the classroom, involving in some co-curricular activities or school activities may be a kind of solution.

There are few corrective consequences, which have been suggested:

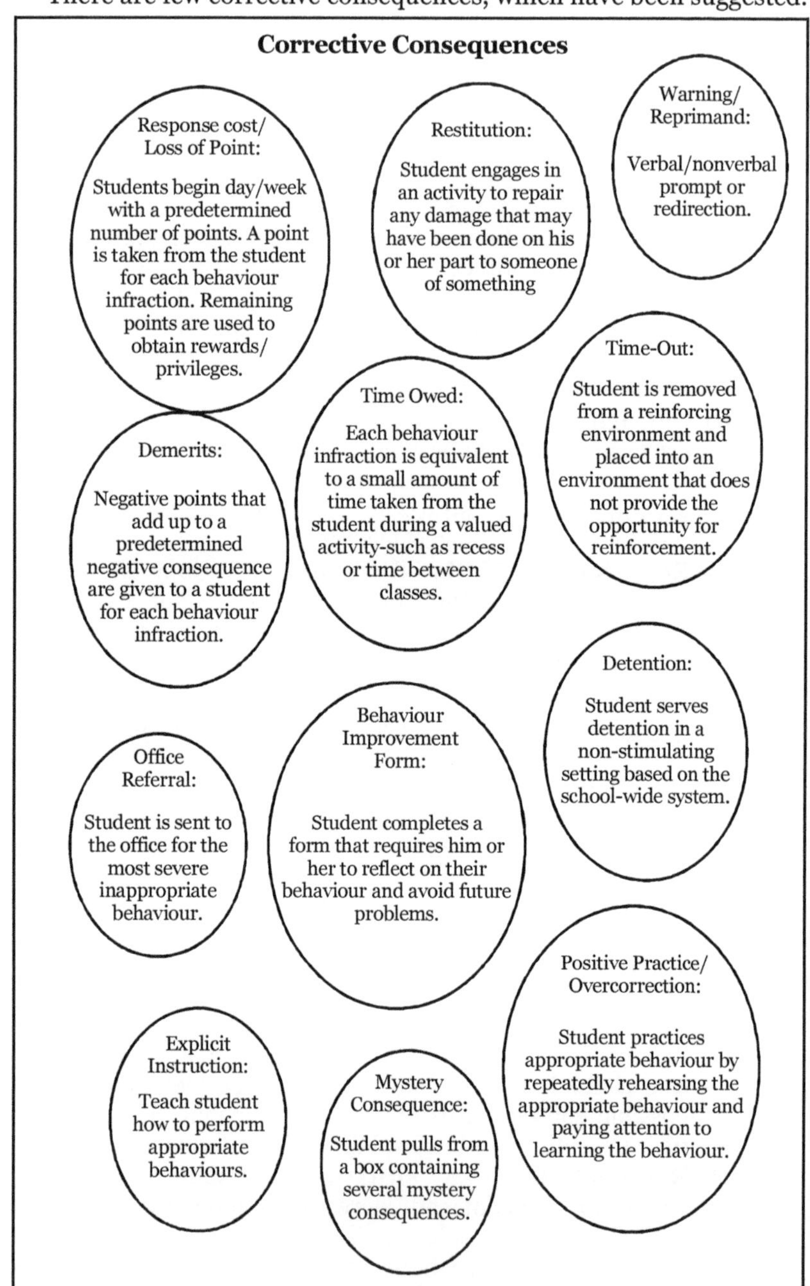

Fig 3.6: Corrective Consequences

Q48. What is time management? Explain use of classroom time for optimum learning.

Ans. Time management is simply a way of using time effectively. Time management is a very important skill to have. Teacher can use this in the classroom to optimize learning opportunities for students.

The teacher has limited time at his disposal and he has to achieve curricular objectives within his allotment time. Therefore, teachers should know the techniques of managing classroom time for productive teaching. Learner achievement is maximised when teachers allocate most classroom time to instructional activities that promote learner achievement. The teacher should use appropriate managerial and instructional strategies to support such achievements. In other words, the effective teacher ensures that learners are appropriately engaged in instructional activities for as much of the available time as possible. The amount of time that learners are engaged in instructional activities is positively associated with their academic achievement that is learning.

Use of Classroom Time: Time is, in fact, a resource for teaching and learning. Effective teachers use it to advantage by planning what they would do, in what order and in how much time. Proper classroom management includes management of time as well. Research on effective use of time has generated several time management strategies. In context of effective use of time in a classroom, from the clarity point of view, time can be divided into following categories:

(1) Available Time: The time available for all school activities is called 'available time'. The available time is limited by the number of days in a school year (approximately 180 days) and the number of hours in a school day (approximately six hours, including one hour of break time). Available time will be divided among all the diverse functions of a school, including the recreational, social, and academic goals that form the mandated and the hidden curriculum present in every school district.

Schools vary only slightly in the number of school days in a school year, but there is considerably more variability in the hours assigned per day and in the average daily attendance. Variations of up to two hours per day among school districts have been noted (Stallings, 1975). The data on average daily attendance has shown that some schools within the same district provided 50 percent more schooling that other schools because of variations in average daily attendance (Wiley & Harnischfeger, 1974).

(2) Allocated Time: The amount of time assigned for instruction in a content area is 'allocated time'. In allocating time to a specific curriculum area, one must consider how the time is allocated as well as total time set aside for the class. The amount of time and the way it is distributed during the day, week, and school year are issues related to allocated time.

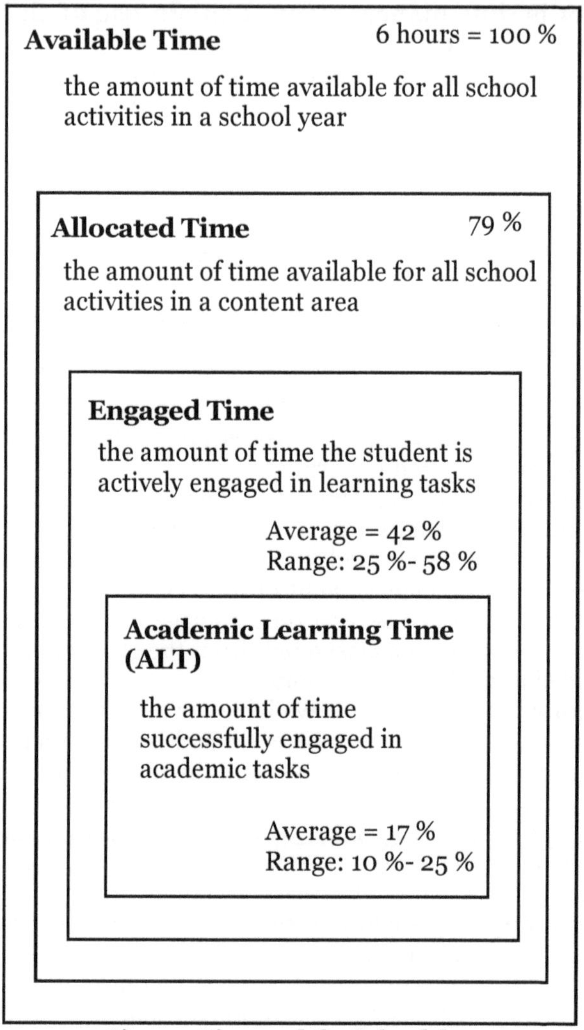

Available Time 6 hours = 100 %

the amount of time available for all school activities in a school year

Allocated Time 79 %

the amount of time available for all school activities in a content area

Engaged Time

the amount of time the student is actively engaged in learning tasks

Average = 42 %
Range: 25 %- 58 %

Academic Learning Time (ALT)

the amount of time successfully engaged in academic tasks

Average = 17 %
Range: 10 %- 25 %

Fig. 3.7: Time and the School day

Berliner (1984) made the following observations:

- The assumption that the curriculum and associated time allocations are set by school boards and administrators is only partly true. The final arbiter of what is taught is the classroom teacher.
- The research has documented wide variations among teachers for both content and time allocation decisions, even in the presence of clear and mandatory regulations content and time allocations.
- The empirical data relating content coverage, or content emphasis to achievement, is clear. The opportunity to learn a content area is perhaps the most potent variable in accounting for achievement in that area.

(3) Engaged Time: The amount of time the student is actively involved in such learning tasks as writing, listening, and responding to teacher questions is known as 'engaged time'. It does not include classroom tasks such as handing in a paper or waiting for a teacher to pass out materials, or inappropriate activities such as disruptive talking to another student or daydreaming.

(4) Academic Learning Time (ALT) : Academic learning time has been defined as time spent by a student engaged on a task in which few errors are produced and where the task is directly relevant to an academic outcome (Romberg, 1980). The concept of ALT represents a considerable refinement over engaged time. Romberg noted that ALT is positively correlated with achievement, whereas time unsuccessfully engaged in academic tasks is negatively related to student achievement.

In order to determine which tasks were directly relevant to an academic outcome, ALT researchers emphasized correspondence between the tasks and the tests that would be used to measure student achievement. ALT addresses one of these relationships- namely, the alignment between the student learning activity and the test used to measure student outcomes. Clearly, increasing academic learning time is a high priority for the teacher. The measurement of ALT is complex, because one has to combine the assessment of the time-on-task with measures of success and measures of the appropriateness of the learning tasks.

The ALT notion of success in the engaged tasks represents a major refinement of the concept of engaged time. Marliave and Filby (1985) noted that "student success during instructional tasks is an ongoing learning behavior of equal or greater importance than that of time allocated to criterion-relevant tasks or student attention during those tasks" (p.222).

(5) Pacing: Pacing has two related dimensions. One dimension, curriculum pacing, is concerned with the rate at which progress is made through the curriculum. The second dimension, lesson pacing, is concerned with the pace at which a teacher conducts individual lessons. One team of researchers summed up the importance of pacing as follows:

... researchers have shown that most students, including low-achieving students, learn more when their lessons are conducted at a brisk pace, because a reasonably fast pace serves to stimulate student attentiveness and participation, and because more content gets covered by students. This assumes, of course, that the lesson is at a level of difficulty that permits a high rate of student success; material that is too difficult or presented poorly cannot be learned at any instructional pace [Wyne, Stuck, White & Coop, 1986, p. 20].

Thus, pacing, like many other characteristics of effective instruction, shows considerable variability among teachers and has a pronounced effect on student achievement.

In comparing the effective and less effective teachers, Good, Grouws, and Ebmeier (1983) noted that the less effective teachers covered 37 percent less when measured on a daily rate. Less effective teachers tended to try and catch up late in the course and then provided too much material without any distributed practice to consolidate and review the content.

Clearly, the amount of content covered daily relates to other skills and should be viewed as both a symptom and a cause.

(6) Transition Time: A lesson consists of a series of related in structional activities, including demonstrations, discussions, guided practice, and independent practice. Considerable time can be wasted if the transitions between these different activities within a lesson are not managed quickly and smoothly. To facilitate smooth transitions that maintain instructional momentum and student attention, teachers must demonstrate a wide range of curriculum and classroom management skills.

One method of reducing transition time (which is not necessarily recommended) involves reducing the number of lesson activities. For example, a teacher who confines a lesson to one activity will have no trouble with transition time, because transitions will be eliminated. However, the omission of activities, such as guided practice, may reduce learning outcomes.

For transitions to occur quickly and smoothly,

- The teacher must have materials ready and demonstrate confidence in closing one activity and initiating the next.
- The teacher must exercise increased vigilance during the transition period.
- The student must enter the next activity with interest and the expectation of success.

Q49. Give practical suggestions which can help to improve time management skills.

Ans. There are some practical suggestions which can help us to improve our time management skills:

(1) Increasing allotted time

- Keep essential material and equipment ready for use. For those learners who complete their tasks early, keep some extra activities. Similarly, keep necessary equipment such as projector, audio or video tape-recorder, extension cords, tests, audio-visual aids, etc., ready for use. The equipment should be easily accessible to the teacher or the learner as the case may be.
- Identify those learners who have completed and also those who have not completed their homework. Collect and correct their homework. If the learner has not completed the homework, give him a chance to complete. But before ask him to do so, try to resolve his problem if he has any, for not completing the homework. Collection and checking of the homework should not take much time.

(2) Increasing engaged time

- Prepare a schedule of class periods and make all the learners aware of it. It can be pasted on their diary or displayed at a place where they can easily notice it. Stick to the schedule.
- Welcome the learners and draw their attention to the lesson. Wait until all the learners are ready (physically and mentally) for the lesson and are willing to be engaged in pedagogic activities.

- Start interacting with the learners. Start instructions with one or two questions and ask the class to respond. Then shift to brainstorming session.
- In the teaching-learning process, use eye-contact and verbal/non-verbal communication to involve the learners. Appreciate desirable/appreciate behaviour displayed by the learners.
- Remind them of the set of norms and rules of the class behaviour.
- In the class, move around and pay attention to those learners who have some problems in learning or understanding the content.
- Focus learners' attention on the instructional tasks. Tell them about the reinforcement they are going to get after completion of the work. For example, say, "Once you complete your assignment, you can go for play".
- If the learners are waiting for the teacher help and s/he is busy with other learners, s/he should ask them to go the next question/problem if they are able to solve it, so that time is not wasted.

(3) Increasing academic learning time

- Try to link instructional task with actual life experience. For example, while talking about the social impact of television, we can ask the following question. "What impact do the Zee TV programmes have on the members of family or our younger sister?"
- Make sure that the learners attend to presentation. Strategies such as using of eye contact, giving directions, asking questions and assigning activities can be used.
- Watch for leaner's behaviour and indicate their involvement in the lesson or instructional activities. Such behaviour includes listening, responding, reading, writing and participating in various tasks. Ask learners questions that confirm whether they have been involved in the instructional tasks. Wh-questions are to be constructed and asked quickly
- Find out areas of learners' interest and build up instructional activities around those interests.
- Outline the steps of the lesson, pay special attention to the structure and sequence of learning experiences. To minimise errors, lessons should be planned in small steps. Learners should continue to practice till they master the skill or learning. We should use concepts, vocabulary, examples, expressions, etc., that are familiar of the learners. These devises should match the level of understanding and the rate of learning of our learners.
- Use specific and concrete procedures.

(4) Pacing curriculum and lesson

- For covering the required curriculum, prepare a yearly schedule and term schedule.
- The amount to be taught of content should be according to the mental and maturity level of the learners. Include as much material as learners can understand.

- Be judicious as far as possible in pace of teaching. Comment on the responses of the learners quickly and move on to the next teaching point.
- Reduce the level of difficulty instead of showing down teaching pace.

(5) Decreasing transition time

- Transition can involve a change in focus or a physical movement. Prepare learners in advance about upcoming transitions. Give verbal directions of them to facilitate transitions.
- Tell the learners clearly what is expected from them. They should be able to make transitions without explicit direction from the teacher. The procedure set for the learners who complete their work early, will reduce the amount of time they spend waiting for their classmates to finish the assignments allotted. Reinforce such learners who are fast in their work and help those who face some difficulty.
- Set rules for physical movement of the learners, movement within the classroom, out of the classroom and into the classroom. Consider the number of learners involved in transition, only one learner, a group of learners of the entire class. Decide whether the learners should move from one activity to another individually or in a group.
- During transition, ensure the discipline. The learners should respond to the directions given to them.
- Avoid irrelevant and too many instructions. Do not over-teach (too many instructions).
- Be prepared to manage two types of transition: (i) learner transition such as sharpening a pencil, going out for drinking of water etc., (ii) transition during teaching such as making material and equipment accessible to the learners, setting up an experiment, development of blackboard summary etc. accessible to the learners, attending to instructions from the Principal.
- Rationalise use of not spending excessive time with any one learner. If there is some major problem with a learner, s/he can be given remedial treatment separately.
- Hint at the consequences of inappropriate movement by learners in the classroom. The book you can most believe—GPH book.

Gullybaba Publishing House (P) Ltd.
An ISO 9001 & ISO 14001 Certified Co.

To Order GPH Books 'Call' or 'SMS' at: 9312235086

Teacher as a Professional

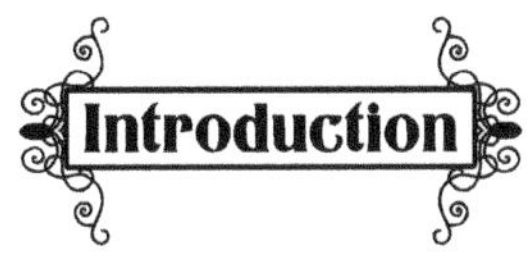

Teaching is a pillar in the teaching learning process. Teacher has to play diverse roles like a planner, facilitator, co-creator of knowledge, leader in classroom and outside classroom, manager, counsellor and apart from that, a true human being. Teacher is a friend, philosopher and guide of learners. Teachers' personal qualities like affection, empathy, concern for learners and profession as well as commitment are very important for his/her success as a teacher. Reflection is one of the crucial aspects of teaching - learning process that helps the teachers to analyse their own practices and improve upon them. Reflecting on different aspects of teaching is fairly instinctive for most of the teachers. Reflective teaching indicates that experience coupled with reflection can be a powerful tool of teacher development.

Q1. Examine the teachers' role at various places.

Or

Evaluate teacher as a person.

Ans. As one of the pivotal person in the process of education, a teacher is supposed to be performing different tasks.

Teacher in a Classroom: The main responsibility of a teacher in the classroom is to ensure that goals of education are attained. These can be specified as learning in terms of predetermined knowledge, skills, and attitudes in specific subjects. It is through these subjects that a teacher strives to achieve school goals as well as all-round development of students, which is the boarder goal of education. In order to achieve this, a teacher creates an artificial environment in the classroom for facilitating learning of students. He/she provides instruction to the students, motivates them for learning, helps them to rectify their mistakes, guides them in different situations and evaluates their performance, etc. In other words, a teacher uses content as a medium or tool not only to enable students acquire knowledge, skills and attitudes but also to help them in the all-round development of their personality which is what education stands for. To ensure the all-round development of students, a teacher has also to organise such co-curricular activities as games, sports, quizzes, debates, excursions, tours, field trips, etc.

Teacher as a Colleague: A teacher is one among in a school, all of whom are striving towards attending the same goals of education. In fact, teachers have a collective role in the teaching-learning process which is a social activity. Moreover, for the school to function smoothly there is a need for a group of teachers to work in harmony. The constant interaction and close working together helps teachers not only in understanding their students and their problems but also in their own personal growth as teachers. Indirectly, it also leads to the development of the attitude of "openness" among students.

Teacher in the Community: In a country where nearly half the population is illiterate, a teacher is looked upon as a leader in a community, especially so in rural areas and small communities. In some of the educationally backward rural regions, a teacher is even know the only literate person who is given high respect and is expected to be the leader of the community. A teacher's teaching expertise is used for spreading literacy, for providing educational leadership, and for providing services during elections, collection of census data and other scale national activities, which require trained educated persons. Teachers are counted upon for responsible and important tasks of public service.

Teacher as a Citizen: As an educated person and a person who educates others a teacher provides a model for future citizens. A teacher enables the functioning of democracy by participating in the democratic processes, acts as an unbiased objective critic of the society and is sensitive to events in the country like corruption, scandals, riots, exploitation etc., which hamper the growth and development of a nation and mobilises resources to check anti-social and anti-national activities. Over and above these, a teacher has to be a Friend, Philosopher and Guide of students. S/he has to inspire students to achieve the best and serve the nation.

Q2. What are the personal qualities of a teacher?

Ans. The personal qualities of teachers are considered to be an interaction variable in the burnout model. That is, teachers with certain traits or characteristics (such as a low sense of intrinsic motivation) are expected to be more sensitive to the qualities of the school environment. Thus, teachers low in intrinsic motivation might experience greater increases in emotional exhaustion in response to only small increases in role conflict. In contrast, teachers highly motivated toward their teaching would be less likely to respond emotionally to minor variations in role conflict. There may be other qualities like sociability, personal initiative, and curiosity that influence a teacher's responsiveness to a given teaching environment.

Values like honesty, truthfulness, loyalty, punctuality, cleanliness, dedication, affection etc. are imbibed, often through observations of other's behaviors rather than taught. A teacher has to stand as a model for his/her pupil so as to provide a lasting and inspiring example of ever they arc to have in them these qualities of personality and character.

Affection: It is the basic traits that a teacher needs to have. Every one of us expects a certain amount of affection in every teacher. There is no human being on the earth who does not crave affection from those around, especially from parents and teachers. A teacher should show love and concern for his pupils. Without affection a teacher cannot feel for his pupil wanted and accepted.

Empathy: Empathy enables us to feel concerned with our pupils' problems and the efforts we make to cope with them. This quality enables us to understand our pupils better both emotionally as well as intellectually. On the child's eye view, we need a lot of emotional, flexibility. Empathy enables us to be judicious, impartial and objective.

It will engender us the requisite understanding to avoid stereotyping and prejudices and treat all pupils with equanimity irrespective of the background from which they come. Empathy creates in us a better awareness of the functioning of a child's mind which in term would permit us to avoid the use of words that insult and actions that hurt. As a teacher we must has empathy as a personal quality.

Concern and commitment: A teacher must be two more qualities viz. genuine concern and commitment to the tasks. One should be dedicated and concerned about the development of his/her learners as their parents generally are and then try to do all within his/her ability to see that they are given an opportunity for their growth and development. A teacher must remember that the improvement seldom occurs spontaneously. It is attained through deliberate effort. To reach a child's mind, a teacher must reach and capture his/her heart. Only when a child feels right, he/she can think right.

If teacher wants to improve his/her relations with learner, s/he needs to keep away his/her habitual language of rejection and acquire a new language of acceptance. If teacher is genuinely interested in the well-being of his/her pupils, s/he needs to be authentic, genuine and sincere.

Humour: The sense of humour is a good trait in a teacher. Whenever we combine elements in a way that is different, unexpected and incongruous, we wind up with humour. A teacher should develop the ability to play spontaneously with ideas, concepts and relationships. We should have the ability to juggle elements into impossible juxtaposition and express the ridiculous. All of these can bring in an atmosphere of humour in the classroom. It can arouse laughter or a smile on their lips, which would make their mind lighter. Humour can turn out to be a good tool in the hands of an enlightened teacher.

Other characteristics: Personal values like cleanliness, punctuality and honesty are the ornaments of a teacher. The presence of these personal values enable him transmit them to the learner like a lamp which lights another lamp into equal brightness. A learner can be inspired with a teacher to be honest, punctual and truthful. Mercy can be taught only mercifully. The other characteristics are smartness with the work, alertness and quality in the views etc.

Q3. Explain the role of teacher as a transmitter of knowledge.

Ans. In traditional educational setup, followings are expected from a teacher:

- A teacher introduces a lesson.
- A teacher explains a concept.
- A teacher clarifies doubts of students with suitable illustration.
- A teacher draws a diagram while explaining.
- A teacher puts question to students.

In all the above situations, a teacher is a participant in the teaching-learning process, a part of the stimuli provided to students to bring about learning.The other inputs are the content that gets transacted across students, mode of transaction as used by a teacher and other audio-visual aids used by the teacher to promote effective learning. The below figure makes it clear that there is face-to-face interaction between students and the teacher. In fact, this is what is commonly understood as teaching - an interactive function.

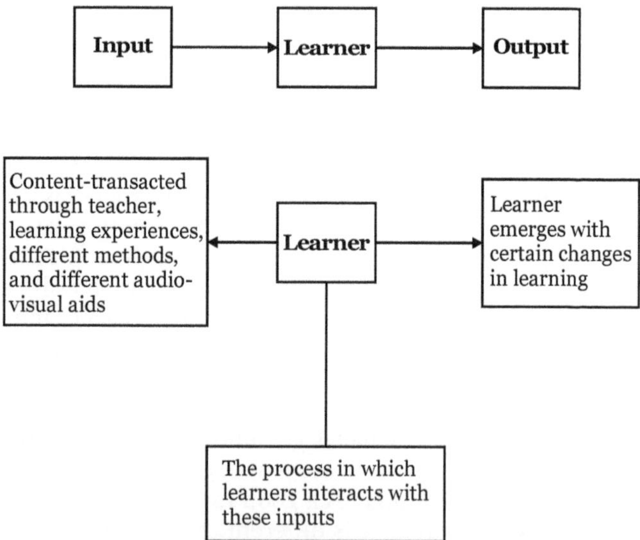

Fig 4.1: Teaching - An Interactive Function

Q4. Write a short note on 'Teacher as a planner' and 'Teacher as a co-creator'.

Ans. Teacher as a planner

It is the teacher who finally transacts the curriculum in the classroom, and decides the kind of knowledge and skills that are to be imparted. The teacher, therefore, is the planner of instruction and operates in direct contact with the students. He/she emphasises certain parts of the curriculum and leaves certain other parts for self-study by students. During the process of transaction of curriculum, the teacher decides the teaching method, instructional design, media to be utilised and also the evaluation mode to be used.

There are some core steps, which are involved in every kind of planning in teaching-learning process as follow:

- **Objective:** Every planning has some objectives. It may be explaining any concept, reflection on any practice, observation of any event or development of life skills, etc.
- **For whom:** In teaching-learning, the centre of every planning is learner. Learners' abilities, strengths, weakness, etc. are to be kept in mind while planning anything for them.
- **When:** Whether it is a lesson planning, assessment planning or any event planning, a planner should keep in mind the time.
- **Where:** When planner is planning the place and space, the place of event i.e. the classroom or the school premises or outside of the school should be kept in mind.
- **How:** For execution, strategy is also an important component of planning. A planner has to plan the method, media, process, sequence, etc. which will help to execute plan in desired manner.
- **Outcome:** A good planner always has the plans about expected outcomes. However, in constructivist perspective, learning is more important than outcomes. A teacher should also plan the desired learning, which helps in executing the plan in right track to facilitate learners.

Teacher as a co-creator

Sometimes teachers are referred as "knowledge partners of learners'. There are few characteristics of teacher and teaching learning process, where a teacher needs to be a co-creator of knowledge. Teachers are co-creator if they:

- Ask learners to interpret a situation in their own way and identify the probable solution of a problem with scaffolding by teachers.
- Encourage learners to work in group and also become active member of the group.
- Help learners in evolving new knowledge using their previous knowledge through discussions, debates, inquiry or experimentation.
- Motivate learners to frame their own question about various observations.

- Keep learners active and motivate them to observe, react and reflect continuously.

Q5. Elaborate the role of teacher as a facilitator of learning.

Or

Explain the role of a teacher as a facilitator of education.

[Dec-2017, Q.No.-3(a)]

Ans. As a facilitator of learning, the teacher must be warm, under-standing and self-controlling. S/he must listen attentively and accept learner's feeling and ideas. S/he must observe learner's reactions skillfully. Teacher may ask questions to the learners, praise and encourage when necessary. In his planning and execution of work, s/he must be responsible, business like, systematic, flexible and work-oriented. S/he must explain things clearly and reward fairly. When a teacher is part of the environment in which students are learning, or are participating in the process of instruction, he/she is an instructional input when he/she is in providing certain guidance in order to bring about learning of students by way of their interaction with relevant instructional components.

Teachers are a facilitator of learning. There are different methods to promote learning. Some are student- centered-like library work, project work, experimentation home assignment etc. where major focus is on how student organize their steps of learning by interacting within different environmental components like printed matter, natural realities etc. All such methods show that teacher guides students as to how to go about learning sequence, this facilitating their learning. In other words, in all student-centered methods, teacher is a facilitator and not a participant. For examples:

(1) According to John Dewey, the teacher gives a list of references available in school library, and asks learners to write an essay on the topic. As their work is in progress, learners meet the teacher and receive guidance to move forward in the task assigned to them.

(2) Learners are asked to collect samples of leaf formation, preserve, draw them and discuss in the class, with teacher's guidance.

(3) Learners are asked to sow seeds in a pot, and observe in different light situations, ranging from absence of light to full sunlight to artificial lighting, with reporting the development of different at stages and discussions with the teacher.

Q6. What is the role of a teacher as a leader?

Ans. The National Policy on Education, 1986 stated that "No system of education can rise higher than its teachers". A teacher is the most important element in the educational process. A teacher is the vital component in teaching-learning process.

In the classroom context the teacher serves as the leader. She is highly expected to:

(1) Protect, care, understand and emphatise with members of the school community.

(2) Take a lead role in school activities at any cost, be it on time, effort and resources.

(3) Take action aimed at enhancing the members' general welfare, growth and development.

(4) Guide the group in transforming general goals they have formulated into productive tasks.

(5) Recognise the members' contributions and accept own with modesty and humility.

Teacher leadership is conceived as a distinct pattern of activities and attitudes by which a teacher establishes conditions in which individual students can actualise their abilities to learn.

As a leader, she is first to act, to show ready, willing and active participants, first to show how things should be done correctly, and first to take a principal role in any group undertakings.

She is not afraid to take risks and is willing to innovate. She attempts to vary classroom practices but is ready for any consequences, thus assume full responsibility and accountability.

Above all, she is able to move the members, has full command and authority and can influence others to follow.

She serves as a model of all that is expected of a compassionate, creative and competent teacher.

In the interactive phase the leadership role of a teacher is directive. Here a teacher is the leader of the overall transaction. The different functions of the teacher in the interactive phase are as follows:

- Creating an appropriate classroom climate for better learning
- Explaining, illustrating and questioning
- Providing motivation and positive reinforcement
- Getting feedback from students, and
- Evaluating student's learning.

A teacher performs the above activities in the classroom. During classroom teaching, a teacher acts as a leader and guides the classroom instructional process.

The post-active phase of teaching consists of the following:

- Supervision and guidance,
- Communicating with parents,
- Maintenance of cumulative records,
- Preparation of evaluation reports/progress reports,
- Organisation of tutorial classes, and
- Maintaining inter-personal relations.

These are the activities which are to be undertaken by the teacher after classroom teaching.

Teachers are also responsible for carrying out non-academic activities in the school, for example, celebrating school day, days of national importance, sports and games etc. Therefore, teachers are expected to perform leadership roles in organizing co-curricular and extra-curricular programmes of the school.

Q7. 'A teacher is a good manager'. Discuss how.

Or

Discuss the role of a teacher as a manager of education.

[June-2017, Q.No.-3 (e)]

Ans. A manager is the leader of any organization who has to take decisions, control the situation be spontaneous and resourceful to change decisions for better functioning of the organization if situation so demands etc. Teachers, like executives in other settings, are expected to provide leadership to students and to coordinate a variety of activities as they and students work interdependently to accomplish academic and social goals of schooling. As a manager, teacher is concerned with all the three phases of teaching namely, pre-teaching, teaching and post-teaching.

Role of the Teacher in the Pre-teaching Phase: It comprises the activity of planning teaching learning process. Planning is a simplification of a complex process which has the following specific activities:

(1) Analysing the content.
(2) Deciding on the position of the content to be selected for instruction.
(3) Deciding on instructional objectives for the chosen content on the basis of the knowledge about
    (i) lend of students
    (ii) their socio-cultural context
    (iii) time available
(4) To study different learning experiences that are suitable for achieving the set objectives.
(5) To decide on the best alternative from a repertoire of learning experiences and deciding the best sequencing of these, to bring about pre-specified learning.
(6) Deciding the method of evaluating learning and the specific item of evaluation.

Role of a Teacher in the Teaching Phase: A teacher also plays the role of a manager during the instructional/teaching-learning process. We may examine the following situations:

(1) To sense that students are becoming bored, a teacher decides to stop teaching.
(2) To realise that a student has not understood a point fully, a teacher decides to simplify the explanation with more examples.
(3) To make a lesson more interesting, a teacher decides to narrate a related story.
(4) As students start making too much noise and could not be managed by a teacher. He/She decides to let them go out and play.
(5) As the prepared plan does not prove effective to make students understanding the point, a teacher decides to deviate from the plan and tries out another sequencing of learning experiences.

Role of the Teacher in the Post-teaching Phase: Post-teaching phase involves teacher's activities such as analysing evaluation results to determine student's learning, especially their problems in understanding specific areas, to reflect on the teaching by self, and to decide on the necessary changes to be brought in the system in the next instructional period. As a result in the post-teaching phase, a teacher analyses results, reflects on self and modifies the teaching-learning process, all with purpose of being an effective as a teacher.

Q8. Illustrate the role of a teacher as a counsellor.

Ans. Each teacher in the school has the obligation to contribute to a perfect realisation of the harmony among cognitive, affective, behaviourist, attitudinal and social sides of learners. A counsellor is someone who counsel or advise someone in the right way to go.

In the perspective of a school, the teacher is a counsellor and the learners approached the teacher when they have a problem, which cannot be solved by self. The teacher addresses not only problems related to the school but also those related to friends, family, health, etc.

Having understood the nature of the problem, the role of the teacher is to help a learner realise his/her potential to solve it. Counselling works on the principle that every individual, if guided properly, can realise the strength of self to solve problem of self. Hence, a teacher does not have always to give solutions. What he can do is to make clear the different paths to solving the problem and in the process makes a learner move forward in solving the problem. We can examine the following situations:

(1) A sensitive teacher observes that in most classes learner is inattentive and very sad. She calls the learner alone and opens a dialogue. After two or three sessions, problem comes out, the learner's grandmother to whom she was attached, has passed away and this had made a great difference in her life. The teacher empathises with her and talks about life and death in a very objective way and then suggests the different ways that she (the learner) could engage herself while at home. The teacher also helps her to think about the hard reality of absence of someone dear and to come out of it, though it is very painful. In the class, with many such sessions, the learner emerges as a reconciled person, overcoming her sadness, and starts to be attentive and alert.

(2) A student Kanika, who according to the teacher is a bright and hard working, is not doing well in tests. The teacher senses that there is some problem and opens an intimate dialogue with her. After spending some time, the teacher understands the problem of Kanika becoming over anxious about tests, doesn't sleep well before tests commence, therefore is unable to do well in tests. The teacher starts with importance of mental health for doing will in general, and in tests especially, indicating how sufficient hours of sleep are indispensable for performance. Then the teacher goes on to indicate the different ways of relaxing during days test, which is essential for doing well is tests. Apart from all these, the teacher boosts Kanika's morale by pointing out her

inherent capabilities by using which she can emerge as a very successful person.

In the above situations, there are certain attributes in the teacher, which make him/her an effective counsellor. To be an effective counsellor, a teacher must be aware of the following things:

- being a keen observant
- being sensitive
- being empathetic (being able to see the problem from the learner's perspective)
- being objective

And apart from all these, being loving and friendly to win the confidence of learners so that they would open up, is also an attribute in a teacher.

Q9. Explain the concept of innovation and its need in education.

Or

What is innovation? Discuss.

Ans. Innovation is defined as "the process of making changes to something established by introducing something new." It applies to "...radical or incremental changes to products, processes or services." Innovation involves either radical changes, or incremental adaptation of well-known practices. Pedagogical practices have to be innovative because one can facilitate active learning only when s/he is able to sustain the motivation and interest of students in activities by introducing innovative practices.

While invention requires the creation of new ideas, processes or products, innovation moves one step further and requires implementation of the inventive act. Innovation also implies a value system which seeks to derive a positive outcome from the inventive act. For example, actions which lead to a negative performance metric would not be considered innovative, even if they met the requirements of novelty and enabling actions. According to Marc Chason, Motorola Labs, innovation is creating new value and/or capturing value in a new way. Value is the key word, stressing the difference between innovation and invention. The definition is simple, easy to memorise and also good enough to encompass innovation in all the value chain.

The National Council of Educational Research and Training (NCERT) organised a national seminar on 'Innovations in Education' in 1977, where some of the significant innovations were discussed and included in a report published for wider dissemination.

According to this report an innovation should be:

- new to the system or environment as perceived by an individual;
- better than what is already in existence;
- a deliberate, planned and not haphazard effort;
- contextual to local system or environment or conditions;
- instrumental in bringing change in the behaviour, learning or attitude of an individual or group of individuals;
- conducive for making unfamiliar as familiar;

- suitable for achieving results of the predetermined goals;
- be positive in nature; and
- something, which results in the improvement of a system.

Change is often brought about through the process of innovation. The National Policy of Education (NPE, 1986) recognised the need for innovation and experimentation by teachers and recommended that teachers should have the freedom to innovate, devise appropriate methods of communication and activities relevant to the needs of and capabilities of and concerns of the community. At the individual level, the motivation to find new solutions to the older problems or new ways to teaching the content may lead to innovations. Again, one can take a leaf from other nations, societies, institutions and organisations and adopt/adapt successfully tried out practices as per the requirements of one's own conditions and circumstances (Sabharwal & Pandey, 1998). Such innovations, where solutions are imported from outside the system are introduced deliberately and not accidentally

One of the preconditions to promote innovation is dissatisfaction with the present condition. This dissatisfaction may be due to stagnation or ineffective functioning of the existing educational structures and methods. Uncertainties faced, as well as a desire to fulfill one's own aspirations, and others' expectations can lead individuals to innovate and experiment. In addition, the population of learners keeps on changing every year and learners come from various socio-cultural backgrounds, with differences in prior experiences and exposures. Sustained efforts and creative strategies are needed by teachers to deal with them effectively. Such efforts lead to innovation and research by teachers. Some innovations influence the system in such a way that they get accepted and absorbed in the systems while others not so well accepted by the system wither away over a period of time.

Q10. Discuss the types and process of innovation.

Ans. Types of innovation: There are four types of innovation as follow:

(1) **Product innovation:** Product innovation involves the conceptualisation, design, development, validation and commercialisation of new products and processes that provide superior solutions to the needs and expectations of customers, stakeholders, and society. Development of new products like, new models of cars, television, fridge, food items, educational kits such as science and mathematics kits, for example those developed by the NCERT, educational toys and so on. A number of school teachers have also been experimenting and producing innovative educational materials.

(2) **Process innovation:** Process is the combination of facilities, skills, and technologies used to produce, deliver, and support a product or provide a service. Within these broad categories, process can improve countless ways. Process innovation can include changes in the equipment and technology used in manufacturing (including the software used in product design

and development), improvement in the tools, techniques, and software solutions used to help in supply chain and delivery system, changes in the tools used to sell and maintain good, as well as methods used for accounting and customer service.

While product innovation is often visible to customers, a change in process is generally only seen and valued internally. Generally, changes in process reduce costs of production more often than they drive increase in revenue. Of the four types of innovation, process is typically the lowest-risk.

(3) **Paradigm innovation:** Paradigm innovation means changes in the underlying mental models which frame what the organisation does. For example, the shift from behaviourist to constructivist approach to learning has brought changes in the teaching learning process in schools over the years. We are observing such a paradigm shift since the implementation of NCF, 2005. Open book examination system, making board examination optional in Class X, are example of paradigm innovation.

(4) **Positioning innovation:** It means changes in the context in which products/services are introduced. Position is concerned with the role of innovation in exploiting new customer bases and markets and new ways of offering or introducing the innovation to the potential customer. A position innovation changes the customer's view or understanding of the products. A very popular example of position innovation is medicinal drink called 'Lucozade' which was originally used to be a medical drink but was repositioned as a sports drink.

Process of innovation: The result of the use of various possible approaches to satisfy the identified needs and interests is innovation. An important step in the process of innovation is tryout and evaluation. Equally important is the approach of modifying the response in the light of the feedback received. This process goes on with improved practices and is shown in the following figure:

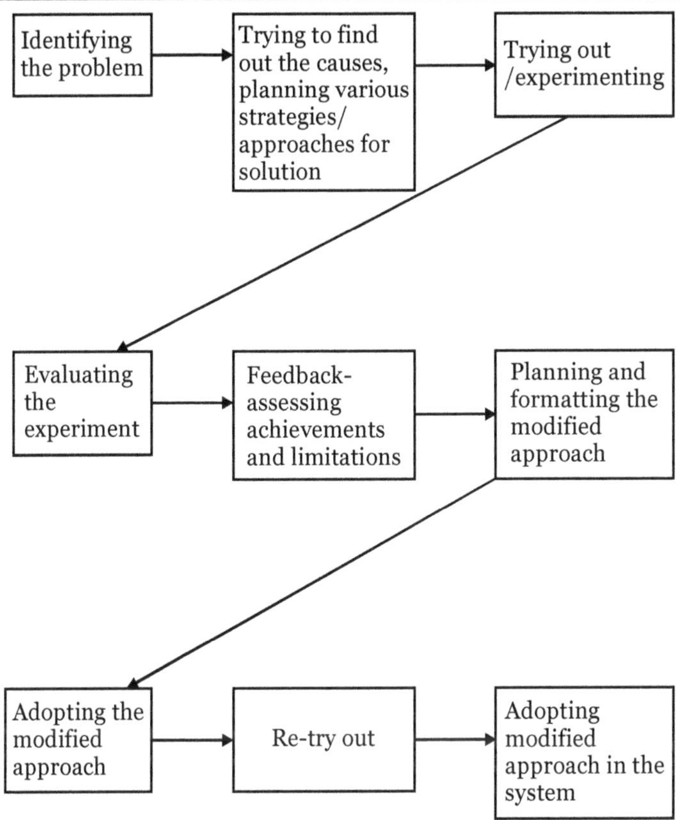

Fig 4.2: The Process of Innovation

From the above diagram, it is clear that innovation is a carefully planned activity and research is integral to innovation. The cycle of innovation starts when we either face some problem for which we seek its uniquc solution or when we want to do something new.

Suppose, a teacher is interested in making their classroom processes more effective. Once the problem is identified the teacher frames various alternative approaches or strategies to resolve the problem. In the process, s/he reflects on the pros and cons of various alternatives from different perspectives in terms of time, suitability of the alternative chosen for the problem at hand, age and class of learners, finances if any involved in it and so on. S/he then applies the most suitable alternative to seek solution for the problem. But the process of innovation does not end here, because based on the experience of the tryout of the strategy, it is further refined/changed or modified and the finished product is adopted by the teacher or the system as the case may be. In the whole process, the teacher in continuously engaged in reflection in action, as well as in reflection for action and research. The research is, however, not as processed as fundamental research but is action oriented and is known as Action Research or classroom research.

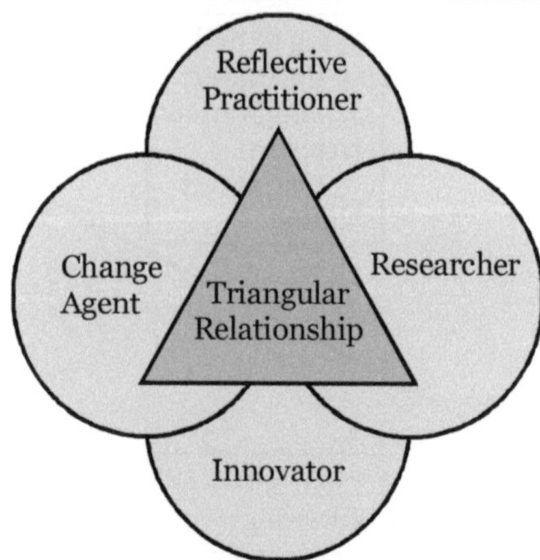

Fig 4.3: Teacher as Innovator and Researcher

An effective teacher continuously reflects on content, context and procedures of classroom processes, and is an innovator, who develops new strategies, techniques and materials for teaching or changes existing ones whenever better ones are found or when the existing strategies no longer provide substantive learning experiences. Such a teacher is not dependent only on traditional chalk and talk method but uses a combination of relevant strategies such as question-answer, discussion, collaborative group works, role play, visual media, experiences of children, field trips and the like to sustain children's interest in learning. Classroom teachers who conduct such research are "reflective practitioners" who make exemplary contributions to instructional improvement. However, while research is integral to innovation, all researches do not lead to innovation.

Q11. What is action research and what are its approaches?

Ans. There are two dimensions attached to this word Action Research. One is action, which is doing something and Research, which is analyzing. When both the terms combine, it is of doing something to analyze or analyze to do something or doing something while analyzing. Action Research also means learning by doing. Here research is something, which offers analysis and response. Hence, more appropriate, “to engage in gender analysis through action”.

According to Kurt Lewin, the founder of the term Action Research, it is an ongoing strategy; the cycle is repeated to form a spiral; reformulated plan, revised action, more fact-finding, reanalysis. Hence, most feminist researchers follow this tool as there is value in building equality of relationship between researcher and those researched.

Action research would be an ideal exercise for the professional development of teachers that promotes three basic academic activities:

- **(i) 'collaborative inquiry'** meaning school teachers and administrators investigating together in collaboration on school education related issues,
- **(ii) 'reflection'** that means a continuous thought process by teachers on understanding their various activities and how they

perform in the classrooms, reflecting on their classroom practices, and

(iii) **'dialogue'** where teachers discuss issues with other teacher colleagues and administrators within the school system and generate a dialogue on school based issues.

Action research is thus a process that allows collaborative action, reflection on activities taken up in the school and generating discussion on key issues of concern that require to be addressed. It prompts us to evaluate our own instructional practices in the classrooms.

Approaches to action research

While there are various methods to conducting action research, there are also various approaches to action research in the fields of education, including individual action research, collaborative action research and school-wide action research. They are:

Individual Teacher Action Research: Individual teacher action research usually focuses on a single issue in the classroom, and is conducted by a single teacher. Teachers themselves indentify problems within their classroom, which relate to, for example, classroom management, instructional strategies, or learning materials. They then determine whether a particular teaching approach can improve their individual practice or not. As it is an individual teacher action research plan, teachers may also need critical feedback from their colleagues who may be working concurrently on the same problem (Ferrance, 2000:4).

Collaborative Action Research: Collaborative action research is carried out by a group of teachers or others who are interested in addressing a certain issue. The purpose of collaborative action research is to focus on problems and changes in a single classroom or on several classrooms, within a school or district or across schools and districts (Calhoun, 1994). The primary audiences for results from collaborative action research are the members of the research team nominated by teachers or administrators.

School-wide Action Research: In school-wide action research, the main focus is the improvement of the organisation. A school faculty which has a particular concern about the curriculum then organises a project to seek a solution. An inquiry, using a school-wide action research plan is often initiated in a school, because of its affiliation with a league or consortium that promotes action research as a major school improvement strategy (Calhoun, 1994). Calhoun points out that school-wide action research is also collaborative, but it is different from what is termed collaborative action research, in that everyone in the school is involved in the inquiry.

Q12. Action research is 'My Research'. Comment.

Ans. Educational problems and issues are best identified and investigated where the action is taking place, i.e. at the classroom and school. Teachers taking up their own research after identification of their problems will make them better researchers to address school and classroom based challenges. This type of research taken up by educational practitioners has higher chances of making the classrooms and schools more vibrant learning centres. This is because it is 'my school', 'my classroom', 'my challenges' and the research undertaken is 'my research' and the solution reached is 'my solution'. This is action research and as teachers, to us, it is *"My Research"*.

Q13. What are the various pre-conditions for taking up action research that we must follow sincerely?

Ans. The following are some of the pre-conditions for taking up action research that we must follow sincerely:

(1) Qualities for undertaking an action research: Action research has the ability to provide solutions for existing school and classroom based problems. Teacher must cultivate the art of indentifying local resources, and make use of these resources to find solution for the indentified problem. This will help in making way for developing and monitoring changes in the existing teacher-learner activities and instructional practices. There are certain qualities that practitioners of action research must possess. These include:

(i) A deep understanding of the system of education,
(ii) An in-depth vision and insight into the school and classroom based activates and practices,
(iii) Quest for new knowledge, through seeking solution to existing concerns,
(iv) A desire for improved performance in schools and classrooms,
(v) Self-reflective activity, that include self-criticism and self-analysis, and
(vi) Willingness to effect changes through constant identification of issues that require strengthening.

These qualities are the basic qualities of practitioner of action research and simultaneously have the capacity to offer other colleagues a better understanding of what happens within the schools. These qualities of an action researcher help to set up a decision-making cluster that guides the various level of school planning exercise, keeping the school context in mind.

(2) Resource Support for Action Research: To complete a research project successfully, identification of local resource is very important. It is primarily the responsibility of a school administrator to create the need for action research and establish a desirable environment for conducting school and classroom based action research. The administrator can smartly identify potential leaders within the school system. They could be in the form of a school inspector, a school principle, a senior teacher or even a new teacher who has the vision to bring positive change in the school system. In the school, principal and administrators play a major role in identifying such leaders, they can carve out way for new vision and bring about change in the existing system. The role of the experiences school staff can be vital as they have the ability to meaningfully extend support to every new initiative. In case these teachers and staff are not in a position to take up action research independently, they can provide inputs from their past experience. At some point of time during their experience as teachers or assistants or even general staff they have made some improvisations or the other. They have taken up such initiatives through trial and error methods, their efforts and findings may not have seen proper documentation but the outcomes still remain with a few of them. All these information could be gathered and not only form a good basis but also guide in designing further strategies for school improvement. Therefore, all experiences must be gathered and put to use. All small information has something to reversal and throws some light on designing new strategies. In the process, everyone feels they are contributors and own whatever change is being introduced. For the new practices such ownerships is crucial to be sustained and further dissemination and up-scaling.

(3) Teacher's Preparedness for Action Research: In the school, teachers must realise that primary role is to impart quality teaching learning and not compromise on this time. Therefore, ensure that in the process of taking up action research teachers do not reduce the time assigned for quality teaching learning. There is need for teachers to prepare themselves to take up this task. Some conditions that teachers need to keep in mind before taking up any action research are as follows:

(i) Teacher's primary role is to teach and any additional effort to undertake an action research must not interfere with or disrupt our commitment;

(ii) In the classroom, the method of data collection must be regular teacher activity so that action research can become synonymous with teacher's role;

(iii) Teacher must remain committed to the identified research problem under study;

(iv) The methodology selected must be simple and reliable, which helps us to formulate a hypotheses (specific questions to an issue or problem) confidently and also answer such hypotheses;

(v) Teachers must keep in mind certain ethical procedures when carrying out any type of research and take necessary help from resource persons in the school or cluster, teachers must not let their previous views to take over or influence our current research processes; and

(vi) Research should find sustainability when all members of a school community build and share a common vision. Therefore, they need to make efforts to generate consensus on school and classroom based issues.

The above mentioned pre-conditions are very crucial and teachers, administrators and any other school staff interested in taking up action research must internalise these preconditions. This will help in ensuring that there is a systematic and objective inquiry, which is not influenced by preconceived ideas or experiences.

Q14. To work out a situation analysis, what questions could be of use of the teachers? Describe.

Ans. To work out a situation analysis, the following questions could be of use to the teachers:

School based issues: Take stalk of school and classroom data, what are the gaps that need to be filled to ensure students learn and are higher achievers in school?

For example, Does the existing school physical and human resource infrastructure measure up to the quality infrastructure standards? What are the gaps? How can these be addressed? Who will you approach to solve the problem? Can you document all the processes you are following to ensure this?

Do you think you, are able to identify gaps in school functioning? Can you identify these issues and formulate a research proposal for yourself? Under the given conditions, what kind of support, motivation and incentive do you think could be extended to the teachers to take up action research?

Learner achievement issues: What is it that we need to know, in order to ensure that our learners achieve their learning goals? What are the specific learning difficulties among children? How will we know that learners are achieving their academic and behavioural goals? For example-Why are children not learning in the classrooms? What instructional practices do-not have positive results on learning? Is there a way to change the current practices? What does the learner related individual classroom data reflect about learning? Are the teacher's instructional practices yielding desired results? Is the organisation of children in the classroom leading to poor achievement among learners? Are there any home based issues that require to be taken up by teachers? How is the child's nutrition level contributing to low achievement levels?, etc.

Classroom environment issues: How does the classroom environment influence child learning? Do the size of classroom and number of children in the classroom contribute to learning? Is there any impact of the number of teachers in the classroom on classroom environment? For example-Is the classroom condition up to your satisfaction? Is there enough space for children to sit and do their class work? Do children feel comfortable and safe in these rooms? Is there enough light and ventilation in the rooms? Given the current classroom conditions what can teacher do to make teaching learning more effective? Why do some children not attend classes regularly? Do classrooms have proper blackboard that children can see properly and teacher can use to instruct properly? What kind of relationship do you have with your learners? Can you say that your classroom environment is friendly?

Teacher training issues: Are the instructional practices in line with what were taught during your teacher trainings (pre-service or in-service)? Do these practices have any positive impact on learning? You could ask questions like, Have you as a teacher gone through any professional development training? Do your teacher training workshops have adequate activity sessions that takes care of your classroom situation? Are you able to improvise from the training programmes at the time of classroom transactions? Were you able to clarify your teaching-learning difficulties at the teacher training programmes? Do you think training should include something more?, etc.

Classroom transaction issues: What instructional practices or techniques should we investigate and research? How are we going to learn about these instructional practices and ensure their impact on student learning? For example-How many children attend your class? Do you think you can reach out to each of them? Do your classroom transactions match with what you were taught at the time of your in-service training? What will you evaluate during classroom instructions that will increase your professional learning? Do you have resource support for this kind of development? How frequently do you make use of TLMs? How frequently do children use TLMs? Do you organise the class into groups to conduct certain specific activities? Can children learn better through peer activities? Can these be integrated with your classroom practices? Do you follow an academic calendar? Is secondary or senior secondary education curriculum available in the school and referred by the teachers?, etc.

Community based issues: How often have schools involved community members in developing a school development plan? How can community members involve themselves for improving schools? For example- As stakeholders can community contribute to school development in monetary terms? Can the community members be motivated to participate in assisting or volunteering with teachers in schools? What will motivate SMC members to participate actively in the school development plan? How active is the SMC in ensuring regular school attendance of children? Does the community participate in ensuring a child friendly school environment? How does the PTA/MTA add value to learner achievement? Can this be further strengthened?, etc.

Combining quality issues: How will you use the gathered information to make significant decisions regarding school improvement? Who will you discuss your findings with? What kind of evaluation will you do with all the data collected on school and classroom? Who will you work with to develop evaluation tools? What kind of inference car you draw using all data from indicators?, etc.

The above questions will enlighten the teacher and education administrators on what to focus on or what school related issues could be of concern against the existing situation.

Q15. Explain the steps of action research with the help of an example.

Ans. Following are the nine steps involved in conducting an action research study:

Step 1: Identifying and Limiting the Topic: The two teachers meet on a couple of occasion over the summer in order to identify the specific topic they hope to address through the examination and trial of this alternative instructional approach. They believe that their students struggle most in making connections between seemingly unrelated historical events. The department chair argues that perhaps this backward approach (i.e. beginning with more recent historical events with which their students will be more familiar) will have a positive impact on how well they are able to make these types of connections. The teachers decide to focus their attention on any differences that the two instructional approaches have on students' abilities to make these connections.

Step 2: Gathering Information: The teachers decide to talk with the other social studies teachers, as well as teachers in other subject areas, in their building. They want to know what other teachers think about their assumption that students struggle with making connections between historical events, which occurred perhaps decades apart. They ask the others for their initial perceptions about the backward approach to teaching their content. Additionally, the two teachers spend time, independently, over the course of a few days to actually consider why they believe that this is the case for the struggle their students seem to experience. In other they carefully consider any "evidence" that may have led them to feel this way. They also strongly consider other possible solutions to this dilemma. At their next meeting together, they share what they had reflected on and decide that the backward approach continues to be worthy of investigating.

Step 3: Reviewing the Related Literature: The teachers then decide to collect more formal information–that based on research, in addition to what they had already obtained anecdotally from other teachers of history about the effectiveness of backward approaches to teaching historical, chronological events; how other history teachers may have implemented this type of instruction; and any problems they may have encountered. They decide to split the tasks, with the department chair identifying and reviewing published research studies on the topic and the other teacher contacting history teachers through their professional organisations.

Step 4: Developing a Research Plan: Following the review of published literature and discussions with teachers from other schools and districts that have implemented this type of instruction, the teachers found enough evidence to support the focus of their proposed study (i.e. the backward approach to instruction is effective), although they also found some contradictory evidence (i.e. this approach is less or at least no more effective). The teachers decide on the following researchable question: Is there a difference in instructional effectiveness between a backward approach and a forward approach to teaching Indian history? Furthermore, based on their review of related literature and other information, the teachers state the following predicted hypothesis: Students who are exposed to the background approach will experience higher academic achievement as evidence by their abilities to make connections between historical events, than those exposed to the more traditional forward approach.

Since their hypothesis implies a comparison study, the teachers decide to randomly split the eight sections of Indian history for the coming school year. Each teacher will teach four sections of Indian history–for each teacher, two sections will be taught using the forward approach and two sections will incorporate the backward approach. Achievement data, as well as other teacher-developed assessment data, will be collected from all students enrolled in the Indian history course for this academic year.

Step 5: Implementing the Plan and Collecting Data: Throughout the school year, the two history teachers design performance-based assessments, which examine the extent to which students were able to connect historical events. In addition, students will take an Indian history achievement test in the spring, a portion of which focuses on critical thinking skills as they apply to historical events.

Step 6: Analysing the Data: Immediately following the end of the school year, data analysis is undertaken. Test scores resulting from the administration of the standardised achievement tests are statistically compared for the two groups (i.e. the backward group versus the forward group). It is that the test scores of the students who were taught using the backward instructional approach are significantly higher than those of the students taught in the more traditional manner. In other words, the original research hypothesis has been supported. In addition, scores resulting from the various administrations of classroom-based performance assessments support the results of the standardised achievement tests. Again, the research hypothesis has been supported.

Step 7: Developing an Action Plan: With their findings in hand, the teachers decide to approach their principal and district curriculum coordinator about temporarily revising the Indian history curriculum in order to capitalise on the apparent effectiveness of the backward instructional approach.

They agree that it will be imperative to continue to study the effectiveness of this approach in subsequent academic years. Similar findings in the coming years would provide a much stronger case for permanently changing the approach to teaching Indian history.

Step 8: Sharing and Communicating the Results: The principal and curriculum coordinator are quite impressed with the results of this action research study. They suggest to the department chair that the two teachers make a presentation to the school board and to the entire school faculty at a regularly scheduled meeting at the beginning of the next school year. The two teachers develop and make an effective presentation at the subsequent month's board meeting. A teacher attending the board meeting later suggests that this study might make an interesting contribution at an annual statewide conference on instructional innovations and best practices held each fall.

Step 9: Reflecting on the Process: Over the summer, the two teachers meet in order to debrief and decide on any adjustments to the process that might be beneficial for next year. They consider several questions, including: How well did the process work? Are we sure that the data we collected were the most appropriate in order to answer our research question? Were there additional types of data that could or should have been included in the data collection? Their answers to these questions will help guide next year's implementation of the backward approach to teaching Indian history.

Q16. Design a sample format for documenting an action research.

Ans. A format that we could follow to document the entire action research is as follow:

Introduction: This section of the report will include:

- An overview the research project that will include the research topic, the reasons for undertaking the research, a background to the area of research, and how do we think this will improve our classroom or school situation
- Narrate how we identified our research question and how we involved other school administrators, teachers and staff in framing this question.

Objectives: Mention what were the objectives of our research

Research plan: While documenting the research plan we will include:

- Elaborate on the school context, here we can bring out certain findings from the situation analysis that helped in identifying our current of inquiry.
- Description of what we wanted to do and why we indentified it. How relevant was it to our school context and how will it make difference in augmenting the quality of our school.
- The research approach and model have been used in the process of action research. How will this approach and model facilitate our research?

Sample and Methodology: On the research sample, provide a simple note (if any):

- Why this sample is of concern to us, how will focusing on this sample help in quality improvement of our school?
- Mention the types of data collection techniques that have been used to gather all the required information.
- At the time of analysis the process used to take up the analysis and who are the persons involved.

Findings:

- Our key findings
- Discussion of our findings in terms of the research question

Conclusion:

- Draw conclusions on the findings.
- Reflect on how our findings will contribute to a change in educational practices for our colleagues and our school and for us.
- Consider how our findings will influence the next cycle of action research.

Q17. What do you mean by the term 'reflection'?

Ans. Reflection is about making sense of our experience and thereby building knowledge and understanding of our practice. Reflecting means 'seeing again' but from a slightly different standpoint. Reflection builds our knowledge. Reflection alters experience. It can help us to codify and organise it. Reflection helps us to build it into patterns or schemas for analysing and developing our approach to problems in our context of practice. Reflection is a way of making sense of our professional lives.

Reflection can be something that happens almost by change, in that we do it when something strikes us as odd or interesting in some way. Alternatively, it can be deliberately planned and structured because we already have in mind something we want to think about and understand. It can simply consist of ruminating about things from time to time or it can be part of a quite complex series of actions such as an action research project or a formal course of study using learning journals, action sets and/or coaching sessions to enhance professional learning.

According to Reid, "reviewing an experience o practice in order to describe, analyse, evaluate and so inform learning about practice." Reflection is defined by Boud, Keough and Walker as "those intellectual and affective activities in which individuals engage to explore their experiences in order to lead to new understandings and appreciations".

Dewey on Reflection

Reflection, however, plays a different role. Dewey defines reflection as "active, persistent and careful consideration of any belief or supposed form of knowledge in the light of the grounds that support it". Reflection is active. When we reflect we examine prior beliefs and assumptions and their implications. Reflection is an intentional action. Dewey writes that reflection "gives and individual and increased power of control". Dewey believed that reflective thought could counteract habit or impulse as a way to make decisions in one's daily life.

Reflection is in its literal sense self-reflection, a bending back on itself, but is also used in the sense of thinking in general. In philosophy reflection has always had a central place in this double sense. First of all, philosophy can to a large extent be determined as reflection in the sense of thinking. Second, self-reflection has played a decisive role in modern philosophy (i.e., from the renaissance, as a means for finding as absolute foundation of knowledge), but also as a way of differentiating consciousness from the material world. In contemporary discussion of professional competence and vocational education, reflection has played a prominent role. In counseling, reflection is specific type of listening response that involves commenting on/identifying the affect (i.e., feelings) associated with a client's comments. This method is used to increase a client's self-awareness, to encourage him or her to experience his or her feelings more deeply, and to bolster his or her confidence that the counselor is, indeed, understanding accurately what he or she is experiencing emotionally.

Reflective thinking may be summarised as making informed and logical decisions on educational matter and then assessing the consequences of those decisions. It is a process that involves more rational and logical problem solving efforts. It also involves intuition, emotion and passion etc. It is performative since the act of reflection can result in some improvement in practice. It may be expected that it leads to some action and change which is a presumptive feature of reflection. Reflective practice involves an objective analysis of the evidence on competing versions of events. Rogers (2002) summarised Dewey's four criteria of reflection they are:

- Reflection is a meaning making process that moves the learner form one experience into the next with deeper understanding of its relationship and connections with other experiences and ideas.
- It is systematic, rigorous and disciplined way of thinking with its roots in scientific inquiry.
- It needs to happen in community, in interaction with others.
- Requires attitude that values personal and intellectual growth of oneself and others.

Q18. Describe reflection as three level progression.

Ans. The three different levels of reflection- technical, practical and critical, originally identified by Van Manen (1977). These levels are differentiated not by the nature of the reflective process as much as by the differing objective of the reflection process and the epistemological perspective informing it, which influence the content of the reflection.

(1) **Technical Reflection:** Technical Reflection is the basic level of reflection that focuses on what works in the classroom. At this level, teachers are concerned with applying knowledge to achieve instrumental outcomes, and actions taken are evaluated on the basis of their success or failure in the classroom.

(2) **Practical Reflection:** Practical reflection is the next level of reflection that focuses on the learning experiences of the student. It goes beyond technical rationality and investigates questions and clarifies end objectives and assumptions held that inform teaching practice carried out to achieve those objectives.

(3) **Critical Reflection:** Critical reflection is the highest level of reflection. It focuses on the value of knowledge in the context that it is formed by. At this level, teachers go beyond and reflect upon the large context of education and critically question their teaching practices connection with ethical and moral issues and societal at large.

According to Schon, reflective practice involves thoughtfully considering one's own experiences in applying knowledge to practice while being coached by professionals in a discipline. Schon has identified three modes of reflection. These modes are as follow:

Reflection-in-action occurs when teachers are in the act of teaching. In order for teachers to be able to reflect-in-action they must, as Schon (1987: 30) has noted "exhibit a kind of knowledge-in-practice, most of which is tacit." knowing-in-practice is analogous to seeing and recognising a face in a crowd without "listing" and piecing together separate features. If anyone had to do this, it would be very difficult. Reflection-in-action begins with teachers experiencing some kind of internal dialogue where they access their thoughts and feelings while they are teaching (Schon, 1987). As Schon (1987:26) points out, "In the midst of action our thinking serves to reshape what we are doing while we are doing it [and] when we can still make a difference to the situation at hand".

Reflection-on-action (Schon 1983, 1987) differs from reflection-in-action as it is more delayed and happens further away from the classroom events. Here teachers reflect on events after the class, such as how instructions were given and understood, the impact of the lesson (what was learned, and what needs to be redone), how classroom communication either provided or blocked opportunities for learning, or many other different aspects of the classroom events that have occurred. Reflection-on-action can be undertaken by teachers with any level of experience and as such will be highlighted in this chapter through the broad lens of classroom observation. As a result of reflecting-on-action, teachers can consider adjusting their practice for future improvement, or their reflections-for-action.

Reflection-for-action is different from the previous notions of reflection, then, in that it is proactive in nature and can be the desired outcome of both reflection-in-action and reflection-on-action. Along with combining the knowledge gained from classroom observations during and after class, reflecting for action can also be facilitated through conducting action research projects on the results of the previous modes of reflection.

The main purpose, then, for reflecting on practice regardless of what stage of the Framework for Reflecting on Practice teachers begin reflections, teachers must know exactly what they do before they try to change anything.

Q19. Discuss the tri-layered reflective thinking model.

Ans. Van Manen (1977), Taggart and Wilson (1998) represented a pyramid model of reflection having three levels – technical, contextual, and dialectical. The reflective thinking pyramid "builds progressively from a basic general premise to a peak of reflection epitomised by individual autonomy and self-understanding".

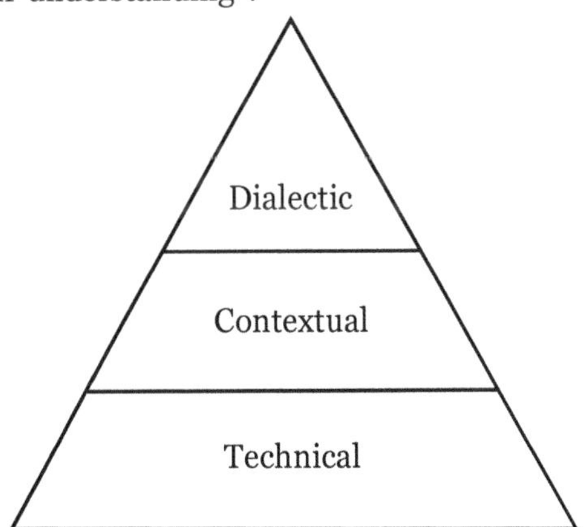

Fig 4.4: Pyramid Model of Reflective Thinking

Technical Reflection: The first level of reflection is technical reflection. When teachers face a problem at this level, they form a non-multiple dimension scheme of the problem. All reflections at the technical level are related to the determined educational outcomes and contain applications relating to teaching methods and behaviors. In their practices, while focusing on reaching the determined goals, they ignore alternative solutions, students' understanding, emotions, will, and characteristics. Through this mode of thinking, teachers can address curriculum, instruction, as well as diagnostic and control issues.

Contextual Reflection: The contextual level focuses on relating content to context and learner needs and the consideration of alternative practices. It deals with pedagogical issues and the non problematic level of technical reflection. Problems at this level motivate teachers to reflect on the contextual situation that may lead to understanding concepts, contexts, theoretical bases for classroom practice. This stage includes:

- Reflection on the context of the problem.
- Reflection on the practices that affect learning.
- Reflection on various alternatives.
- Reflection on relating theory to practice.

The contextual reflection deals with the pedagogical issues and relationship between theory and practice. An outcome for practitioner reflecting at this level may be context understanding with theoretical bases for classroom practices, then implementing those practices and articulating their relevance to learners' growth.

Dialectical Reflection: Van Manen (1977) highest level of reflection is the dialectical level. The dialectical-level of reflection is better than others. To reflect at this level means that educators are thinking critically about their practice including moral and ethical considerations, in order to make decisions. Evidence of reflection at this level includes systematically questioning one's own practice, suggesting convergent and divergent theories, reflection of both the decisions and the consequences of those decisions during action, considering moral, ethical, and sociopolitical issues on one's own practice, and the ability to express one's self with efficacy and self-confidence both verbally and in written communication. Dialectic reflection, therefore, includes:

- Reflect on decisions and consequences during the course of action.
- Suggest alternatives and competing theories.
- Bring moral, ethical, and socio-political issues for discussion.
- Systematically questioning practices.

Q20. Explain the approaches to reflective thinking.

Ans. Literature on reflective thinking describes three general approaches, which are given below:

(1) Cognitive Approach: The cognitive approach emphasizes decision-making based on information gathering and processing. Shulman (1987) has indentified six categories of knowledge; content pedagogy, curriculum, characteristic of learners, context and educational purposes, ends and aims. Later on, Shulman added a seventh category of teacher knowledge i.e. pedagogical content knowledge which encompasses the first three categories and refers how teachers portray important specific to their content. The cognitive approach emhasises how knowledge base is organised into networks of related facts, concepts, generalisations and experiences. These organised structures called Schemata', constitute the individual's comprehension of the world. Research findings indicate that the development of schemata is related to the experience of teachers and consequently the experienced teachers have more developed schema than the novice teachers. These schemas are, therefore, constructed through experiences of teachers with the help of the process of assimilation accommodation.

(2) **Critical Pedagogy Approach:** The critical approach focuses on problem framing using ethical and moral reasoning. Teacher experiences, values, sociopolitical implications, and goals from the benchmarks for decision-making. Critical approach is often considered in terms of critical pedagogy. Mc Larne (1989) stated that "critical pedagogy attempts to provide teachers and researchers with a better means of understanding the role that school actually play within a race, class and gender divided society." Teachers therefore need to visualise teaching as a process of inquiry and think about the long term effect of the techniques adopted for teaching for teaching on students' values and perceptions.

(3) **Narrative Approach:** The narrative approach uses personal narratives naturalistic inquiry, case studies, and action research to focus on circumstances under which decision-making takes place. Teachers create their own pedagogical principles as they describe, analyse, and make inferences about classroom events, from this experience the information gained is often tacit and difficult to analyse.

Q21. How can the teacher educator promote reflection when working with large group of trainee teachers?

Ans. Among teachers, reflective thinking may be promoted in different ways, like teacher narratives, maintaining reflective journals, discussions, collaborative group works, role-play, action research, thinking aloud, group buzz, questioning and brainstorming, etc.

Amongst these techniques, questioning is perhaps one of the oldest techniques that facilitates learners and teachers to meaningfully reflect on various aspects of issues under discussion which is otherwise ignored, assists learners in identification of issues, helps in value clarification and facilitates in development of deep insight into the problem etc.

(1) Teacher Narratives: According to Bruner, 1996, narrative has been considered as a mode of thinking and particularly valuable for presenting the richness of human experience. Through narratives human being play an active role in their knowledge construction. Teachers' own narratives on their experiences in the classroom are significant in developing reflection. Ershler (2001) accepts that one of the important learning models is to reflect on one's own experiences. One way of collecting 'data' about one's own experiences is by writing about daily experiences in the classroom. However, this reflection is not in a disroganised manner; Ershler has described the methodology of narrative reflection. The trainee teacher may be asked to describe different events or instances of his/her teaching practice. These experiences are shared with their peers who are part of learning group. In the next step, these narratives are discussed with the group members at length. Usually the teacher focuses on specific event that is being narrated and then effort is made to establish connections and observe the isolated event within a larger context. By listening to the experiences of others, the trainee teachers can live some experiences, while the narrators get an opportunity to 'step outside' of their own personal experiences and analyse themselves as any other teacher in a particular teaching learning situation. It helps them to see clearly their own strengths and weaknesses more objectively and improve accordingly. Narratives, by nature are social and rational and cannot be separated from the socio-cultural context in which they emerge. According to Syrjala and Estola (1999), narratives help pre-service teachers to connect their past, present and future selves with the hope of nurturing and strengthening their teaching voices.

(2) Reflective Journals: Reflective journal is a means of communication and conversation with oneself and the material, tutors, and peers. It helps to develop critical thinking, provides feedback and a platform to synthesis one's ideas and knowledge. Reflective journal, like the diary record experiences and event over a period of time. It provides opportunity for trainee teachers to reflect on their own classroom behavior as well as other minor incidents of their School Experience Programme (SEP). Reflective journals are important tools for helping trainee teachers to better understand their pedagogical reasoning in relation to teaching and learning experiences. Journal writing helps them to:

- highlight critical issues that may not have been considered by them at the time of the class.
- reflect on and develop insight into the purpose of school experiences programmes.
- reflect on one's own strengths and weaknesses.

Reflective journal helps trainee teachers to become aware of the gaps in their knowledge and skills, and provides feedback, as well as future directions based of one's experiences. There is no single way of writing a journal and that can be evolved in numerous ways and the entries in the reflective journal may include:

- Make note of the concepts, and questions and confusions which are coming in mind.
- Record new insights and problem solving strategies in a creative and innovative way.
- Explore possible solution to problems being raised in the classroom.
- Some thoughts that are not fully conceptualised and need further clarification.
- Brief summary of lecture, practice teaching, lab activity, group discussion, or reading material, etc.

- Reflect upon these activities record our own thoughts, ideas, responses, and reactions to these.
- Important events of school experience/internship.

One can augment learning when trainee are encouraged to reflect on learning event and use their own judgment about the content and process of learning. If reinforces reflection-in-action as the trainee teachers develop better understanding of integration between theory and practice. It also develops self-awareness or meta cognition, orientation toward open-mindedness, and willingness to accept responsibility for self-directed learning besides developing a keen sense of observation, critical thinking, and reasoned analysis. Some of the useful phrases of reflective writing include I think...I felt...I was aware...I now think...I was uncomfortable about... and looking back, etc.

(3) Discussions: It is a basic tool of teaching, in which the teacher tries to create understanding by providing opportunity to student teachers for exchanging information, opinions, or experiences while working towards a common goal. The facilitator (teacher educator) observes and encourages group discussion without being directly involved. One of the approaches in discussion that is useful in developing reflective thinking among learners is *Brainstorming* which helps the trainee teachers to freely share their views and encourage uninhabited participation of learners.

(4) Cooperative Learning: Cooperative learning is a successful teaching strategy in which small teams, each with students of different levels of ability, use a variety of learning activities to improve their understanding of a subject. It can improve individual's achievement more than the traditional approaches of instruction, if implemented effectively, which also ensures high learner motivation, active involvement and more time on various tasks. However, in order to be effective it has to be well planned and systematically executed by the teacher. In cooperative group, every learner has a specific task and everyone is involved in learning. The essential components of cooperation are positive interdependence, face-to-face interaction, individual and group accountability, interpersonal and small group skills and group processing. Therefore, it is essential to judiciously structure these elements in cooperative group work to ensure learning. To be effective cooperative learning must include group goals, individual accountability, and equal opportunity for success. Cooperative learning helps to produce:

- Higher achievement.
- Increased retention.
- More positive relationships and a wider circle of friends.
- Greater intrinsic motivation.
- Higher self-esteem.
- Greater social support.
- More on-task behavior.
- Better attitudes toward teachers.
- Better attitudes toward school.

(5) Role play: Role play *is* a technique that allows students to explore realistic situations by interacting with other people in a managed way in order to develop experience and trial different strategies in a supported environment. It is a part of reflective teaching. The idea of role play in its simplest from is that of asking someone to imagine that they are either themselves or another person in a particular situation. They are then asked to behave exactly as they feel that persons would. As a result of doing this they, and rest of the participants learn something about person or situation. Situations for role play may be simple or elaborate, familiar or strange. They may be described in detail or left to the imagination of the role player. Participants in role play can be made to relive a particular work situation, so that they can get the real feel of the roles they are called upon to play. The experience enhances their knowledge and helps them understand the behaviour of others as well as their own emotions and feeling. Some advantages of role play are as follows:

- Students immediately apply content in a relevant, real world context.
- Students take on a decision making persona that might let them diverge from the confines of their normal self-imposed limitations or boundaries.
- Students can transcend and think beyond the confines of the classroom setting.
- Students see the relevance of the content for handling real world situations.
- The instructor and students receive immediate feedback with regard to student understanding of the content.
- Students engage in higher order thinking and learn content in a deeper way.
- Instructors can create useful scenarios when setting the parameters of the role play when real scenarios or contexts might not be readily available.
- Typically, students claim to remember their role in these scenarios and the ensuing discussion long after the semester ends.

Q22. Define a profession. What are its important characteristics? Discuss.

Ans. The word profession has been defined as an occupation that can claim exclusive technical competence and also adheres to ethics of professional conduct. Elsewhere, a profession is being defined as a calling in which one professed to have acquired special knowledge used by either instructing, guiding or advising others or serving them in some art. Examples of professionals are lawyers, doctors, engineers, accountants, architects, quantity surveyors, etc. These professions have quality control measures and compulsory registration of their members.

Profession is an essentially contested concept. According to Saundres, "A profession is based upon specialised intellectual study and training, the main purpose of which is to supply skilled service and advice to others for a definite fee or service." To quote Cogan, "the profession, serving the vital needs of man, considers its first ethical imperative to be altruistic service to the client." From this, we can say that a profession requires a high degree of a general and specialised knowledge along with it a specialised intellectual training to provide a unique social service.

Hoyle and John (1995) suggested that there is considerable evidence that 'professions are more easily instanced than defined'. Further, Hoyle and John state that in reality then term 'professional' hides a multiplicity of perspectives:

"The unitary notion of a 'professional community' masks a vast array of competing positions which characterise a service profession such as teaching. In this sense, the role of a teacher is never static but is constantly changing according to the particular educational traditions that predominate at any particular historical juncture."

The term profession is seen and understood as both a concept-in-use and a theoretical underpinning. Hoyle defines a profession as the one that:

- performs a crucial social function;
- demands considerable skills for use in routine and especially non-routine situations;
- required its members to draw on a body of systematic knowledge;
- requires its members to undertake a lengthy period of study which inculcates professional values;
- focuses on clients' interests and has a code of ethics;
- enables professionals to make their own judgements vis-a-vis appropriate practice; and
- rewards training responsibility and client centredness, with high prestige and high levels of remuneration.

According to Hema Raghavan, professional is one who extends his chosen pursuit to benefit fellow beings and his work is marked by humanistic values and devotion to human development and welfare. Garrett and Bowles (1997) also focused on the following three aspects of being professional in education:

- a professional will have undergone a lengthy period of professional training in a body of abstract knowledge (Goode 1960; Hughes 1985; Coulson 1986) and will have experience in the field;
- a professional is controlled by a code of ethics and professional values (Barber 1963, 1978; Huges 1985; Coluson 1986); and
- a professional is committed to the core business of the organisation, i.e. the quality of student learning (Coulson 1986).

Characteristics of a profession: A true profession must have the following characteristics:

(1) Knowledge acquired after a period of specialized intellectual study and training essential for the practice of an occupation.

(2) Controlled entry into the occupation.

(3) A code of conduct to guide the behaviour of the members of the profession.

(4) A strong professional organisation, which guides the interest of its members as well as codifies the entire professional framework.

(5) Independence and freedom a practice without any interference.

A professional must possess knowledge required to practice his occupation. This knowledge must be of a specialized type, which is acquired after a specified period of training. Furthermore, entry into the profession must be controlled. This is done by specifying the pre-requisite for entry into training, the probable duration of training, the basic knowledge required for the practice of the occupation and the minimum qualification for one to be admitted into the occupation.

A profession generally has some ideals. There is therefore a code of conduct clearly defined for members. Such code of conduct includes standard of practice taken as good by the profession. These ideals are expected to be strictly abided by the members. This means a professional must not only be professionally competent but must also be of unquestionable character. The professional is not expected to exploit the ignorance of his students but to use his knowledge to benefit them in the practice of his occupation. On the whole, a profession is a service occupation, where public interest supersedes that of the individual.

Houle has suggested that there are at least fourteen characteristics of profession. These are:

(1) Clarifying the defining function of the profession;
(2) A mastery of theoretical knowledge;
(3) The capacity to solve problems;
(4) Use of practical knowledge;
(5) Self-enhancement beyond professional specialism;
(6) Formal education and training;
(7) Credentialling;
(8) Creation of a subculture;
(9) Legal reinforcement;
(10) Acceptance by the public;
(11) Ethical practice;
(12) Penalties;
(13) Establishing relations to other occupations; and
(14) Establishing relations to clients.

Mcfarland has given five characteristics of profession as the existence of a body of knowledge or techniques, formalised methods of acquiring training and experience, the establishment of a representative organization with professionalisation as its goal, the formation of ethical codes for the guidance of conduct and the charges of fees based upon services but with due regard to priority of service over the desire for monetary reward.

Q23. Write down the characteristics of a teaching profession.

Ans. The characteristics of a teaching profession are following:

(1) **It essentially involves an intellectual operation:** Since teaching involves arousal of interest in teaching learning process, it requires an intellectual operation. The teacher evolves a suitable plan of action to carry out teaching by creating a conducive and supportive learning environment to

achieve the pre-specified objectives, i.e. bringing desirable changes in the behaviour of the learners. All the above are intellectual operations on the part of teacher. Therefore, teaching is essentially an intellectual operation and exercise.

(2) **It draws material from science:** Teaching is not only an art but also a science. As an art, it propels teachers to acquire some skills which are called "tricks of the trade". As such, a teacher needs to be trained properly in order to achieve some objectives. As a science, it goes through certain steps which are followed in the training of a teacher. He/she is well versed with the steps of teaching which go in a systematic way. Therefore, teaching is not a haphazard affair. It requires proper planning to reach the goal. It is a goal directed process.

(3) **It transforms raw material into a practical and definite end:** Learners are prospective raw-materials in teaching profession. They are prepared to teach with efficiency and effectiveness for the larger interest of society which has varied expectations. They are trained into a practical and definite end by means of providing right knowledge and practical training in teaching and other pedagogical courses.

(4) **It possesses an educationally communicable technique:** An important characteristics of teaching as a profession is its nature of science. As teaching is a science, teaching techniques are systematic and have certain steps to be followed. It is easily communicable for its wide application.

(5) **It tends towards self-organisation:** It demands sensitivity of personnel involved in teaching activities towards growth and development of profession. So they are self-organised by evolving a definite mechanism to sustain and promote the standards of teaching profession.

(6) **It essentially performs a social service:** A nation or a society marches forward on the track of development if teachers serve in a better manner to effect changes in various ways. Teaching infuses a sense of service in the minds of teachers, because teaching is essentially a social service. Self-interest recedes giving way to general interest. It accords high premium on social service-the crux of profession.

(7) **It has a lengthy period of study and training:** Another chief characteristic of teaching is that this profession requires a lengthy period of study and training. In other words, a person willing to take up this profession has to study for a number of years and acquire mastery over the contents of the subject matter. After this, he/she has to pursue training in teaching skill and method.

(8) **It has a high degree of autonomy:** Autonomy is free from any form of intervention. Any form of intervention in teaching activities is not brooked right from planning of activities,

identifying instructional objectives, development of curriculum, and transaction of curriculum, evaluating student's performance, framing of admission and promotion rules to organisation of co-curricular activities.

(9) **It is based upon a systematic body of knowledge:** Knowledge springs from different layers and spheres of life—social, political, historical, psychological, economic, cultural and religious. Teaching as a profession is based upon systematic body of knowledge emanated from different spheres of human life and activities.

(10) **It has a common code of ethics:** Teaching profession has a common code of ethics which guides the behaviour and conduct of teachers in their institutions and outside. A code of professional ethics is a charter of rights and duties for the protection of professional autonomy and freedom. This can ensure development of a high degree of recognition, regard and social status of the profession so that true professionalism emerges in the long run. He/she is committed to his/her profession in a true perspective.

(11) **It generates in-service growth:** In teaching profession, a teacher always learns at all stages of teaching. Learning does not stop. An extra-ordinary literary genius R.N. Tagore says, "A lamp can never light another lamp unless if continues to burn its own flame; a teacher can never truly teach unless he is still learning himself".

Q24. Define professional development. What are its needs for teachers?

Ans. Professional development refers to many types of educational experiences related to an individual's work. Doctors, lawyers, educators, accountants, engineers, and people in a wide variety of professions and businesses participate in professional development to learn and apply new knowledge and skills that will improve their performance on the job. In education, research has shown that teaching quality and school leadership are the most important factors in raising student achievement. For teachers and school and district leaders to be as effective as possible, they continually expand their knowledge and skills to implement the best educational practices. Educators learn to help students learn at the highest levels.

In India, NCF-2005 has brought radical changes in teaching-learning process. This has influenced role of teachers also. Many such policy changes have influenced teachers' role. Professional development of teachers does not include giving them only an opportunity to learn a new concept or adopt a new teaching learning methodology, rather it also focus on developing their competencies to deal with changing scenario of teaching learning process and adopt the best for the benefit of learners. Professional developing brings changes in teachers' approach, attitude, understanding and practice to enhance level of learning.

For teachers, a definition of professional Development is given below:

"The process by which... teachers review, renew and extend their commitment as change agents... and by which they acquire and develop critically the knowledge, skills, planning and practice... through each phase of their teaching lives." (Day, 1999:4)

Teacher's professional Development "is the body of systematic activities to prepare teachers for their job, including initial training, induction courses, in-service training and continuous professional development within school settings." (OECD, 2010)

Need of professional development for teachers are as follow:

- Focus of use of ICT
- Due to changing pedagogy
- Meeting demands of society and nation
- Increasing involvement of media
- Expanding knowledge domain of subjects
- Enactment of policies and schemes

Q25. What do you mean by the term continuous professional development? What are the needs of it?

Ans. Continuing professional development (CPD) is a process by which individuals take control of their own learning and development, by engaging in an on-going process of reflection and action. This process is empowering and exciting and can stimulate people to achieve their aspirations and move towards their dreams.

CPD combines different methodologies to learning, such as training workshops, conferences and events, e-learning programs, best practice techniques and ideas sharing, all focused for an individual to improve and have effective professional development.

The needs for continuous professional development are as follow:

(1) Updating Knowledge: Continuous professional development (CPD) as new knowledge helps teachers is being gained and used for improvement of knowledge. Not only in our subject areas, but also in teaching methodologies and technologies, new knowledge is emerging continuously. For example, teaching-learning process from behaviourist approach to constructivist approach. There are many more such new trends and developments. New discoveries and innovations are leading to increase in the corpus of knowledge base in various subjects. Knowledge domain of subjects ranging from languages to science, arts to social sciences is increasing day by day and a teacher has to be aware of these developments. Teachers cannot remain oblivious of these developments in our subject area. A well informed feels confident and is respected by his/her colleagues and the learners. A teacher can respond to the queries raised by learners in a better way in his/her field if s/he keeps him/herself abreast of the developments.

(2) Improving Classroom Practices: A good teacher is not only a facilitator of learning but is also a good communicator. S/he not only teaches but also learns from classroom experiences. S/he also tries to apply the emerging innovations, techniques and technologies to the teaching-learning process and thus improves his/her teaching learning process.

(3) Dealing with Emerging Challenges: Today, teachers are advised to use new methods of teaching and learning. They are also urged to integrate technology into the teaching and learning process. All these trends pose challenges to teachers. Managing the classroom without resorting to corporal punishment as a means for maintaining discipline, carrying out formative evaluation, teaching in inclusive classrooms and the like are also challenging. Challenges like dealing with diversity of learners in the classroom, ensuring gender, caste, class, ethnic, religious equity, making classroom inclusive, adopting positive discipline instead of corporal punishment, inculcation humane values and ensuring social justice, are to be faced by a teacher in today's classroom. Many teachers find it difficult to adopt these new practices. For example, some teachers who are into the traditional educational system for a long time do not feel comfortable with new technology and reluctant to shift to technology mediated teaching learning process.

(4) Professional Networking: Nowadays, it is the age of collaboration rather than competition and individual working. Teamwork, sharing of resources and networking enhance the capacity of individuals rather than grappling alone with problems. CPD also implies that teachers gain the ability and the attitude for cooperation and collaboration. Hence the ability for technology mediated networking for sharing information, ideas, and experiences, collaboration on projects, and so on is required. Professional networking is needed not only for educational benefits but also for discussing and reflecting collectively on professional issues. In such networked systems, more experienced knowledgeable colleagues can provide effective guidance and facilitation. Opportunities of CPD provide us with the ability for creating technology mediated network and using the network for benefitting professionally. Today's self-initiated efforts for professional development as life-long learning are also required.

Q26. Elaborate ICT for access to resources.

Ans. In teaching-learning process, Information Communication Technologies (ICTs) have become an essential part. ICT enhances learning opportunities and provides the user the flexibility regarding time and pace of learning.

The use of ICT for providing opportunities for CPD is described bellow:

Portal for Educational Purposes: SAKSHAT: Sakshat is a landmark initiative of the Ministry of Human Resource Development (MHRD) to develop a One Stop Education Portal for addressing all the education and learning related needs of students, scholars, teachers and lifelong learners. The portal envisages providing one stop solution to educational requirements of learners ranging from K to 20 covering all fields of study including vocational education and learning for life skills.

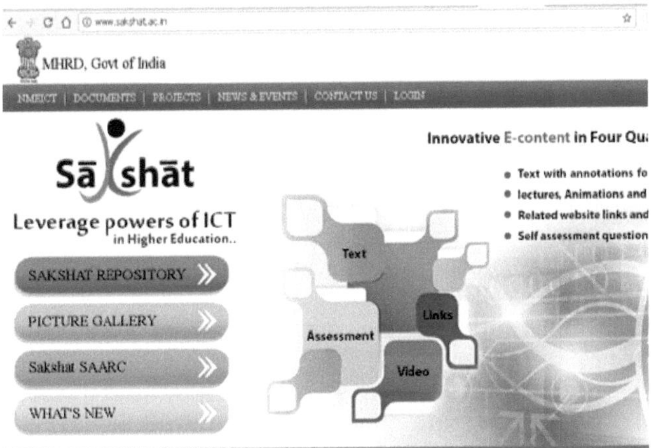

Fig. 4.5

The vision is to scale up this pilot project 'SAKSHAT' to cater to the learning needs of more than 50 crore people through a proposed scheme of 'National Mission in Education through Information and Communication Technology (ICT). The scheme is to provide connectivity to all institutions of higher learning to world of knowledge in the cyber space, to leverage the potential of ICT, in providing high quality knowledge modules with right e-contents, to address to the personalized needs of learners, in order to take care of their aspirations. These modules are to be delivered through 'SAKSHAT'. The scheme may also have a provision of certification of competencies of the human resources acquired through formal or non-formal means as also to develop and maintain the database of profile of human resources.

MOOCs for Teachers: MOOCs are open access courses that can be used for many purposes. They cover range of topics and often have thousands of students. In ICT based teaching learning one of the recent innovations are MOOCs. The philosophy underlying MOOCs visualises teaching and learning as a lifelong process. MOOCs are ICT based initiative in distance training programme, which have vide scope in teacher education, which provide ample opportunities for many people including teachers to get education. In developing countries MOOCs based teacher training is in initial stage like India and most of the initiatives are being taken by individuals and not by organisation. Most of the MOOCs teacher training programme are of capsular in nature and focused on basic ICT skills or Content enrichment issues but MOOCs have potential to develop as full-fledged teacher training medium in near future.

In 2016, MOOCs platform called SWAYAM has launched by MHRD and Government of India. SWAYAM stands for Study Webs of Active-learning for Young Aspiring Minds. MOOCs can best be utilised for continuums professional development of teachers. Organisations can initiate such projects or teachers can participate in any such course individually.

Using OER Repositories and NROER: India has launched a new learning repository for open educational resources (OER). OERs are basically the teaching and learning materials made available freely for everyone to use. Anyone, whether he/she is a teacher, a student, an educator, an educational administrator or a freelancer can get benefited by the content provided as OERs. Variety of content including texts, article, lesson plans, techniques and tools of learning and assessments, teacher made designs, laboratory manuals, text and reference books, pictorial quizzes, and many more resources in audio/video forms, picture graphs, etc., are available as OERs.

In teaching and learning the ideology of OER is in tune with collaborative and cooperative nature OREs are providing an opportunity to assess quality content to learners and teachers without much investment of time and money. There are many OERs platforms in various institutions but two indigenous models of OERs are One is of National Institute of Open Schooling (NIOS) and other is the National Repository of Open Educational Resources (NROER) being managed by NCERT, New Delhi. For various purposes, teachers can use these OERs.

Q27. Discuss the use of ICTs for interaction and collaboration.

And. Today, ICTs are being used for interaction and collaboration in following manner:

Wiki: Wikipedia is a free online encyclopedia with the aim to allow anyone to edit articles. Wikipedia is the largest and most popular general reference work on the Internet and is ranked among the ten most popular websites. The nonprofit Wikimedia Foundation owns Wikipedia.

It is very interesting and useful web application where people can add, modify, or delete content in collaboration with others. Teachers can use a number of wiki pages available for knowledge updating in their specific field.

WiKi provides opportunity to not only share content but also can post audio, video, pictures, graphs and can give hyperlinks also to other WiKi pages as well as other websites.

We can start an article at http://en.wikpedia.org/wiki/Wikipedia:Starting_an_article or we can attend some WiKi Tutorials. We can practice on some freely available pages like Create our wiki now at http://www.wiki-site.com/index.php/Create_your_wiki_now or at http://www.wikia.com/Special:CreateNewWiKi. There are some good tutorials for editing, formatting, links, citation, etc. available at http:/en.Wikipedia.org/wiki/Wikipedia:Tutorial. We can read and practice after that.

Blogs and Discussion Forums: For people blogs provide a great way including teachers to share experiences, ideas and content like lesson plans, classroom management tactics and other helpful tips. There are blogs on various issues related to teaching and teacher. Some of them focus on specific issues or subjects while some are comprehensive in nature.

Today, we can many Blogs on ideas for classroom management, sharing of learning material, for engaging learners, etc. Subject focused blogs helps us to keep updated on particular topics, allowing teachers who need a refresher to quickly glean important facts about historic events and figures.

There are many popular blogs on various aspects of education. If we visit these blogs, we will find that teaches from all around the globe are sharing their experience, content, methods and teaching learning experiments through these blogs with teaching community. Make a habit to visit and follow such blogs, which are beneficial for us not only in knowledge updating but also in sharing and experiencing new ideas and innovation in teaching and learning.

Discussion Groups and Forums: Another use of ICT is for creating discussion groups and forums. Some discussion groups focus on a theme like problems of teachers, or that of teachers of specific subject groups. Online discussion groups and forums are dedicated online platforms where in closed group people post, share and discuss some issue.

People by posting a block add their comments of text to the group. Others can then comment and respond. Discussion groups differ from chartrooms and instant messaging because they usually deal with one topic and personal exchanges are typically discouraged. Discussion groups are often archived. These archives may be organised by thread, which means all the messages that reply to a starting message can be read in some order.

In common platform these discussion groups are providing to like-minded teachers to share, debate, discuss and enrich their knowledge and sharpen their skills.

Q28. Write short note on followings:

(i) Social networking

Ans. Social networking is the use of internet-based social media programs to make connections with friends, family, classmates, customers and clients. Social networking can occur for social purposes, business purposes or both through sites such as Facebook, Twitter, LinkedIn, Classmates.com and Yelp. Social networking is also a significant target area for marketers seeking to engage users. In present times, Social media is one of the most influential innovations.

(ii) E-conferences and Webinars

Ans. In professional development, teachers are aware of role of seminars and conferences. Such events to interact with other people of our field not only provide us opportunity but also provide us an opportunity to share our experiences and get benefited from experiments and experiences of our colleagues from various institutions.

Traditional conferences and seminars have transformed accordingly with the advancement of ICTs. Now-a-days E-conferences and Webinars have been replacing traditional ones. There are a number of web portals providing opportunity to participate in e-conferences and webinars.

There are major benefits of E-Conferences and Webinars as follow:

- Participant can contribute from their work place.
- No restriction on number of participant due to virtual space.
- Every participant can share his/her views with all and get immediate feedback, comment on the post.

- The whole proceeding for future use could be archived.
- Synchronous and asynchronous communication is possible. Recorded Sessions are available for future reference.
- People of their own benefit can figure and the activity.
- Boundaries and limitations through these events like regional, national or international are dissolved. Teachers and educationists from many countries can contribute and share their work at one platform.

The main aim of GPH book is to provide knowledge as well as good marks in exam.

HERE, 'WILL' is THE ONLY THING NEEDED TO BECOME AN 'AUTHOR'
We, at Gullybaba, will guide you at every step of self-publishing of your book and promote this at Global level.
amazon.in amazon.com flipkart.com
SHOPCLUES.com paytm kindle direct publishing
Call: 8130886000 or Visit: Gullybaba

Question Papers

BES-123: LEARNING AND TEACHING
June, 2017

Note: All questions are compulsory. All questions carry equal weightage.

Q1. Answer the following question in about 600 words:

What do you understand by "approaches to learning"? Discuss any one behaviourist approach and its classroom implications.

Ans. Refer to Chapter-1, Q.No.-9 and Q.No.-12

Or

What are they key factors of motivation? Discuss the role of motivation in promoting learning.

Ans. Refer to Chapter-2, Q.No.-13 and Q.No.-15

Q2. Answer the following question in about 600 words:

What do you mean by "reflection"? What techniques would you suggest to develop reflection among teachers?

Ans. Refer to Chapter-4, Q.No.-17 and Q.No.-21

Or

Why is it important to manage behavioural problems in a classroom? Discuss some supportive and corrective measures to overcome the behavioural problems that you would like to adopt in your classroom.

Ans. Refer to Chapter-3, Q.No.-47

Q3. Answer any four of the following questions in about 150 words each:

(a) Explain the various types of intelligence identified by Gardner with suitable examples.

Ans. Refer to Chapter-2, Q.No.-9

(b) Discuss the various ways to foster creativity among learners.

Ans. Refer to Chapter-2, Q.No.-18

(c) Explain the nature of learning.

Ans. Refer to Chapter-1, Q.No.-1

(d) How does situated learning take place? Give suitable examples.

Ans. Refer to Chapter-1, Q.No.-31

(e) Discuss the role of a teacher as a manager of education.

Ans. Refer to Chapter-4, Q.No.-7

(f) How does ICT support in professional development of a teacher?

Ans. ICTs have become an essential part of whole teaching learning process. ICT enhances learning opportunities and provides the user the flexibility regarding time and pace of learning.

We are now increasingly witnessing 'second-generation' ICTs in schools programmes, in which the programme design and implementation is being done by teachers and educationists, keeping in mind larger educational aims over narrow technology literacy goals. Such programmes duly consider the educational contexts as well as principles of curriculum and pedagogy, and have been able to obtain the ownership of schools and the commitment of teachers to integrate digital processes and methods into their own professional development as well as in their transactions with students. These programmes support the agency of the teacher and the learner, by enabling a social constructivist digital environment founded on the use of free software and digital content.

Various educational portals like SAKSHAT, MOOCs, etc. have also been launched which help at greater level in professional development of a teacher. ICTs are also playing important role in interaction and collaboration in education. Social networking and Blogs and discussion forums have importance place in professional development of teachers.

Q4. Answer the following question in about 600 words:
As a teacher at the secondary level, what factors would you consider for instructional planning? Prepare a unit plan on any topic of your choice from secondary level using concept map.

Ans. **Sample of a Unit Plant**

(1) Subject/Course : Social Studies (Geography)
(2) Unit : The Solar System
(3) Class/Target Group : 6th
(4) Entry Behaviour of Students:

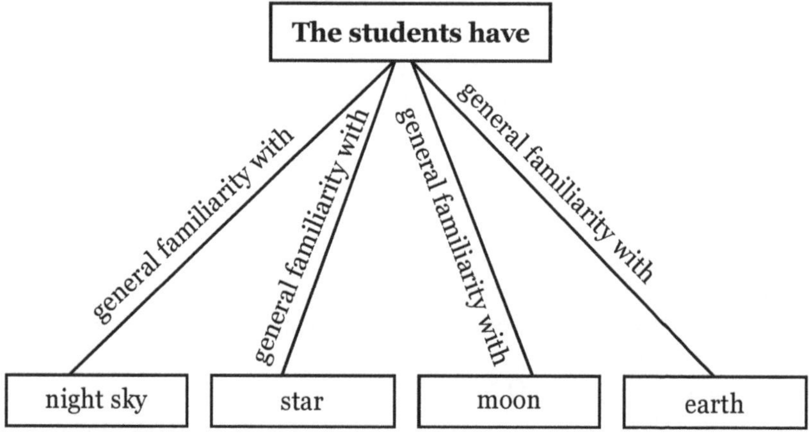

(5) Major objective of the Unit:

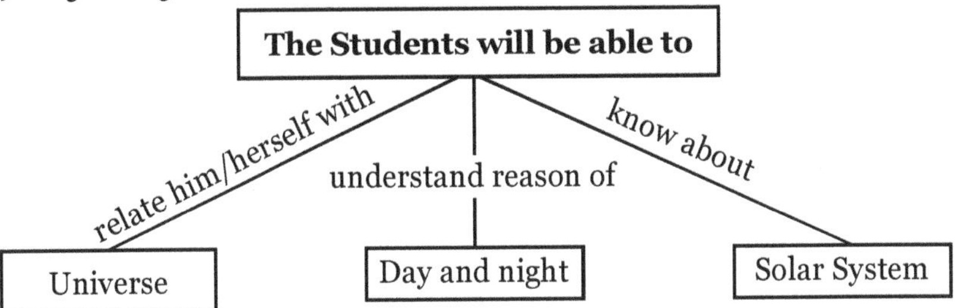

(6) Overview of the theme of the Unit: The sun, eight planets, satellites and some other celestial bodies known as asteroids and meteoroids form the solar system. We often call it a solar family, with the sun as its Head.

(7) Details of the Unit Plan

(8) References

Foundation Course, FST-1: Foundation Course in Science and Technology, Block-3, Universe and Life: The Beginning, New Delhi: IGNOU

GPH Panel of Experts (2014), Lesson Plan, Social Science, New Delhi: Gullybaba Publishing House, Pvt. Ltd.

(9) Evaluation/Assignment

(i) What do Solar System consist?
(ii) What is the distance of the sun in km away from the sun?
(iii) Why is Venus considered as 'Earth's-twin'?
(iv) Why the Earth is called a blue planet?

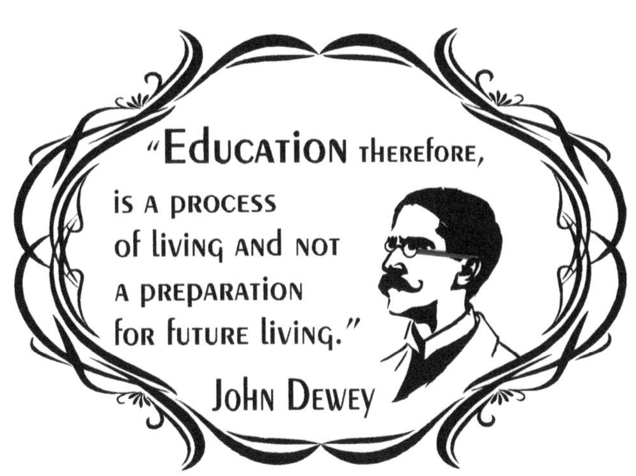

BES-123: LEARNING AND TEACHING
December, 2017

Note: All questions are compulsory. All questions carry equal weightage.

Q1. Answer the following question in about 600 words.

What do you understand by 'Cognitive approach to learning"? Discuss various steps suggested by Jean Piaget for learning.

Ans. Refer to Chapter-1, Q.No.-13 and Q.No.-15

Or

What is aptitude? How does it differ from attitude? Why should a teacher know about learner's aptitude?

Ans. Refer to Chapter-2, Q.No.-16 and Q.No.-17

Q2. Answer the following question in about 600 words.

What do you mean by classroom management? Discuss various factors influencing classroom management.

Ans. Refer to Chapter-3, Q.No.-41 and Q.No.-43

Or

Discuss characteristics and stages of inquiry based instruction with suitable examples.

Ans. Refer to Chapter-3, Q.No.-21 and Q.No.-22

Q3. Answer any four of the following questions in about 150 words each:

(a) Explain the role of a teacher as a facilitator of education.

Ans. Refer to Chapter-4, Q.No.-5

(b) Explain the various types of differently abled learners.

Ans. The various types of differently abled learners are as:

(i) Learners with mental retardation

(ii) Learners with hearing impairment

(iii) Learners with visual impairment

(iv) Specific learning disabilities

Now, Refer to Chapter-2, Q.No.-4, Q.No.-5 and Q.No.-6

(c) Discuss various learning styles with suitable examples.

Ans. Refer to Chapter-1, Q.No.-5

(d) Explain various elements of observational learning.

Ans. Refer to Chapter-1, Q.No.-30

(e) "Teaching is a complex activity". Justify the statement.

Ans. Teaching is a complex activity that is challenging both intellectually and emotionally. It requires knowledge about the subject being taught, the curriculum, appropriate teaching and learning strategies and about the abilities, interests and personalities of the learners. Teachers' practice is informed by the many and varied events that they will have experienced. The knowledge used in practice often becomes 'second nature' as individual teaching styles that depend on both routines and flexibility are developed. Knowledge about teaching is also distributed amongst members of the profession with individuals adopting different positions in their approaches to teaching and learning.

It follows that supporting student teachers as they learn to teach is also a complex and challenging activity. Developing expertise ('knowledge in practice') in teaching involves analysing experience and values which make it very different from other forms of learning in academic life which focus on more abstract types of knowledge. Student teachers will bring with them much experience of 'being taught' and will conceptualise 'learning to teach' in various different ways.

(f) Mention the steps of 5-E Approach of lesson planning.

Ans. Refer to Chapter-3, Q.No.-16

Q4. Answer the following question in about 600 words.

Explain various steps of action research with the help of a problem that you have faced in your class. How will you conduct this action research?

Ans. Same as Chapter-4, Q.No.-15 and Q.No.-16

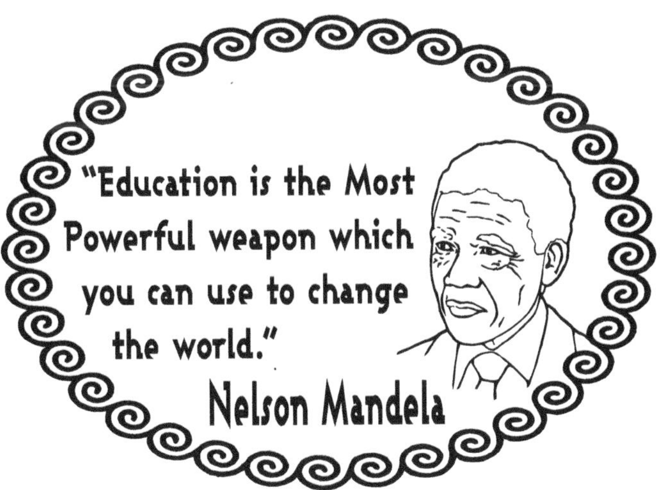

BES-123: LEARNING AND TEACHING
June, 2018

Note: (i) All questions are compulsory. (ii) All questions carry equal weightage.

Q1. Answer the following question in about 600 words.
What do you understand by transfer of learning? Discuss various types of transfer of learning. Support your answer with suitable example and also discuss their classroom implications.

Or

What is aptitude? How does it differ from attitude? Discuss various components of aptitude. Give suitable examples also.

Q2. Answer the following question in about 600 words.
What are various learner centred methods of teaching-learning? Discuss any one in details and explain how will you use it in your classroom.

Or

What do you mean by "Action research"? Identify a problem and develop an action-research proposal.

Q3. Answer any four of the following in 150 words each:

(a) What are various learning styles? Explain briefly with the help of suitable examples.

(b) How will you create a constructive learning environment in your classroom?

(c) Discuss role of a teacher as motivator.

(d) What are important characteristics of teaching profession?

(e) Discuss need of continuous professional development for teachers.

(f) Discuss various factors influencing classroom management.

Q4. Answer the following question in about 600 words.
What do you understand by 5-Es? Select a topic of your choice from class IX and write a lesson plan based on 5-E approach.

BES-123: LEARNING AND TEACHING

June, 2019

Note: All questions are compulsory. All questions carry equal weightage.

Q1. Answer the following question in about 600 words:
How is learning different from teaching and imprinting? Discuss the nature of learning with suitable examples.

Or

What do you understand by active learning? Discuss various strategies for promoting active learning in your class.

Q2. Answer the following question in about 600 words:
Discuss the role of a teacher as a manager in different phases of teaching.

Or

Explain the concept of reflection. Discuss the techniques you will adopt to develop yourself as a reflective teacher.

Q3. Answer any four of the following questions in 150 words each:

(a) Discuss various factors affecting socio-cultural diversity among learners.

(b) Discuss the role of intelligence in learning.

(c) How do individuals differ in creativity? Discuss with suitable examples.

(d) Explain 'teaching' as a morally laden activity.

(e) Discuss various criticisms of behaviourist approach to lesson planning.

(f) Discuss various supportive measures for managing the behavioural problems of learners.

Q4. Answer the following question in about 600 words:
Identify a topic, which you would like to deal by using problem solving approach.
Explain the various steps of problem solving approach by taking the example of the topic identified by you.

BES-123: LEARNING AND TEACHING
December, 2019

Note: All questions are compulsory. All questions carry equal weightage.

Q1. Answer the following question in about 600 words:

What is Motivation? Explain various approaches to motivation and discuss its role in learning with suitable examples.

Or

Highlight the recommendations of various policies for in-service education of teachers. Discuss the role of in-service teacher training as professional development activity for teachers with the help of suitable examples.

Q2. Answer the following question in about 600 words:

How will you use cognitive apprenticeship as constructivist tool for developing higher order skills in your learners? Discuss with suitable examples.

Or

How will you use collaborative learning strategies in your classroom? Discuss with suitable examples.

Q3. Answer any four of the following in about 150 words each:

(a) Explain various types of transfer of learning.

(b) What are the various types of learners?

(c) Explain Tri-layer reflective thinking model'.

(d) Discuss the role of a teacher as planner.

(e) Discuss various factors affecting use of ICT in classroom.

(f) Differentiate Unit planning and Lesson planning.

Q4. Answer the following question in about 600 words:

Identify a problem based on your classroom experience and prepare an action research proposal on it.

BES-123: LEARNING AND TEACHING
June, 2020

Note: All questions are compulsory. All questions carry equal weightage.

Q1. Answer the following question in about 600 words:
Why is it important for a teacher to manage time in the classroom? Suggest some ways to improve the time management skill.

Ans. Refer to Chapter-3, Q.No.-48 and Q.No.-49

Or

What is team teaching? Discuss its characteristics, advantages and disadvantages.

Ans. Refer to Chapter-3, Q.No.-20

Q2. Answer the following question in about 600 words:
Differentiate between intrinsic extrinsic motivation. Discuss the ways you will adopt to motivate your learners in your class.

Ans. Refer to Chapter-2, Q.No.-13

Or

Define Creativity. How can you faster creativity among your learners? Explain with the help of examples.

Ans. Refer to Chapter-2, Q.No.-18

Q3. Answer any four of the following questions in about 150 words each:

(a) Explain VARK model of learning styles with suitable example.

Ans. Refer to Chapter-1, Q.No.-5

(b) Explain Maslow's hierarchy of needs.

Ans. Refer to Chapter-1, Q.No.-19

(c) Discuss spiritual intelligence.

Ans. Refer to Chapter-2, Q.No.-8

(d) Explain the leadership roles of teacher.

Ans. Refer to Chapter-4, Q.No.-6

(e) Explain the need of professional development for teachers.

Ans. Refer to Chapter-4, Q.No.-24

(f) Discuss the context specific approach to instruction.

Ans. Refer to Chapter-3, Q.No.-31

Q4. Answer the following question in about 600 words:

Identify problem from the subject of your choice from secondary level curriculum. Explain, how problem solving approach that can help you deal with that problem.

Ans. Refer to Chapter-3, Q.No.-23 and Q.No.-24

BES-123: LEARNING AND TEACHING
February, 2021

Note: All questions are compulsory. All questions carry equal weightage.

Q1. Answer the following question in about 600 words:
Explain various types of differently-abled learners. Also discuss your role as a teacher in helping such learners.

Ans. Refer to Dec-2017, Q.No.-3(b)

Or

What do you understand by curiosity? Discuss strategies to promote curiosity among your learners.

Ans. Refer to Chapter-2, Q.No.-21

Q2. Answer the following question in about 600 words:
How do group-centred techniques facilitate learning? Discuss the process of brainstorming method with help of a classroom example.

Ans. The classroom normally connotes to a group. It means, as a regular feature, teacher adopts group centered method of instruction rather than individual centered. As a result, majority of times instead of facilitating the classroom interactions, teacher takes control over it and transmits the information to the learners without having any understanding whether learners are able to absorb it. What are the needs of the learners? Do they already possess some knowledge related to the content which has been delivered? This mistake often takes place when we equate our classroom as a group of learners which is actually not true.

Teachers who are of the view that they are teaching to group of learners (classroom) have mistaken the very concept of group. Group always connotes set of individuals that have special characteristics and are limited in numbers. When we say group centered instruction, it means teaching-learning process takes place within the few members who are part of the group. In group centered instructions teacher has the minimal role. Teacher assigns the activity to learners, which needs to be completed by them. It is the responsibility of the group members to plan, organize, manage and execute all the tasks. The role of teacher is to act as more of a facilitator, mentor or guide. The task will be completed under teacher direction. It does not mean that teacher regularly interferes in the activity. The autonomy and the accountability of the learner is key for group centered instruction. Depending upon the task or activity, the group can be small or big in size. Within the group centered instruction following are commonly used in the classroom by teachers and are described below:

Now, Refer to Chapter-3, Q.No.-25

Or

Why is it important to understand learners' need for classroom management? Explain various principles of classroom management with suitable examples.

Ans. Refer to Chapter-3, Q.No.-41 and Q.No.-42

Q3. Answer any four of the following question in about 150 words each:

(a) Explain Pavlov's Classical Conditioning.

Ans. Refer to Chapter-1, Q.No.-11

(b) Discuss Social Constructivism with the help of an example.

Ans. Refer to Chapter-1, Q.No.-21

(c) Define the concept of Intelligence Quotient.

Ans. Refer to Chapter-2, Q.No.-8

(d) Explain Jigsaw technique with the help of an example.

Ans. Jigsaw: A Jigsaw is a puzzle type activity (like rubrics) where learners are grouped into teams to solve a problem. This strategy involves learners becoming "experts" on one aspect of a topic, and then sharing their expertise with others. These can be done in one of two ways – either each team works on completing a different portion of the assignment and then contributes their knowledge to the class as a whole, or within each group, one learner is assigned to a portion of the assignment (the jigsaw comes from the bringing together of various ideas at the end of the activity to produce a solution to the problem). First divide a topic into a few constitutive parts ("puzzle pieces"). After that, form sub-groups of 3-5 learners and assign each sub-group a different "piece" of the topic (or, if the class is large, assign two or more sub-groups to each subtopic).

Each group's task is to develop expertise on its particular sub-topic through brainstorming, developing ideas, and if time permits, researching. Once learners have become experts on a particular sub-topic, shuffle the groups so that the members of each new group have a different area of expertise. Learners then take turns sharing their expertise with the other group members, thereby creating a completed "puzzle" of knowledge about the main topic. A convenient way to assign different areas of expertise is to distribute handouts of different colours.

For the first stage of the group work, groups are composed of learners with the same colour of handout; for the second stage, each member of the newly formed groups must have a different colour of handout. The jigsaw helps to avoid tiresome plenary sessions because most of the information is shared in small groups.

This method can be expanded by having learners develop expertise about their sub-topics first through independent research outside of class. Then, when they meet with those who have the same subtopic, they can clarify and expand on their expertise before moving on to a new group. One potential drawback is that learners hear only one group's expertise on a particular topic and don't benefit as much from the insight of the whole class. To address this issue, you could collect a written record of each group's work and create a master document—a truly complete puzzle—on the topic. The advantages of the jigsaw include the ability to explore substantive problems or readings, the engagement of all learners with the material and in the process of working together, learning from each other, and sharing and critically analyzing a diversity of ideas.

(e) Explain the use of ICTs for interaction and collaboration.

Ans. Refer to Chapter-4, Q.No.-27

(f) Discuss various approaches to reflective thinking.

Ans. Refer to Chapter-4, Q.No.-20

Q4. Answer the following question in about 600 words:
Identify a classroom problem on which you can conduct an action research. Prepare an action research proposal on it.

Ans. Refer to Chapter-4, Q.No.-15 and Q.No.-16

BES-123: LEARNING AND TEACHING
June, 2021

Note: (i) All questions are compulsory. (ii) All questions carry equal weightage.

Q1. Answer the following question in about 600 words:
What is cognitive approach to learning? Discuss stages of cognitive development suggested by Piaget.

Ans. Refer to Chapter-1, Q.No.-13 and Q.No.-15

Or

Explain the process of cognitive apprenticeship with an example from your classroom situation.

Ans. Refer to Chapter-1, Q.No.-25

Q2. Answer the following question in about 600 words:
How will you use classroom as learning resource for teaching-learning? Explain with the help of an example.

Ans. Refer to Chapter-3, Q.No.-35

Or

What do you understand by Reflection? Discuss modes of reflection suggested by Schon with examples.

Ans. Refer to Chapter-4, Q.No.-17 and Q.No.-18

Q3. Answer any four of the following questions in about 150 words each:

(a) How can you use OERs for professional development?

Ans. Refer to Chapter-4, Q.No.-26

(b) Discuss various types of learning disabilities.

Ans. Refer to Chapter-2, Q.No.-6

(c) How does personality affect learning?

Ans. Refer to Chapter-2, Q.No.-10 and Q.No.-11

(d) Explain various types of transfer of learning.

Ans. Refer to Chapter-1, Q.No.-8

(e) Discuss elements of observational learning.

Ans. Refer to Chapter-1, Q.No.-30

(f) How can you manage your classroom time?

Ans. Refer to Chapter-3, Q.No.-48

Q4. Answer the following question in about 600 words:
How is behaviourist lesson planning different from constructivist lesson planning? Prepare a lesson plan on any topic of your choice using constructivist approach to lesson planning.

Ans. Refer to Chapter-3, Q.No.-14 and Q.No.-16

BES-123: LEARNING AND TEACHING
December, 2021

Note: (i) All questions are compulsory. (ii) All questions carry equal weightage.

Q1. Answer the following question in about 600 words:
Explain learning as a social construct. Discuss various modes of learning with suitable examples.

Ans. Refer to Chapter-1, Q.No.-4 and Q.No.-7

Or

Enlist major tenets of humanistic approach to learning. Discuss contribution of Maslow towards humanistic approach.

Ans. Humanists think learning as the way in which the individuals develop a unique way of controlling their environment and attaining the best potential. Humanistic approach is based on humanism, which is a philosophy of Man-ism or Human being-ism, concerned with human and humane interests, characteristically human, not supernatural belonging to human beings and not to external nature, raising a human being to his/her greatest potential or giving him/her as a human being, the greatest satisfaction.

The major tenets of the humanistic approach are given below:

- Humanistic psychologists view learning as a process that is inevitable and unique for every individual
- Human beings concerns -what a human being ought to be
- An individual can distinguish between herself/himself and her/his environment and is inherently capable of taking responsible decision and learning effectively
- A child is capable of learning. Let it learn with love and peace (without any external pressure).
- Human beings possess the power or potential of solving problems through reasons courage, reason vision and human virtues.

Now, Refer to Chapter-1, Q.No.-19

Q2. Answer the following question in about 600 words:
What is creativity? Discuss various strategies to foster creativity among your learners.

Ans. Refer to Chapter-2, Q.No.-18

Or

Discuss the need of Continuous Professional Development (CPD) for school teachers. How ICT can be used for CPD? Explain.

Ans. Refer to Chapter-4, Q.No.-25 and Q.No.-26

Q3. Write notes on any four of the following in about 150 words each:

(a) Role of socio-cultural context of learners in teaching-learning process

Ans. Refer to Chapter-2, Q.No.-1

(b) Factors affecting learning of learners

Ans. The diversity among learners is not only in their social conditions or cultural backgrounds but also in their learning styles, needs, aspirations and attitude. How did this diversity emerge? This question needs to be answered by the teacher; as a teacher, you should be aware of the factors which may make a difference in the learning of learners. A few are as follows:

Family Structure

Diversity in family structure also affects the learner's learning. For example, the learners who belong to nuclear families may have lower learning outcomes. It is assumed that in nuclear families, increased responsibilities on learners such as childcare roles, domestic duties impede in the time available for school work and the parents also have less time to spend with their children and to supervise their school work. As a result, they may show low learning performances. Whereas in a joint family, parents spend more time with their children as they have helping hands in their family. So the learners who belong to joint family may show higher learning performances.

Type of School

Apart from the family structure, type of school also influences the learner's learning outcome. A private school has a number of learners from high class families whereas a government school has a number of learners from middle and low class families. Private schools select learners with high academic abilities and they also have financial support. The learning environment in a private school is also quite different from a government school. Due to greater financial support in a private school, the classrooms and laboratory are well-furnished and well equipped with new technologies, while in government schools the classrooms are not well equipped. We read news regarding the real picture of our government schools where there are no classrooms in most of the schools and learners learn in the open. As a result of lack of appropriate learning environment, learning outcome of learners in government schools is sometimes lower than the private schools.

Geographical Location

Geographical location also affects the learning outcome. Due to lack of appropriate learning facilities in the rural and remote areas such as cost, transport facilities, low family income, new technologies such as computer, mobile, internet etc., the learners from these areas remain disadvantaged. We may say that learners who belong to non-metropolitan areas may have lower learning outcome in comparison to the learners from metropolitan areas.

Socio-economic Status

The socio-economic status of family also plays a crucial role in the learning of a learner. A learner who belongs to a family of lower socioeconomic status, does not get intellectual stimulus from his family and as a result, he remains lazy and inactive in the classroom. On the other side, the learner who belongs to a family of medium socioeconomic status, gets full motivation from his family, has high level of aspirations and as a result he remains active in classroom. We may say that his/her learning outcome is may be higher than the learner who belongs to lower socio-economic status.

Cultural Background

Learner's cultural background has an impact on learning. Learners from different cultural backgrounds learn in a different manner. You must have observed in your classroom, when you ask a question, some learners of your class could be able to make eye contact with you while they were responding but there may be some other learners too, who felt shy and could not make eye contact with you while they were responding. It generally happens in our classrooms and it is just because of cultural diversity. Cultural backgrounds impact the way the learner participates in various activities of school. A learner from collectivist cultural background prefers to learn in cooperation with others, while a learner from individualist cultural background prefers to learn independently. The important aspect for the teacher is that s/he should be aware about the differences between the school environment and cultural background of a learner. The teacher must work to understand the learner's cultural background and in this task the learner herself/himself could be a valuable source of information to the teacher. As a teacher, we may encourage the learners to talk about his/her family and cultural background etc., so that we can organise the learning environment accordingly.

Language

The linguistic diversity also affects a learner's learning outcomes. Have you ever thought about the situation when you get sick and go to consult a doctor? Just try to think for a moment, if in this situation four different doctors who speak different languages, would inform you about your health status, how would you feel? The same is the case with the teachers. In our classrooms we have diverse learners including many non-Hindi or non-English speaking learners. Learners who belong to those families whose language do not match with the medium of instruction of the school find themselves disadvantaged. Linguistically diverse learners sometimes show lower learning outcome and higher dropout rates. To ensure educational equity, we may appoint qualified teachers to reach the linguistically diverse learners. As a teacher, we should start language programmes for the learners with specific languages and during parent teacher meetings, we should try to present all the information in the parent's native language.

(c) Teacher as a facilitator

Ans. Refer to Chapter-4, Q.No.-5

(d) Tri-layered reflective thinking model

Ans. Refer to Chapter-4, Q.No.-19

(e) Gagne's nine steps of instructional process

Ans. Refer to Chapter-3, Q.No.-3

(f) Principles of classroom management

Ans. Refer to Chapter-3, Q.No.-42

Q4. Answer the following question in about 600 words:
Develop a plan to utilise community as a learning resource in formal education.

Ans. Refer to Chapter-3, Q.No.-36

www.ingramcontent.com/pod-product-compliance
Ingram Content Group UK Ltd.
Pitfield, Milton Keynes, MK11 3LW, UK
UKHW041827200726
13854UKWH00002BA/643

9 789386 276636